Defying the Inquisition in Colonial New Mexico

Pasó Por Aquí

Series on the Nuevomexicano Literary Heritage
Edited by Genaro M. Padilla,
Erlinda Gonzales-Berry, and A. Gabriel Meléndez

Frontispiece. Zambullo door, Penitente morada, Arroyo Hondo. The door is four feet, eleven inches high; the roughly hewn panels are one and a half inches thick. Probably made as recently as 1852, but the technology employed here is characteristic of the colonial period. Courtesy of Museum of New Mexico, Santa Fe. Neg. no. Pict 000-385-LL34.

Defying the Inquisition in Colonial New Mexico

Miguel de Quintana's Life and Writings

EDITED AND TRANSLATED BY

Francisco A. Lomelí and Clark A. Colahan

FOREWORD BY LUIS LEAL

University of New Mexico Press

Albuquerque

Printed in the United States of America

First paperback printing, 2018
Paperback ISBN: 978-0-8263-3958-4

Library of Congress Cataloging-in-Publication Data
Lomelí, Francisco A.
Defying the inquisition in colonial new mexico : Miguel de
Quintana's
life and writings / Francisco A. Lomelí and Clark A. Colahan.
p. cm. — (Pasó por aquí)
Includes bibliographical references and index.
ISBN-13: 978-0-8263-3957-7 (cloth : alk. paper)
ISBN-10: 0-8263-3957-3 (cloth : alk. paper)
1. Quintana, Miguel de, 1677–1748.
I. Colahan, Clark A. (Clark Andrews), 1945–
II. Quintana, Miguel de, 1677–1748. Works. English & Spanish. 2005.
III. Title. IV. Series.
PQ7079.Q56Z84 2006
861'.4—dc22

2005032420

Research and publication of this book was aided in part by support from the College of Letters and Science at the University of California at Santa Barbara.

Publication of this book was supported in part by the Center for Regional Studies at the University of New Mexico.

DESIGN AND COMPOSITION: Mina Yamashita

Contents

List of Figures

Foreword

The reconstruction of Chicano literary history has been a laborious undertaking carried out by a few critics who have persistently reconstructed a tradition that extends back to the period of exploration and settlement of the Southwest. Like archaeologists, they have recovered neglected texts piece by piece and demonstrated that the community producing them was not an illiterate society lacking the most essential literary skills.

Why was this search for lost Hispanic texts necessary? As Francisco A. Lomelí and Clark A. Colahan state in the introduction, in the case of New Mexico (and this applies to other regions of the Southwest), its literary history "has been innocently, surreptitiously, or systematically overlooked, dismissed, or ignored by the subjectivity of cultural bias and linguistic blindness."

The reconstruction of a Chicano literary history by Chicanos and Chicanas themselves had a modest beginning in 1959, the same year, according to some critics, that Chicano literature was born with the publication of the novel *Pocho* by José Antonio Villarreal. Although we now know that literature has existed in the Southwest since the sixteenth century, it was necessary to wait until 1959 for the first summary history of Chicano literature to appear, the brief pamphlet, *Breve reseña de la literatura hispana de Nuevo México y Colorado*, by José Timoteo López, Edgardo Núñez, and Roberto Lara Vialpando, published in Ciudad Juárez that year. This work had little influence upon the development of Chicano literary history, for it was not well formulated and too limited in scope, but it nonetheless represents an important early critical assessment of a body of literature that was still unconceptualized at that point in time.

It was not until the decade of the sixties and El Movimiento that an interest in Chicano culture, education, literature, folklore, and the arts was awakened. At the same time, a theory of cultural nationalism was formulated simultaneously by Luis Valdez and his followers in California, Rodolfo "Corky" Gonzales in Colorado, Reies López Tijerina in New Mexico, and José Angel Gutiérrez in Texas. Meanwhile, in Berkeley in September 1967, Nick C. Vaca, Octavio Romano V., and other Chicanos at the University of California published *El Grito: A Journal of Contemporary Mexican-American Thought*. One of the results of this awakening was the training of Chicano/a scholars at the universities. In 1971, an important year in the development of Chicano literary historiography, the space the history of Chicano literature occupied began to expand rapidly, as the first doctoral dissertations dealing with the history of Chicano literature were accepted at leading universities. Philip D. Ortego presented a well-researched dissertation, "Backgrounds of Mexican American Literature," in which for the first time an extraordinary amount of information on Chicano literature in the nineteenth century was collected. He dated the birth of Chicano literature to 1848, since, he argued, the Chicano community was born that year with the signing of the Treaty of Guadalupe Hidalgo. In 1973 I proposed that Chicano literature had begun in the sixteenth century with the *cronistas* (chroniclers), the first to document life and culture in the Southwest. Since then, several books and many articles dedicated to early periods have appeared, among them the edited volumes from Erlinda Gonzales-Berry, *Pasó Por Aquí: Critical Essays on the New Mexican Literary Tradition, 1542–1988* (1989), and María Herrera-Sobek, *Reconstructing a Chicano Literary Heritage: Hispanic Colonial Literature of the Southwest* (1993).

The reconstruction of Chicano/a literary history is now enriched by Francisco A. Lomelí's and Clark A. Colahan's study dedicated to a single eighteenth-century author, Miguel de Quintana. They begin the study of Quintana's poetry by placing the author and his works in the context of New Mexico's heritage and cultural development from its origins during the sixteenth century to the end of the Mexican period in 1848. They emphasize what contributed to make Mexico's northern colony become "a cultural hub or epicenter of colonial literary expression." They then examine the causes for the neglect of literary writings of the Nuevomexicanos, pointing particularly to mainstream critics, who consider them to be nonexistent or belonging to the oral tradition or ignore them altogether, despite the existence of such important literary works as Gaspar Pérez de Villagrá's *Historia de la Nueva México* (1610). The main body of Lomelí's and Colahan's introduction reconstructs the literary history of New Mexico, both written and oral, beginning with the earliest manifestation of that literature in order to place Quintana's writings in a New Mexican literary tradition going back to the earliest *cronistas* of the sixteenth century.

After establishing the proper literary-historical context in their introduction, the authors examine the subject of the book, Miguel de Quintana, at length, looking first at his overall significance in the sections entitled "Miguel de Quintana: A Barometer of a Writer's Options in Colonial New Mexico" and "Miguel de Quintana: A Missing Link in Hispanic Literature." "Miguel de Quintana: From Colonizer and Scribe to Defendant," where his life and works are delved into in greater depth, follows. Quintana's dramatic life in northern colonial New Mexico is for the first time made available in its entirety to the English-speaking world. This biographical study is enriched with an interpretive analyses of firsthand sources, such as the original manuscripts kept in Mexico City in the archives of the Inquisition, the infamous institution to which, ironically, we owe this information. The University of New Mexico's Zimmerman Library and the Archivos Franciscanos in Mexico City have preserved other documents about Quintana's life. Much more important is Lomelí's and Colahan's piecing together of Quintana's complete literary works, consisting of handwritten poetry, essays, and letters, thus eliminating some of the haphazard organization of the original materials. This reconstruction has been done in the context of social, religious, and cultural struggles of the time.

Quintana's frontier life in the northern New Mexico town of Santa Cruz de la Cañada, where he lived with his family after his arrival in 1694 with the Diego de Vargas caravan of colonists, is thoroughly and meticulously pieced together. There he became a farmer and participated actively in community affairs beginning in 1705, the year he became town scribe, and later as a clerk and secretary of the *alcalde mayor*, while at the same time writing poetry and religious plays. His downfall began in 1732, when the Inquisition accused him of being a heretic.

This book on Miguel de Quintana brings to light an early case in American thought and poetic expression dealing with perennial issues such as conformity, freedom of speech, censorship, and other humanistic topics that the theorists of frontier life seldom analyze or discuss. For this, we are all indebted to Lomelí and Colahan.

—Luis Leal
University of California at Santa Barbara

Acknowledgments

A study of this nature could not have been completed without much perseverance and collaboration. The varying stages of the project's development brought new challenges in every phase. Twenty-five years in the making, the work demanded creative strategies of compilation, transcription, translation, documenting literary history, pinpointing archival materials with multiple interdisciplinary approaches, and deciphering socioliterary content. We received considerable assistance and some leads along the way, along with many dead ends. First and foremost, Fray Angélico Chávez deserves our sincerest appreciation for the clue and insight he provided to pursue such an endeavor in the first place. An informal conversation with him in 1979 about recovering Nuevomexicano literary heritage fortuitously led to this investigative study. After consulting the microfilm collection of Inquisition documents in the Coronado Room of the Zimmerman Library at the University of New Mexico, we felt compelled to locate the original Miguel de Quintana papers in the Inquisition section of the Archivo General de la Nación, located at the Lecumberri Library in Mexico City. Here we managed to cross-check and compare with considerable precision our transcriptions with the original documents. It was truly exhilarating to review the actual letters and poetry Miguel de Quintana wrote along with the accompanying documents from other ecclesiastical sources. The staff at the Archivo General de la Nación was most helpful in answering questions about certain obscure eighteenth-century abbreviations and other formulaic expressions from the Inquisition period. We also sought information at the Archivos Franciscanos at the Universidad Nacional Autónoma de México, where by a stroke of luck we located Quintana's last letter of recantation written in 1737 to the bishop of Santa Fe, Dr. don Martín de Elizacochea. This was the last reference to the poet except for his death certificate in 1748.

Following the extensive transcriptions and recreation of the documents as complete as we could determine came the arduous task of formulating comparative and interdisciplinary approaches, mostly literary and religious studies; examining genealogical sources; contextualizing historical data; analyzing various literary traditions such as mysticism; and organizing the manuscript in the form of a critical edition on an early New Mexican writer. We then proceeded to explore the many realms Quintana would reveal about himself, the historical period, and his social environment. To this end we must mention the contributions of many institutions that helped advance our work through funding, staff support, or allotted space: the Recovering U.S. Hispanic Literary Heritage at the University of Houston; the SCR43 Project within the Center for Chicano Studies at the University of California, Santa Barbara; Whitman College; the Southwest Hispanic Research Institute at the University of New Mexico; the Affirmative Action Office at the University of California, Santa Barbara; the Chicano Studies Program at the University of New Mexico; and the Spanish Archives of New Mexico in Santa Fe. Many individuals contributed in some capacity, for which we are eternally grateful: Dr. Felipe Gonzales, Charlie Martínez, Dr. Luis Leal, Dr. Denise Segura, Dr. Carl Gutiérrez-Jones, Raymond Huerta, Larry Miller, Orlando Romero, and Dr. Eduardo Chávez-Hernández. To our families and spouses, who allowed us to indulge in such a project for so many years, we offer our deepest thanks for their unwavering patience and support.

We wish to thank Fray Angélico Chávez for his tip on Miguel de Quintana and Tom Steele, SJ, for his enthusiastic encouragement and expert guidance when we began this project twenty-five years ago.

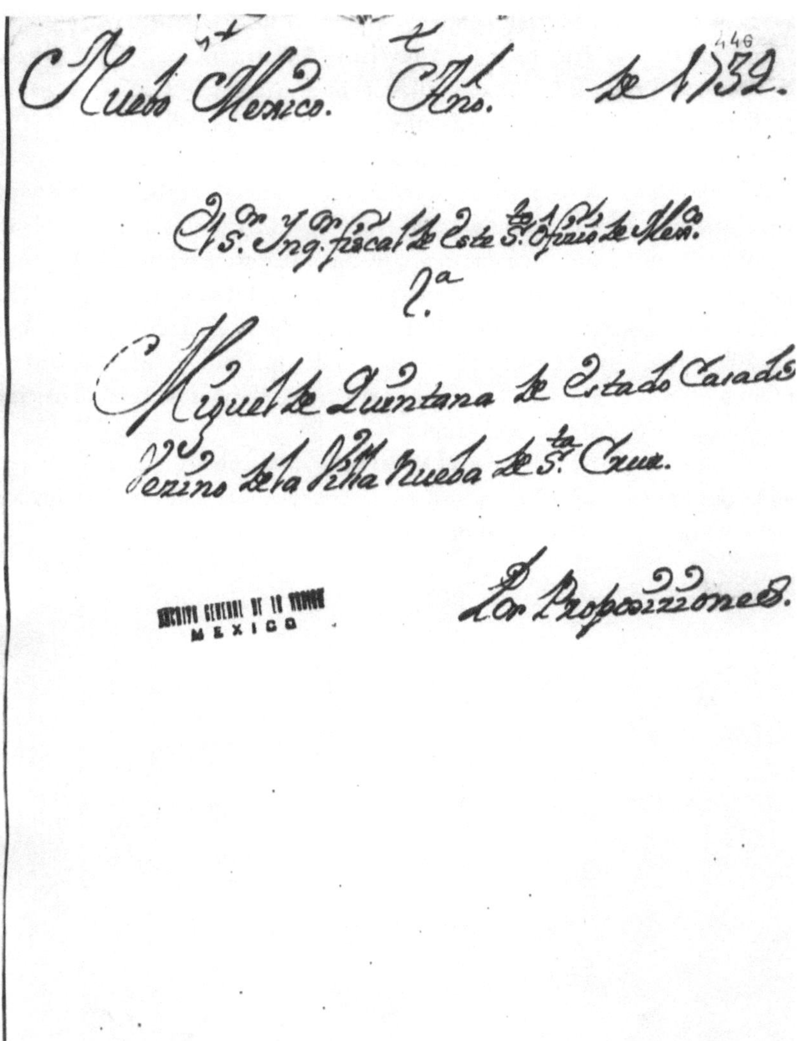
446

Nuevo Mexico. Año de 1734.

El Sr. Inqr. fiscal de este Sto. Officio de Mexco.

contra

Miguel de Quintana de Estado Casado
Vezino de la Villa Nueva de Sta. Cruz.

Por Proposiziones.

ARCHIVO GENERAL DE LA NACION
MEXICO

Fig. 1. This is a photograph of the title page of the Inquisition process against Miguel de Quintana as it appears in the Archivo General de la Nación in Mexico City. It reads as follows (folio 446r):

New Mexico. The Year 1734.
The Honorable Prosecutor for the Inquisition for This Holy Office of
Mexico City against Miguel de Quintana, Married, Resident[3]
of Villa Nueva de Santa Cruz
For Heretical Assertions[4]

PART ONE

Introduction

New Mexican Poet in a State of Disenchantment

1. Santa Cruz, New Mexico, 1737

The inquisitor's Christian charity and brotherly love were as stone-cold as the icicles hanging from the Palace of the Governors. The January weather had stabbed like a driven nail when the Most Reverend Joseph Antonio Guerrero set out from Santa Fe to ride north to Santa Cruz de la Cañada. When he got there and met Father Joseph Yrigoien, priest at the Santa Clara mission and the Holy Office's notary for New Mexico, they warmed themselves primarily in one way—over the fire of their simmering anger and a burning zeal to compel respect for their authority. In his old farmhouse they found Miguel de Quintana, who was now far from young himself and had been ill in bed for more than a month, but whose exceedingly rare ability to read and write had served as the basis of a career of some prominence as clerk of the civil and church courts, author of community Christmas plays called *coloquios* (also meaning "dialogues"), and scribe for the letters and documents of his neighbors for many miles around. Intriguing controversy seemed to swirl around Miguel de Quintana in this small northern New Mexico town, setting the stage for this humble David to face the Goliath of the Inquisition.

The Mexican Inquisition's commissioner and notary were on a mission of warning. They would have preferred one of chastisement, as they had formally accused Quintana of heresy, but their superiors in Mexico City, overruling the insistent claims of their New Mexico agents that he was a sly old fox and perfectly sound in the head, had reached the conclusion that his mind was wandering with age. The orders from above were not to punish, but to admonish and assign him an understanding confessor. The threat of damnation was to be linked only to any continuing obstinacy, a refusal to obey orders, a failure to give up writing poems and essays that cited divine words of encouragement specifically for his freedom to write.

There was little Quintana could do in the face of an official visit backed up by the authority of the Holy Office, whose operatives the church empowered to command his obedience. He had already irritated Guerrero and Yrigoien further by failing to respond to their summons to go to Santa Fe for this interview, alleging illness, so he acquiesced. They demanded he write out on the spot for the bishop a statement of recantation, a promise of compliance, and even an endorsement of the rectitude with which his accusers had acted in the whole affair.[1] The declaration he provided them with was so self-denigrating, and its praise of his enemies so extravagant, that it is hard to read it today as anything but biting sarcasm.

Miguel's behavior in the following weeks supports this interpretation. The rebellious poetry and prose, urging him to fight the good fight and calling down divine sanctions against his oppressors, continued to bubble up from within him. Seeking support within his network in the Santa Cruz area, he delivered these new compositions, too, to his friends. Before long an outraged Yrigoien was in hot pursuit, collecting the papers and sending them off to the inquisitors far to the south. There was no response, though, only new additions from the writer's pen to a file that two and a half centuries later allows us to look into an anxious but representative New Mexican mind that those jealous of their power sought to bury in silence.

As we shall discuss more fully later, the importance of his voice lies partly in the crisis that it describes from within. Among the big questions being contested in the three-way correspondence among Quintana, the Inquisition agents in New Mexico, and the Inquisition authorities in Mexico City were issues we read today in the intellectual context of the Enlightenment: individual conscience versus social conformity, freedom of speech versus censorship, personal religious experience versus dogma, and, in the final analysis, the embedded hegemonic values of the Spanish empire versus comparatively humanistic, liberal values in a frontier community moving toward greater democracy. Lest we mistakenly look for the influence of French rationalist philosophers, however, it is important to keep in mind a native Hispanic variety of individualism, existing since the Renaissance and expressed in the writings of classic Spanish mystics such as the reformer St. Teresa of Avila.[2] As we shall see, both she and other religious figures of the sixteenth and seventeenth centuries sought to change balances of social power in favor of the marginalized by appeals to the divine court of justice, not to science. That spiritual activism was part of Quintana's grassroots cultural heritage. The resolute resistance he offered to abusive authority is precisely the type of Hispanic writing in the American Southwest that the discipline of Chicano Studies has often endeavored to recover and foreground.[3]

Quintana and his writings are important for more than his role as a religious nonconformist and defiant writer, however. His story, and even more so his way of understanding and visualizing it, has the equally significant value of contributing to fill a large empty space in the *intrahistoria* of colonial

Fig. 2. La Iglesia de Santa Cruz de la Cañada. Photograph by H. T. Hiester. Courtesy of Museum of New Mexico, Santa Fe. Neg. no. 37007.

New Mexico.[4] As we shall see, the period is rich in church and government documentation, as well as oral literary expression that has come down to us, but very little personal writing has survived from a largely illiterate community without a single printing press. In most cases the extant documents lack the personal, nuanced expression of an individual's emotional and intellectual life made possible by the capability to put one's changing thoughts down on paper, and with the expectation of reaching more than one's family and friends.

While Quintana's subject matter speaks to us more intimately than most of the early New Mexican writings previously available, they are difficult to understand as fully as one might hope. The simple fact is that many of the things he said or assumed about the nature of writing and religion sound strange to modern readers, especially for those with an Anglo and/or Protestant cultural background. His vocabulary is drawn from Hispanic, Roman Catholic traditions that must be at least somewhat familiar to the reader if his ideas are to make sense. In short, some cultural contextualization is necessary. To contribute to that orientation we have included in the later sections of this introduction basic information on parallel Hispanic writers, particularly those addressing religious themes, with whom Miguel shared traditional concepts and images.[5] For similar reasons of cultural context, before documenting what is known about Miguel's early life we begin with an overview of the types of colonial writing that have by and large guided historians of New Mexico's Hispanic past.

2. New Mexico as a Hub of Early North American Writings

New Mexico has enjoyed a long-standing and particularly rich tradition as a source of written inscriptions, including the many Native American petroglyphs as the first human registers. The wealth of recorded documents, however, was greatly shaped by the extensive Hispanic presence during the colonial period (1540–1821) and the Mexican Period (1821–48). Their legacy extended well into the Territorial Period (1848–1912). The cultural diversification of the region has flourished from a unique interaction unlike any other region in what is now the continental United States. A distinctive identity in the annals of frontier life has developed here within the framework of a crossroads of cultural agency among Native Americans, *españoles mexicanos,* and later Anglo Americans. Consequently, New Mexico stands out for a variety of reasons, the most compelling being its peoples of diverse backgrounds and world views having merged in a syncretic manner to create a regional ethos.

A by-product of such an intercultural matrix is visible in the early writings. In terms of sheer volume, this region has produced the greatest mass of written documents prior to 1848, as well as the most ancient records, far exceeding any other geographical area in what is now the United States. In addition to chronicles of exploration, many samples of writing by known individuals dot the archival landscape, particularly within official colonial documents. In regard to colonial literature in California, Luis Leal observes what is also true for New Mexico in the period:

> In general it can be said that California colonial literature is didactic in nature. It consists of diaries, letters, memoirs, *memoriales,* chronicles, histories, travelogues, *relaciones,* essays and a few scattered poems and plays. Written first by the explorers themselves and then by the missionaries, government officials, military men, and other non-professional writers, its immediate end is seldom aesthetic.[6]

As his list makes clear, though, we cannot judge this literary production by modern classifications of genre and narrative points of view, since literary form was less of a concern than the story being told. The magnitude of the action intrinsic to exploration, conquest, and colonization made those subjects the central protagonists rather than the writer.

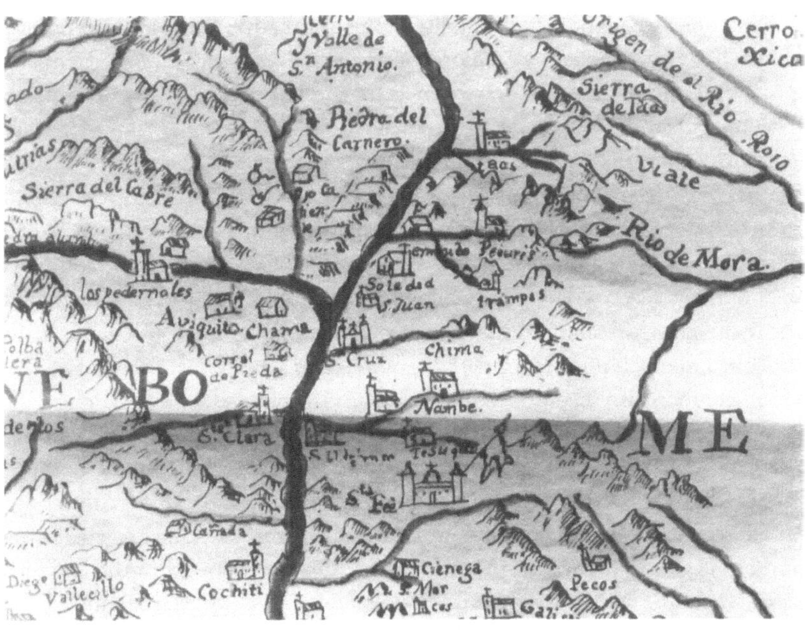

Fig. 3. Portion of 1778 Bernardo Miera y Pacheco Map.

Often perceived in the Hispanic world as a cultural backwater, New Mexico has not altogether been able to overcome its original reputation of forlorn remoteness, what came to be known as terra incognita, that is, the furthermost northern frontier of the Viceroyalty of New Spain (Mexico, including present-day California, Nevada, Arizona, New Mexico, Texas, and the southern tips of Oregon and Colorado).[7] In these two ways, then, New Mexico as a cultural entity has attracted much attention, on the one hand praised in the United States for its unique makeup and on the other disparaged elsewhere for its purported backwardness and repeated conflicts and setbacks.

The goal of many failed expeditions and explorations, this region produced virtually nothing profitable except illusions of grandeur. While testing Spaniards' tenacity to the limit when they set claims to some unprecedented discovery, it generated only unfortunate tales of returning empty-handed with broken spirits and unfulfilled promises. Early accounts contradicted reality; the news brought of the various attempts at discovery titillated the imagination with fantastic places, especially through hyperbolic stories that spread like wildfire. Any tale, no matter how absurd, attracted a number of gullible followers. Not coincidentally, a long list of adventurous but seemingly mesmerized and enchanted explorers crisscrossed vast expanses of territories and in the process created important texts combining wide-eyed description with unbridled inventiveness.

From another point of view, the chronicle as a literary genre predominated for its mixture of quasi-journalistic reporting: unrestricted, subjective, and sometimes tangential confabulations blended in with the narrator's personal observations. Indeed the reading public's appetite had thrived on the countless tales of danger, accounts of the incredible, adventures into the unknown, and the many fantastic renditions of discoveries. The explorations and expeditions provoked as much interest, or perhaps more, than space travel does today. The chronicle therefore served multiple functions: it made accessible descriptions about faraway events, often with a seasoning of hyperbole and marvel, while at the same time informing a public predisposed toward assimilating news about worlds that defied the real—and sometimes even the imaginings of fiction. In addition, the discourse often cloaked self-interest, seeking to win favors and privileges on the writer's behalf (though this was not true in the frequent cases when the writer was primarily a scribe). From the standpoint of the visual imagination, as photography had not yet been invented, such writing performed the role of creating images, frequently projecting stimulating scenes better, larger, or stranger than life. In sum, the chronicle had both stirred up and then quenched a nearly insatiable thirst for fantastic details to fill a void in what was known about the lands beyond the northern Mexican provinces.

Among some of the more salient chronicles are the following: Alvar Núñez Cabeza de Vaca's unbelievable wanderings on foot into the unknown from Florida to New Mexico and back to Mexico City in his *Relaciones* (1542);[8] Francisco Vázquez de Coronado's search for the Gran Quivira from 1540 to 1542 in Pedro de Castañeda's *Relación de la jornada de Cíbola, poblados, ritos y costumbres* (1596);[9] Fray Marcos de Niza's quest for the seven golden cities of Cíbola in *Descubrimiento de las siete ciudades por el Padre Fray Marcos de Niza* (1539);[10] Padre Gerónimo de Zárate Salmerón's recounting of fabulous exploits in *Relaciones de todas las cosas que en el Nuevo México se han visto y sabido de 1538 hasta 1626*;[11] Fray Francisco de Escobar's stunning stories about unusual human species in *La relación de Fray Escobar de la expedición de Oñate a California* (1605);[12] and much later, in William G. Ritch's concept of the Aztec mythic homeland, in *Aztlan: The History, Resources, and Attractions of New Mexico* (1885).[13] All these, to a considerable extent, were foundational chronicles, accounts, and/or landmarks of inflated fancy.

This penchant for the marvelous was later ingeniously reinscribed in the region's culture at the turn of the twentieth century, when the commercial interests of land developers and an aggressive tourist industry promoted the "Land of Enchantment" state nickname. Fictional accounts masquerading as real and even claiming to date back to the sixteenth century have propagated an image, rather, a vision, of the region as an elusive promised land with utopian qualities. Similarly, the name Nuevo México, generally found as Nueva México until early in the nineteenth century, originally evoked an element of wishful thinking for another "new" Mexico that either duplicated or exceeded the extraordinary riches of the Aztec empire. "Nueva" as a feminine modifier can either allude to *provincia* or *ciudad* (the latter implying Tenochtitlan or Mexico City, clearly the most dominating cultural center of New Spain), and that changed into a masculine modifier, "Nuevo," when the region acquired its own more prosaic identity as such.[14] The motivation behind the first modifier was the hope for locating another strategic civilization center of indigenous peoples that would naturally draw conquistadors and colonists toward the outer fringes of the frontier and beyond; anything even remotely within the realm of possibility boggled the mind of many. Such a mythical place was suggested once and for all by Gaspar Pérez de Villagrá in his famous epic poem, *Historia de la Nueva México*, as early as 1610. Myth and legend clearly played key roles in shaping the popular view of the region that was influencing the collective consciousness of those in New Spain, where a zeal for conquest of new lands reigned supreme. The string of sedentary indigenous settlements along the Río Grande from time immemorial, called pueblos after the conquest by the Spaniards, fascinated fortune seekers to the point of frenzy because explorers equated permanent communities with wealth. Such a milieu presented a propitious nucleus of elements from the Spaniards' point of view around which to fantasize about the establishment of a federation of pueblos, or the blueprint of a potential small-scale empire state. It was recognized that there was a problem stemming from the lack of a single urban center with numerous independent communities and of a single leader like Moctezuma—two key conditions the Spaniards considered indispensable to conquer, coerce, or co-opt the indigenous peoples. From the outset, though, land, laborers, and resources seemed plentiful enough to make the area self-sufficient, especially if rich minerals such as gold and silver could be found to stimulate colonization. Spaniards, then, introduced their Mediterranean world of beliefs, which had been greatly fashioned by medieval-era traditions, and it combined with a Mexican reservoir of folklore that was strongly Indian. The two blended and borrowed from each other freely to produce an amalgam of bicultural invention.

In short, the region incited countless unconfirmed tales of riches while confabulating an "imagined frontier" out of what Clark A. Colahan terms "the enchantment of the unknown."[15] New Mexico's apparently fantastic qualities, growing from a myth-based perception, continued to make imaginations run wild, in spite of the failure of sixteenth-century expeditions. Lofty dreams of power, faith in a "rags-to-riches" paradigm, and notions of knightly achievement fanned interest among prospective colonizers in central Mexico. This prompted a number of expeditions northward, including two large, family-based colonizing endeavors: that of Juan de Oñate from Zacatecas in 1598 and of don Diego de Vargas Zapata Luján Ponce de León from Mexico City in 1693.[16] A crescendo of growing excitement contributed toward a steady flow of colonizers who marched north to risk their fate on the new frontier.

The experience of the first Spanish settlements in the region proved to be a greater challenge than anticipated, however, as some were ravaged by the elements or the scarcity of food, others by plagues or hostile natives, or a combination of all four. Remoteness in itself made the exchange of basic goods slow and difficult. The fertile fascination from the initial stages of conquest quickly succumbed to the constant struggle for survival. A hardy ability to endure was required, given the demanding physical environment and the region's limited resources. So, setting their laurels as conquerors aside, the settlers had to become adept at learning how to negotiate forms of coexistence with the local indigenous peoples. Close contact between the two peoples often proved mutually beneficial as a survival tool during times of poor crops and food shortages. For nearly three hundred years that interaction evolved into a unique regional ethos of *mestizaje*, or social hybridization, which established the foundation of an unparalleled cultural network, New Mexican style, consisting of Hispanic-Mexicans and Native Americans. It in turn much later contributed to the formation of a distinctive tripartite cultural fabric with the addition of the Anglo American element. This amalgam appeared early. Whereas recruitment policies for expeditions before 1695 admittedly favored those of Spanish origin, followed by the criollos, cultural mixing as well as crossbreeding became the norm for recruitment by 1695.[17] This was clear from the muster list of Juan Páez Hurtado's expedition, when a preference for those from Spain was deemed impractical to uphold if the ultimate objective was the colonization of the far reaches of northwestern New Spain.[18] By 1700, the era of spectacular conquests and discoveries had come to a virtual end, gradually freeing the enterprise of expansion from its sentence to the gallows of unsustainable fantasy. The alternatives for the colonists became relatively clear-cut: either fend for themselves, adopting Native American techniques of survival and working out policies of interaction with them, or perish or retreat in total defeat to Mexico.

New Mexico's resiliency is partly attributable to the hardy strain of settlers who remained to endure the kinds of obstacles that afflicted them constantly. Despite such hardships, some areas of literary creativity flourished in the region, leaving a lasting imprint of aesthetic expression. The settlers did depend on writing to some extent, but their folklore, like that of the indigenous peoples, primarily increased orally, as new collective experiences were articulated, and proportionately, as new motifs, symbols, and narrative models were transferred from one culture to another. Much like the Native Americans before them who had captured elements of their environment through the inscriptions of petroglyphs and other pictographs, some colonial settlers also left their impressions on stone walls, such as Morro Rock, and other artifacts to represent their presence. The deep-rooted Spanish inclination for documenting every phase of official and unofficial activities, including impressions and observations, made the settlers faithful recorders of life on the frontier. Cleve Hallenbeck has observed: "Spaniards had the passion for preserving attested memoranda of every event, however insignificant."[19]

This tendency was fleshed out in the inscription of the colonial Hispanic imagination in a corpus of documents, including individually refracted versions of what the explorers and settlers saw or imagined and felt or thought. New Mexico therefore represents what we might call a cultural hub or epicenter of colonial literary expression. In some cases it has stirred stories of high drama and distinctive appeal, even though much of its import survived only by accumulating dust—much like archaeological artifacts—in monograph form, personal ledgers, family chests, scattered newspaper collections, or other preserved archival sources. Few works from the colonial period, however, have survived in proportion to the enormous quantity of written documents that were produced. A major problem has been preservation because of the harsh physical conditions. Furthermore, Cleve Hallenbeck stresses that

> [m]ost of the provincial documentary material dealing with the Spanish period in New Mexico has forever disappeared. Complete records once existed in the archives at Santa Fe. . . . All the archives in the province . . . were destroyed in the great Pueblo Revolt of 1680. Then most of the archives covering the period 1693 to 1846 were burned or otherwise disposed by the early Anglo-American officials, who could not read Spanish.[20]

Many of the archival documents that were not eliminated suffered the indignity of being used as wrapping paper or packing material, consequently minimizing their value as historical sources. Most of the early literature has been innocently, surreptitiously, or systematically overlooked, dismissed, or ignored by the subjectivity of cultural bias and linguistic blindness. When it has not been relegated to oblivion in these ways, this Hispanic literary production tends to be considered part of oral tradition and therefore "subliterary." Fortunately, through references found in better-known materials or the discovery of empirical evidence, numerous literary samples have survived despitte the long odds associated with hostility or indifference.

Consider these examples. In 1598 along the banks of the Río Grande near present-day El Paso, Capt. Marcos Farfán de los Godos presented a play entitled *Los moros y cristianos.*[21] Its purpose was to celebrate military success as well as religious zeal—the two arms of conquest—along with putting to use a sense of aesthetics. Villagrá's *Historia de la Nueva México* from 1610, mentioned above, an often-undervalued epic poem that functions as a chronicle or treatise on the Oñate conquest of New Mexico, rivals and might even eclipse aspects of Alonso de Ercilla y Zúñiga's famous *La Araucana* (1569–89) from Chile for its scope, historical veracity, and post-Renaissance flamboyance. This voluminous poem of thirty-four cantos is the product of a particularly New Mexican social context and clearly defies the general notion that the Hispanic borderlands did not produce any worthwhile texts.

Some critics of American letters still regard the overall Southwestern literary scene as a wasteland or what Russell Martin terms a "sagebrush school of literature."[22] Only recently has this seminal work by Villagrá assumed its rightful place in the canon, thanks in part to a recent translation and a number of critical studies.[23] The text's poetic exuberance seems to contradict the region's negative reputation as a place of aridness and privation, especially for its time, through insightful descriptions, a skillful portrayal of a drama of epic proportions, a copious account of details on Oñate's expedition, a wide spectrum of personalities (both Spaniards and Native Americans), the mentality of conquest and search for glory, and the classical framework of the battle at Acoma and its tragic destruction. It is clear from this text that literary sophistication appeared early along with popular forms of expression. This foundational text confirms the fundamental role and importance that the early colonial Hispanic voice—through the discourse of an imaginative lens—played in the construction of what eventually became the American Southwest.

In addition, in most cases early documents were neither written nor saved for their value as a writer's personal expression. Some, such as Vargas's letters written home to his family in Madrid and Cabeza de Vaca's *Relaciones*, do offer glimpses of deeds and events imbued with elements of literary imagination, but they rely primarily on divulging facts and real-life experiences, regardless of their seemingly incredible nature, instead of depending on a creative, personal artistry.[24] Villagrá's epic likewise generally represents depersonalized accounts about a wide-ranging set of actions and exploits within an epic mode, but only secondarily focuses on the author as a poetic voice. The text well defines a geopoetic view of history and the cultural transactions between indigenous peoples of the Río Grande and the Hispanic-Mexican explorers, thereby providing an elucidating glimpse into a broad panorama of things to come in the subsequent colonization. Nonetheless, little is revealed about the author himself within the literary formulas he imitates and the grandeur of the historical events of the conquest in process.

The harsh conditions and widespread illiteracy of frontier life did not encourage much writing about one's own personal preoccupations any more than about flights of fancy focused on the unknown. The act of writing thus became an official gesture that recorded basic necessities or ceremonial events such as baptisms, proclamations of the banns of marriage, deaths, litigation, and criminal records. Incursions into original meditations, humorous exchanges, or aesthetic embellishments are rarely found on the written page of the period, though to a certain extent these forms of personal expression became incorporated into the oral tradition, which continued to flourish. Literary expression in written form remained a rarity during the colonial period.

Several causes led to the dearth of written literature in the colonial period. Aside from the widespread illiteracy of most colonial New Mexicans, the dwindling excitement over new discoveries and geographical remoteness isolated the populace. This produced an ignorance of emergent ideas and trends in the larger world, while those with intellectual inclinations tended not to remain in the region. Cultural creation recorded in writing, within the context of a pastoral society, required education and leisure that were simply too much of a luxury to cultivate. In addition, a number of strictures, prohibitions, and fears that did not tolerate freedom of expression guided much of colonial life. The Inquisition, the best known of several formal and informal social institutions, enhanced its inhibitory effect through its secrecy and strove to control any form of either religious or political dissension. Orthodoxy represented the hegemonic ideology. Furthermore, as mentioned above, the absence of a printing press before 1834 alone represented a major obstacle or deterrent—not to be underestimated—to recording any form of literary expression. Its appearance revolutionized the writing in the region, opening the possibility for popular Hispanic voices to express themselves, regardless of what the official authorities did or did not sanction.

Of course, much oral literary expression existed in rituals, such as plays, celebrations of saints, symbolic reenactments of battles or commemorative dramas of conquest (*Los moros y cristianos* and *Los Comanches*), other religious holidays and social events (like fairs and festivals), or informal round-the-fire gatherings. It also passed from generation to generation through improvisational transmission for the sake of amusement, including moments when the speaker aimed to exhibit prowess in storytelling or verbal dexterity. New Mexico possesses a rich reservoir of anonymous folklore in both these categories.

Its voluminous outpouring did not occur like some sort of "spontaneous combustion" in a vacuum.[25] On the contrary, New Mexico's wealth of oral tradition developed within a long cultural context of imaginative interaction (including humor) in a diverse social environment of Native Americans, Hispanics with a filtered acculturation in Mexico, and subsequent contact with Anglo Americans. These cultures have all contributed a wide range of experiential points of view; legends and stories, including popular archetypes and symbols (such as *el poeta negrito*, a ubiquitous folkloric figure from Mexico, and the coyote); ballads of intrigue and romance; military conflicts; a variety of linguistic nuances and concepts; and a sense of religion and place that have combined as in no other region. Among other forms, the *romance* (a legendary ballad with distinctly medieval qualities), the *décima* (a standardized ten-verse poem), the *pastorela* (a Christmas shepherds' play), the *cuento* (short story), the *indita* (a dance-song popular at the turn of the nineteenth century that resembled a *corrido*, but sung to an Indian rhythm), and the *alabado* (religious hymn) are all vestiges of a deep-rooted oral tradition that has survived through the centuries, despite all the material obstacles that have hindered its preservation.[26] They clearly attest to a living culture that continues to be dynamic in reaffirming itself and retelling its stories from its own testimonial standpoint.

3. Miguel de Quintana: A Barometer of a Writer's Options in Colonial New Mexico

One clear exception to the category of depersonalized writings is a work of modest but discernible literary content by Miguel de Quintana. As mentioned above, he was a humble farmer, poet, town scribe, and writer of coloquios (plays in the form of extended dialogue). He was an assistant to both the civil and ecclesiastical authorities from Villa Nueva de Santa Cruz de la Cañada in northern New Mexico during what some historians have called the darkest era of the colonial period. His story took a sudden turn toward notoriety when he was investigated by the Santo Oficio (the Holy Office, or Inquisition) between 1732 and 1737. His life story, including these five years of conflict, serves as a telling testimonial about church and society—the internal administrative apparatuses as well as the related attitudes and practices—at a specific time and place when Hispanic settlements were still taking root on the frontier. His dramatic personal history, filled with fascinating controversy, represents an example of someone who tested the restrictions and limitations of free thinking, expression, and tolerance, and whom the ecclesiastical authorities perceived to be defying social norms for philosophical and religious decorum.

Our purposes in studying Miguel de Quintana and his writings are several. Perhaps above all, we have sought to recover his story without the compromising entanglements of his time and in the process reconstruct his manuscripts in their entirety (handwritten poetry, essays, and letters), including those from various participants and sources in order to show a creative, literary mind at work in colonial New Mexico. The history of such legal and/or ecclesiastical investigations has made an extremely interesting yet little-known chapter in North American historiography. We have also been committed to rescuing from oblivion the saga of a writer confronting censorship and social stigmatization; documenting the inner workings of a social institution, the Inquisition, in its treatment of an individual in the remote context of the struggling frontier; and explaining the various social, ideological, and religious doctrines of the time that make his struggles and conflict understandable today. By examining a person's writings, we hope to unfold some of the layers of literary and cultural meaning in colonial Hispanic writings from *el vasto norte,* the seemingly infinite stretch of land of endless proportions. Of even greater value is the insight he provides about himself, his era, and his region through an intimate self-portrait, one that renders elements of a particularized personality, a corresponding psychological state, and a spiritual snapshot, along with an individual's response to the hierarchical machinery of the much-feared Inquisition.

A great deal of the literary interest Quintana evokes lies in the difference between what he and the church authorities expressed in writing and what was probably meant. More than likely a bit of posturing and self-righteousness influenced the two sides. Irony and outrage glint between the lines in a battle of words as each side wielded the weapons available. The root cause was Quintana's defiant challenge to restrictions on both his religious and artistic freedoms to express himself and his struggle to hold his place in society at the same time that he questioned how social deviancy could be used as a label against him. Both sides claimed rights to which they believed themselves inalienably entitled.

Among the questions being contested in the three-way correspondence between Quintana, the inquisitors in New Mexico, and the Inquisition authorities in Mexico City were issues of individual conscience versus social conformity, freedom of speech versus censorship, personal mysticism versus dogma, and finally, the embedded values of hegemony of a Spanish colony versus the emergent values of a modestly enlightened humanism in a nascent community. More succinctly, Quintana's writings reveal a struggle between structural powers and the determination of an individual's free will. He reflected a new attitude of acute individualism that was taking shape at the grass roots within the grandiose backdrop of don Diego de Vargas Zapata Luján Ponce de León's epic "recuperation" of New Mexico in 1693.[27] In this way, Quintana's writings provide insight into a number of intrahistorical happenings in the newly developing frontier villages, perhaps intimating the Penitentes' sense of being a cultural broker for a strongly independent people.[28] Not by coincidence, Quintana was an active member of the Third Order of St. Francis, the precursors who not only evolved into Penitentes, but who also demanded a degree of autonomy with respect to their religious practices in light of having been the gatekeepers of Roman Catholicism when the church was virtually unable to keep its places of worship open because of the scarcity of resources and priests.

4. Miguel de Quintana: A Missing Link in Hispanic Literature

One may well wonder how someone like Miguel de Quintana could remain hidden in the manuscript pages of the Spanish Archives of New Mexico and the Inquisition Archives in Mexico City. Such a life history of presumably unspectacular events between 1677 and 1748 was unlikely to survive through time. He never published a single work of literature, nor did he perform any military deeds except as an unsung participant in the epic expedition don Diego de Vargas led in 1693 to reconquer New Mexico. He does, however, embody a fundamental change in early Spanish history in New Mexico, going from colonizer to farmer in an ordinary, almost humdrum, life of frontier routine. Considered an isolated case, his profile nonetheless unveils hidden aspects of social dynamics lost in the pages of history: namely, the obstacles to being a creative writer and free-thinker. In addition, he stands out as the first identifiable Hispanic poet from the region after Gaspar Pérez de Villagrá from the colonial period. That in itself is a distinction worthy of scholarly consideration, except that Quintana deviated from the epic focus to an intimately personal one.

Whether through luck or serendipity, we came across this distinctly tragic, somewhat perplexing, but certainly unpretentious figure while perusing early colonial documents, hoping for new, revealing clues to a Hispanic literary past in the Southwest. Beginning about 1980 we combed libraries and archives in search of writers from the colonial period who had been ignored, new voices to be added to the familiar chroniclers. This almost archaeological undertaking unearthed a few gems but was not truly successful until it included a personal interview with Fray Angélico Chávez in Santa Fe. Himself a perennial traveler through the largely uncharted waters of colonial New Mexican church documents, he pointed out a forgotten writer about whom he had in the

1940s written a preliminary study entitled "The Mad Poet of Santa Cruz." Our search redirected, we read the microfilm copies of the relevant Inquisition documents at Zimmerman Library at the University of New Mexico and shortly thereafter proceeded to compare the primary materials at the Archivo General de la Nación in Mexico City in the form of forty-seven folios, or pages, sewn as one document.[29] From our transcriptions, whose accuracy we checked with later trips back to the original source, we then translated the Inquisition's file on Quintana. Supplementary materials came to light upon our searching the Archivos Franciscanos at the Universidad Nacional Autónoma de México. In this manner, we have attempted to fill in historical and biographical gaps in order to make possible a fuller portrait of Miguel de Quintana, the church authorities involved in his case, eighteenth-century New Mexico, and the developing consciousness of a frontier writer.

What did Fray Angélico Chávez mean in 1948 when he called Quintana a mad poet? Curiosity teased us, not knowing whether he was suggesting Quintana was demented, delusive, lunatic, fanatical, unorthodox, nonconformist, unbalanced, strange, or quixotic. Upon closer examination, what emerged instead was an educated man, an important missing link in a literary legacy and tradition that by the late nineteenth century had become seemingly irretrievably lost or at least forgotten. Along with Gaspar Pérez de Villagrá, who holds a special place in literary history with his epic *Historia de la Nueva México,* Quintana is one of only two early New Mexican writers to escape from anonymity by leaving his name and life story together with his poetry and essays. It is indeed ironic that the Inquisition, the highest order enforcing conformity, which sought to silence him, made all this possible. The meticulous, systematic method by which the Inquisition investigated each case shows a vigilant institution that, although guilty of such denouncements, was also wary of arbitrary or unscrupulous accusations made under the guise of religiosity or other righteous pretexts. Within this context it seems conceivable that similar kinds of texts may have failed to survive the intervening three centuries.

Despite the personal hardships he suffered, including intimidation and religious persecution, Quintana stood his ground, rarely wavering in his convictions. His poetry and prose do not demonstrate a highly polished style, and his ideas are not particularly original. Nonetheless, thanks to the local agents of the Inquisition, a thorough investigation was conducted to examine every bit of evidence to determine the weight of accusations of heresy leveled against him. To make sense of the case, the ulterior motives of his accusers are as relevant as the character of the accused, so the episode speaks to the nature of New Mexican colonial power as much as it does to the personality of a "mad poet." Virtually every paper written in the case, both in New Mexico and at Inquisition headquarters in Mexico City, was compiled, filed, and saved for posterity.[30] Curiously, none of the experts on the New Mexican Inquisition—France V. Scholes, John L. Kessell, Robert J. McCue, or Richard E. Greenleaf—makes mention of Quintana's case, possibly because of its lack of epic proportions, its unequivocally ambiguous nature, and the final exoneration.[31] The conflicting arguments and strikingly subjective points of view of the interested parties, including the defense Quintana himself formulated, have not previously been analyzed. They only appear in forty-seven folios sewn into Inquisition documents located in the Archivo General de la Nación in Mexico City at the Lecumberri Collection.

In more general historical terms, Quintana's case sheds light on the least-known century of Spanish New Mexico, particularly as it relates to the inner workings of the Inquisition. It may also represent the tip of an iceberg in the relationship between church and state, which had been heated for some time and continued to be so through most of the century.[32] Our aim has been to provide analysis of the vested interests and prejudices in play at that time and place. A sense of the dynamics of hierarchy and hegemony and of the period's usual discourses helps to make sense of Quintana's understanding of his own literary production. Without that introduction his poetry strikes us today as strangely "mad," intimately religious, or overly driven by self-justification, somewhere between simpleminded folk poetry and mystical exaltation, with some Illuminist religious overtones. It echoes in the unfamiliar minor modes of the Penitente hymns, the *alabados,* and the heretical *alumbrado* religious sects, whose orgiastic appropriation of divine approval for personal satisfaction had brought the wrath of the Inquisition down on them like the temple roof on Sampson. Church officials, especially those of the Inquisition, were concerned that some illegitimate forms of unorthodox beliefs and practices might be taking root in faraway places difficult to administer and preside over. Vigilance was the order of the day to corral unauthorized modes of conduct. We also wonder, though, if the local priests took some liberties in checking so-called prohibitive comportment thanks to this ambience of surveillance.

5. Miguel de Quintana: From Colonizer and Scribe to Defendant

Miguel [Mathías] de Quintana [y Valdés Altamirano], at the young age of sixteen in Mexico City, joined a caravan of colonists, part of the second group of settlers to participate in Vargas's reconquest of New Mexico (Preston and Esquibel, *The Royal Road: El Camino Real from Mexico City to Santa Fe,* 151–53), making his inauspicious entry into the kingdom of New Mexico the following year. This was at the conclusion of the Pueblo Revolt of 1680 that had driven the Spaniards out for thirteen years, most settling temporarily in El Paso and awaiting the subsequent reconquest. Quintana was recruited by the viceroy Cristóbal de Velasco and Fray Francisco Farfán among one of 67 families or 275 resettlers,[33] together with a sizable contingent of soldiers[34] who later joined forces in El Paso with returning exiles from the Indian expulsion—totaling no more than "800 souls."[35] He was accompanied by his young bride, Gertrudis de Trujillo, together with his new in-laws: father-in-law Nicolás Moreno de Trujillo, his wife María Ruiz de Aguilar, and their three daughters (María de Guadalupe, Juana Teresa, and Micaela Antonia). Originally from a middle-class family from Mexico City with some noble lineage on his mother's side, Quintana's compelling motives for embarking on such a venture were probably an attempt to improve his and his family's fortune, a desire to raise their social status, and an urge to make a fresh start on the dangerous but alluringly unknown frontier.[36] No documents regarding Quintana's life prior to his experience in New Mexico exist, except for baptismal records, although we do know his family provided him with a formal education and some relatives and family friends enjoyed socioeconomic stature in Mexico City. Quintana seems to have risked this comfortable social environment for the captivating life of the frontier, thus demonstrating a degree of courage and determination as he set out with his young wife to begin a new life.

Considerable mystery surrounds Miguel de Quintana's true identity, which requires explicating and unraveling. This is partly attributable to the repetition of names among his siblings, Gabriel García Márquez–style, the unreliability of record-keeping, people's inexact memory, and the tradition of guesstimating age. Miguel came from a family with two sets of brothers and sisters because his father, don José de Quintana Peralta from Mexico City, remarried when his mother, doña Nicolasa de Valdés Altamirano, a native of Toluca, died around 1681, possibly from childbirth complications. There is no way of knowing from the sketchy records if any of these events in his family influenced his decision to move north. According to José A. Esquibel, a pivotal genealogist of the Quintana family, the first set of siblings consisted of: Sebastián Francisco (1670), José Miguel (baptized March 24, 1672, probably a week after his birth, as dictated by custom), Juan I (1673), Miguel Mathías (baptized on November 28, 1677, and more than likely born around November 21), José (baptized on November 12, 1678), María de San Diego (1679), and Juan II (1681) (Esquibel and Colligan, *Spanish Recolonization of New Mexico: An Account of the Families Recruited at Mexico City in 1693*, 564–65). The other siblings from his stepmother, Feliciana de Andrada[e] Ramos, were: Francisco Antonio (1683), Joseph (1685), Manuela Ursula (1688), and Miguel (1689). The issue, then, is which one is the true Miguel de Quintana, as he was commonly known and referred to in all the later documents from northern New Mexico?[37] The answer is unfortunately not clear-cut because arguments can be made in favor of at least two of the brothers. Varying references compound the confusion. For example, José Miguel is a likely candidate, as we originally claimed, because being born in 1672 would make him twenty-one (instead of twenty-two as he is described) at the time of signing on Vargas's muster list.[38] The official list from 1693 describes the real Miguel in the following manner, though one should keep in mind that factual precision was not a science, in light of the liberties taken to meet quotas of eligible colonists.

> Miguel de Quintana, son of José, native of Mexico, twenty-two years old, able-bodied, round face, small forehead, large eyes, and a mole in the chin.[39] (Twitchell, "Spanish Colonization," 36)

The true identity becomes clouded when we realize two brothers shared the first name José, one born in 1672 and the other in 1678. Nothing guarantees that the first José Miguel, the older of the two, would have the edge to consider such a drastic move. Besides, it is believed that the younger one later followed his brother Miguel to New Mexico, probably in 1695, where he, too, lived for the rest of his life, married Antonia Luján in 1696, and made a livelihood mainly in Santa Fe and Bernalillo, just as Miguel did, as a scribe. For José Miguel to be the "mad poet," then, he would have had to drop his first name to become known only as "Miguel," which would consequently complicate his namesake with his other brother Miguel Mathías.

More than likely the real poet from Santa Cruz is none other than Miguel Mathías, born in 1677, according to the baptismal records at Ascención church in Mexico City.

> On February twenty-eighth of sixteen hundred and seventy-seven as authorized by Father Semo I baptized Miguel Mathías, son of José de Quintana and Doña Nicolasa de Valdez [*sic*] Altamirano. His godfather was Captain D. Agustín Flores Urrutia de Vergara, Gentleman of the Order of Santiago. Chief Constable of the Tribunal Dr. Antonio de la Torre y Arrellano (Rubric)[40]

Since the custom of dropping the second name was more common than dropping the first, his final identity as simply Miguel de Quintana—also eliminating the string of surnames that indicated a degree of nobility—does not seem farfetched, especially in New Mexico, where pretentiousness would seem absurd and impractical in a stark place where everyone knew everyone else. The aforementioned discrepancy about his age in the muster list of 1693 seems at first difficult to reconcile if in fact he was only sixteen, but reliability is questionable. In a hearing before Governor Vargas in June 1698 where Miguel signed his name, he declared his age to be "twenty-four, more or less" (Spanish Archives of New Mexico, Series II, no. 71, frames 640–43), which would suggest a birth date of 1674, somewhere between José's and Miguel's. On another occasion on November 8, 1734, when the chief inquisitor from Santa Fe interrogated Miguel, his age was estimated at "fifty-six years old, more or less"—the only reference to his age in the Inquisition documents—approximating Miguel Mathías's birth date of 1677 by one year. Coincidence or not, when he died on April 9, 1748, his listed age in the burial records, "seventy, give or take a few," is again closer to Miguel Mathías's (1677), but José Miguel figures as too old.[41] Even his wife was cited as being fifteen in the muster list although her baptism was on June 23, 1675, making her eighteen in 1693. Determination of exact age obviously operated loosely in those times because fewer rites of passage were dictated by age.

Other considerations can support the Miguel Mathías theory. Since married status was a requirement for joining the ranks of colonists and his future in-laws, including many other relatives, had already enlisted, it seems plausible that young Miguel either lied about his age—if an age requirement was in place—or stretched the truth a little in order to become doubly eligible himself, based on status and age. In any case, Miguel's motivation might have stemmed from one or two reasons: to participate in this life-changing event of historic implications, or because his love for Gertrudis,[42] whom he married about a month[43] before the caravan departed, was too strong to risk losing her. The marriage may have been conveniently timed to keep both his dreams intact.

Excitement about great feats was still in the air in the 1690s, even though the peak period for discoveries and explorations of mythic proportions was past. The power of publicity and propaganda, however, cannot be underestimated when Carlos de Sigüenza y Góngora published his impassioned edition of *Mercurio Volante* in Mexico City precisely in 1693, "a suitably laudatory account of the longed-for recovery of New Mexico" (Kessell, Hendricks, and Dodge, *To the Royal Crown Restored*, 6). It invoked epic deeds while embellishing some points and polishing Vargas's "own tortured syntax and military preoccupations," thus rendering the rhetoric of colonization more palatable to those who already possessed some social standing they dared not risk. As the editors Kessell, Hendricks, and Dodge explain further:

> Though the publication of the *Mercurio Volante* was not an element in the early recruitment of potential colonists for New Mexico, it may have served to bolster the confidence of those who had already

> decided to enlist and sway the opinion of some who were wavering. (*To the Royal Crown Restored*, 6)

Aside from his recent marriage, another prominent reason contributing to Miguel's decision was the extended family with whom they would travel, including both relatives and family friends.

> This marriage placed Quintana within the largest kinship group to travel among the colonists from Mexico City to Santa Fe, which included the families of Ansures, Atienza (Atencio), Fernández de Atienza, and Moreno de Trujillo. (Esquibel, "The People of the Camino Real: A Genealogical Appendix," 163)

Without suggesting that the caravan of colonists was one big family, the evidence clearly reveals common bloodlines in many cases, for nine distinct kinship groups represented nearly half the total number of recruited colonists (Esquibel, "Mexico City to Santa Fe," 7). This was a social network that potentially prescribed greater benefits, resulting in a unique pattern of colonization described as a "colony of cousins" (Kessell, Hendricks, and Dodge, *To the Royal Crown Restored*, 9).

Although concrete evidence is lacking to explain Quintana's sudden uprooting, his recent marriage suggests that the young couple was enticed by the royal decree's offer of land, a 300-peso subsidy, special privileges—such as being granted the title *hidalgo*, an official title carrying a higher social status—and transportation free of charge.[44] Both more than likely belonged to the small, seventeenth-century middle class of modest means, judging from their parents' position in the social circles of the Mexican capital and Quintana's own formal education. Neither was associated with the Mexican aristocratic class, an automatic disqualification for the expedition, nor did they fit the profile of racially mixed people, those with Indian ancestry, who were excluded. The basic requirements he and his wife met consisted of being of Spanish descent, legitimately married, law-abiding citizens, and of good Christian character. The organizers' stated preference for selecting craftsmen and those who could build and create things raises the question of what practical trade Quintana had to offer, but his writing skills almost assuredly gave him a skill that could be put to good use.[45]

After many delays, contretemps, and complications, the arduous trek on the Camino Real through the central plateau of Mexico finally ended when the settlers reached New Mexico successfully in 1694, whereupon the tired travelers eagerly anticipated laying claim to plots of land or land grants by virtue of royal promises. The first order of business, according to Vargas, involved reinstating Santa Fe as the capital in order to fortify strategically its social, economic, and military position for the reconquest to take full effect. Given the delicate balance of diplomacy required to avoid alienating the local Native American populace, a group of settlers, the Quintanas included, was forced to wait patiently before finally proceeding to found another important political center, thereby expanding and solidifying Spanish dominance further north.

With due pomp and ceremony, including speeches and public proclamations, La Villa Nueva de Santa Cruz de la Cañada de Españoles Mexicanos del Rey Nuestro Señor Carlos Segundo (the New Villa of Santa Cruz de la Cañada of Mexican Spaniards under the king, our lord, Charles II),[46] today known as Santa Cruz, was founded on April 22, 1695, just north of Santa Fe.[47] It was to become the young couple's permanent home until their deaths. After Santa Fe, the Villa Nueva de la Santa Cruz de la Cañada enjoyed the distinction of being the most prominent villa in New Mexico through 1848. Its importance in the early stages of recolonization was as headquarters of the northern district of the territory—also considered the edge of "civilization"—located close to only semipacified Indian country. In this valley of widely dispersed agricultural settlements, the Quintanas built a simple dwelling, plotted their allotted land grant, plowed the soil, grazed their animals, and built acequias for irrigation.

Confronted with the daily struggles of hard pioneer life, they initially managed to eke out an existence by farming, thanks to a few farm animals, rudimentary equipment for cultivating the land, and the *fanegas* of corn and wheat the original royal decree granted them.[48] Most ranch families in the region also raised cows and a flock of sheep. As part of the livestock distribution to the settlers of Villa Nueva de Santa Cruz de la Cañada, the Quintanas in 1697 were granted "4.5 varas of wool, 3.75 of baize, 9 mantas, 20 sheep, 2 cows, 1 bull."[49]

Quintana's responsibilities in establishing his rural settlement, as his foremost priority, took up most of his time and energy; he later added a second job as town scribe beginning around 1705. For a while he figures simply in the period's documentation as one more settler in the area, engaged entirely in farming, thus fulfilling his obligations to the crown under the contract for resettling the area. No detailed portrait exists of his life during this period, just bits and pieces concealed in the early archives from which a sketch can be drawn. His signature, for example, figures notably on many official documents ranging from banns of marriage, legal suits, or as a witness. Most of his perceptible activity exhibits a quality of officialdom, rarely displaying individual reactions to show his personality or psychological makeup. His participation in town life, on the other hand, reveals a central community member with important political ties, such as when he joined twenty-nine other Santa Cruz residents on

Fig. 4. Farms, hills, and distant mountains at Santa Cruz de la Cañada, as seen from the church about 1980. Courtesy of Clark A. Colahan.

September 25, 1695, to petition Vargas in an emergency meeting, demanding a greater distribution of food supplies, livestock, and seeds in order to survive the winter.[50] Upon closer examination, what begins to form is the impression of an outspoken person whose deep sense of fairness moved him toward action, even if it meant confronting figures of high stature such as Governor Vargas, against a backdrop of social instability, danger, and uncertainty for the colony.

Later in June 1698, another event sheds further light on others' high regard for Quintana. As a well-established settler and head of a large family, he was selected as one of the colonists summoned to provide testimony at a hearing concerning Governor Vargas's administration. He demonstrated restraint and equanimity by not taking sides, as many did. Six years later, with Villa Nueva de Santa Cruz de la Cañada in disarray and in danger of disintegration, a number of residents met with Vargas, partly expressing their frustration, but principally to revalidate their land grants on February 13 and 14, 1704. In the survey Vargas conducted to assess both continuing occupancy and abandonments by the 1695 residents (and of the latter there were many), Quintana is well accounted for as a stable permanent resident of the community, two necessary conditions that made possible his growing social stature.[51]

Quintana's personal profile began to broaden little by little by the turn of the century when his activities and roles multiplied. His lifestyle took a dramatic change in 1704, with favorable news of his appointment as scribe for both local government and the ecclesiastic court of Santa Cruz, but his in-laws' petition to return, disillusioned, to Mexico on March 24, 1705, quickly overshadowed this. Documents contained in the Archives of the Archdiocese of Santa Fe support his expanded role in local affairs, especially serving in the capacities of witness and scribe for many prenuptial investigations, called *diligencias matrimoniales*, the clergy conducted in Santa Cruz, occasionally in Santa Fe, and three times in Albuquerque. His involvement extended from 1704 well into 1736, to the ripe age of fifty-eight, "more or less."[52] In addition, his signature also figured in a number of civil cases.[53]

Despite this apparent change of fortune or better yet, opportunities, his main preoccupation continued to be what he termed "extreme poverty," constantly struggling to provide for his growing family, which eventually totaled up to ten children.[54] Making a living was difficult for almost everyone. Colonists at the time of the crop failure in the late 1690s were "obliged to eat dog, horse, and mule meat; toasted skins; & foul-smelling weeds and grasses" (Esquibel and Colligan, *The Spanish Recolonization of New Mexico*, 12). Such concern seemed to demand Quintana's full attention, so much so that it figured prominently in a suit he brought against a neighbor, Capt. Joseph Trujillo, "for a theft of two horses by Indians, one of whom was his [Trujillo's] servant."[55] The incident represents a most telling glimpse into his circumstances, certain attitudes of justice and honesty, and his knowledge of frontier law. In a well-articulated legal statement, he appealed to the authorities for rightful restitution, given that "eran mis pies y manos los otros (dichos?) dos caballos" (the other [said?] two horses were my hands and feet).[56] He added: "Pues después de hallarme como me hallo, cargado de siete hijos, tenía en dichos dos caballos el alivio de conducir un poco de bastimento y leña y salir a mis diligencias" (Since I am in the situation where I find myself [i.e., extreme poverty], burdened with seven children, those two horses provided me some relief by carrying a few supplies and firewood and allowing me to run errands). Visibly fixated on his family, he repeated the "burden" of his many children at least twice. No final outcome can be ascertained in the archives, but presumably he won handily. What emerges unmistakably is the hint of an eloquent writer who uses language with considerable legal sophistication and the ability to convey his sense that justice is on his side, that of the victim.

Once the rustic pomp and grandiloquence of the reconquest faded into the routine details of implanting the necessary colonial infrastructure, life on the frontier became a round of activities focused on a hand-to-mouth existence. "The level of subsistence was so minimal as to leave little margin for experimentation or chance. The colonists held on by their fingernails. The result was a cultural crystallization" (Bunting, *Early Architecture of New Mexico*, 4). Such dire living conditions during the colonial period have been well chronicled by many researchers, but we sometimes overlook the degree of poverty that consistently plagued the settlers, oftentimes exacerbated by the natural elements. One poignant, unforgettable example involves the occasions when they found themselves eating leather as a last resort. Besides, conditions worsened before improving, consequently putting a great deal of pressure on the fragile social fiber. It is no wonder that historian Hubert Howe Bancroft remarked somewhat disdainfully about the overall climate: "From 1700 New Mexico settled into that monotonously uneventful career of inert and non-progressive existence" (*History of Arizona and New Mexico, 1530–1888, 225).* The primitive economy, based on agriculture and stock-raising, and the region's isolation did not, however, imply complete stagnation. More recent historiography has corrected the tendency to dismiss the period, attempting instead to unearth information in order to better understand its nuances and dynamics.

Such a remote life of hardship demanded sustained, determined action, not simple resignation, for the colonists to survive. Quintana clearly embodied this spirit of self-reliance, perseverance, and mettle in his remote farming community. His resourcefulness and gumption exemplified the kind of backbone required to endure such conditions. The governing of new towns, including Santa Cruz, put a premium on the organizational skills needed to create functional local administrations. Similarly, individuals with any skill in writing were valuable commodities on an illiterate frontier bereft of schools. Edna Fergusson points to lack of education as one of the conditions that plagued the region and directly affected its development: "In 1681 [*sic*] only 3 out of 147 recruits for the reconquest of New Mexico could sign the muster roll. Of New Mexican women appearing before the Inquisition in Mexico, none could write her name" (*New Mexico: A Pageant of Three Peoples,* 190).

In the midst of such a rustic setting, with fellow ranchers and former militiamen, Quintana was one of the few who could claim a formal education in Mexico City. It opened up new opportunities for him to supplement his family's earnings. He was apparently quite capable of conducting record-keeping duties, carrying out politically sensitive activities, and filling posts that were usually reserved for the clergy and judicial bureaucrats. As Fray Angélico Chávez so aptly notes: "His clear even script and his adept use of the language in writing attest to the fact [of his suitability for being a court clerk]" ("Mad Poet," 11). He must have seemed ideal for a position that otherwise might have been hard to staff: *notario*, or court clerk, for local *alcaldes mayores* (district administrators with extensive political and judicial authority). As clerk and secretary to such an official, he had a direct hand in presiding over local affairs.

Unsalaried and serving at the governor's pleasure, the alcalde mayor had wide powers, including the following:

> He administered petty justice, settled minor disputes over land and water, supervised the use of Indian labor, rallied the local militia, and helped the friars maintain discipline in the missions—any or all of which could be turned to his own profit and that of the governor. An *alcalde mayor* could be the missionary's best friend or his worse enemy. (Kessell, *Kiva, Cross, and Crown*, 177)

In addition, Quintana held the post of clerk of the ecclesiastic court (not to be confused with the Inquisition), an honor contributing further to his social prominence. He was, by this time, well positioned to gain an inside view of the local workings of church and crown and was clearly well versed in civil, criminal, and religious matters. He was probably a key player in the politics of Villa Nueva de Santa Cruz de la Cañada, and his signature can be found on a variety of official documents going between Santa Fe and his adopted town. Despite the exclusive circles within which he moved, and the measure of influence he must have acquired, he does not seem to have fallen victim to arrogance. He consistently referred to himself as a "humble servant" of God, his community, and his family, and the phrase strikes the reader as more than a formula or pose. That impression is all the more striking when one knows from depositions in the Inquisition case that his social prominence was more than just official. He also became much sought after by his neighbors for his multiple talents and services. He was often consulted about both legal questions and personal matters, acting as notary public and public scribe. He composed prayers for personal situations, such as invitations for weddings and eulogies for wakes, and sometimes worked as playwright for parish and community dramatic productions, writing coloquios for Christmas and other religious holidays.

The accusations against him sent to the Inquisition in 1732 revealed another literary ability: he was credited with the composition of mystical verse. For all these reasons, Chávez argued that the writing of such important popular works as the traditional Christmas play, *Los pastores*, or at least one version of it, can plausibly be attributed to his pen ("Mad Poet," 11).[57] These are indeed words with which to reckon. Quintana therefore stands out among his peers as a landmark figure for his special place in literary history, having enjoyed considerable importance and recognition derived from his literary and legal activities.

6. Shepherds' Plays

Yrigoien's testimony that Quintana had a reputation for piety in his writings leaves open the question of what other sorts of religious pieces besides coloquios he may have composed. That he said he had been prohibited specifically from writing Christmas plays, however, further strengthens the argument that the Franciscans viewed him as an interloper on their professional domain. Juan Rael has documented the origin of the Mexican shepherds' plays in the missionary colleges of the central highlands.[58] They were a characteristic tool for conversion the friars took throughout the north of New Spain. While the evolution of the texts in New Mexico leaves no doubt that at some point over the centuries lay persons made local changes and additions—and Quintana seems to have done complete new adaptations of his own—these plays began as performances the Franciscans composed and organized. The pastorela by Father Florencio Ibáñez confirms that this was still the case in the younger California missions as late as the beginning of the nineteenth century.

A native of the province of Aragón, Ibáñez worked seventeen years at the missionary college in Querétaro, as well as serving as choirmaster at the College of San Fernando in Mexico City. Volunteering for the missions in Alta California, he directed Soledad from 1803 until his death in 1818. He enjoyed teaching the soldiers to read and write, as well as instructing the neophytes in music. Owen Francis Da Silva, OFM, writes: "The welcome he gave his friend, Governor Arrillaga, with vocal and instrumental music, and with verses composed by himself, has come down in history.[59] He is also remembered as a dramatist. His *Pastorela*, or Nativity play, was a great favorite in Old California, and was usually performed on Christmas Eve."[60] Hubert Howe Bancroft provided further evidence of the play's popularity: "Pío Pico [who was the last Mexican governor of California] used to play the part of Bato, the chief shepherd, and the [wealthy] Vallejo's frequently took part. But the best player, and the one who used to get most applause, was Jacinto Rodríguez, who used to go to the seashore to practice his part, uttering fearful shouts, and making all kinds of crazy gestures, to the great amusement of the boys who hid nearby and watched him."[61] It is reasonable to suppose that Ibáñez's friendship with Governor Arrillaga and the prominence of his play were paralleled to some extent in New Mexico by the position of esteem that Quintana held. This sort of social as well as religious influence held by one of their parishioners, instead of one of the missionary priests themselves, may well have been another source of anxiety for Sopeña and Yrigoien.

7. Hispanic Mysticism as Liberation

While there is no reason to question Quintana's sincere belief in the authenticity of the heavenly voices that encouraged him, still it must be admitted that this new situation did offer two very practical advantages in his struggle for freedom to write. First, he was now in possession of a higher and traditional authorization allowing him to disregard the directives of the parish priests. The lives of Spanish mystics like St. Teresa and St. John of the Cross, whom the Inquisition investigated but later vindicated (something that did not prevent their canonization later), were well known in New Spain. The church at Santa Cruz, for example, constructed from 1733 to 1744 and so contemporary with Quintana's writings, has had on its altar screen, very likely from the time of its original dedication, four Mexican paintings flanking the central crucifix; one of these shows St. Teresa receiving inspiration from the dove of the Holy Spirit. The possibility of direct communion with God and the other heavenly personages was, and still is, a living part of Hispanic Roman Catholicism. New Mexico folklore records the frequent intervention of the saints in daily life in a visible and talkative manner, as Fray Angélico Chávez's stories remind us.

When seen in the context of traditional New Mexican Roman Catholicism, Quintana was correct in insisting he was not a heretic, but, as he said, "a Catholic Christian." Even most of the defiant elements in his writings, and certainly nearly all his ideas and ways of expressing them, are squarely within the Franciscan variety of Roman Catholicism established in New Mexico. The Franciscan origin of most of the ideas and images in his writings becomes clear by a comparison with those of two mystics associated with that order whose ideas were well known and respected in New Mexico at the time: St. Francis himself and a seventeenth-century Spanish nun known as María de Jesús de Agreda (1602–65). One need read only these two authors to find echoes of most of the images and concepts Quintana used.

Probably the most basic characteristic doctrine of Franciscanism is the importance of poverty and humility. St. Francis was known as the *poverello*, the poor little fellow, and his humility was expressed in statements like, "Those saintly and most holy eyes of God have not seen a greater, stupider, more despicable sinner among all the wicked people than me. . . ."[62] Similarly, Quintana often referred to his poverty and used the same word to describe himself, *un pobrecito.* He was also quick to recognize, at least in general terms, his own sinfulness, as when he said, "Soy un hombre ingrato y pecador" (I am an ungrateful and sinful man; 134). Both writers, in order to convey their own insignificance, used the familiar comparison of themselves to a little worm, taken from the Psalms.

Poverty and humility, in the Franciscan world view, are not allowed to go without divine reward. Apart from what is received in heaven, St. Francis and similar mystics talk about divine "favors" granted in this life, tokens of future glory, experiences such as St. Francis's own stigmata. The ritual commemorating that miracle includes the phrase "Francis, a poor and humble man, enters into heaven rich and honored by celestial hymns."[63] Quintana, who frequently referred to his divinely inspired verses as favors, immediately articulated in the first extant poem from this period of conflict the same idea, that his verses are a reward: "Es locución muy segura / la que el gran poder te ha dado / por humilde, que al humilde / Dios se inclina y se ha inclinado" (Very sure are the words that the great power has given you because of your humility, for God draws near, and has drawn near, to the humble; 122).

Individuals who feel themselves to be so favored often consider themselves to be a vehicle for the direct communication of God's will to men. St. Francis, like Quintana, threatened with divine punishment those who did not heed the words or instruction that God entrusted to him to convey to others. In his "Letter to All the Faithful," St. Francis underlined that that same document should be read and obeyed, while the illiterate should have it read to them often, since "those who fail to do this shall be held to account for it before the judgment seat of Christ at the last day."[64] Quintana, whose fundamental concern is writing and being known as a writer, naturally emphasized this point, too. At times, often in the earlier poems, he was optimistic that Yrigoien would recognize the importance of his writings and reward them: "Podrá ser, Miguel, que el padre, / a vista de tus letritas, / te dé alguna recompensa / de azúcar y unas tablillas" (It may be, Miguel, that the father, seeing your writings, may reward you with sugar and some candy; 126). As the situation dragged on, he looked more to God to vindicate him and confound his enemies: "Cree que tus letras han de causar a los que te han mofado horror, confusión" (Believe that your verses will bring horror and confusion to those who have mocked you; 166).

Because giving such importance to one's writings suggests a proclamation of self-worth at odds with the ideal of complete humility, we find the idea of the writer as only a weak, obedient instrument in the hands of his master. St. Francis's saying, "Make me an instrument of peace," is well known. Quintana referred to himself as a "docile instrument" several times, sometimes expanding the phrase so as to bring out the underlying idea of God's power acting through him: "Su divina majestad . . . se vale de los instrumentos más débiles y de los pobrecitos a quien el mundo abate y persigue por instrumentos de su Divino Justicia" (His divine majesty . . . makes use of the weakest instruments and the poor people trampled underfoot and persecuted by the world to be instruments of his divine judgment; 167).

Three other important elements of Roman Catholicism to which St. Francis gave special importance were worship of the Virgin Mary, compassion for Christ's suffering in the crucifixion, and reading the Psalms. He viewed the Virgin as the celestial advocate of his order and prescribed daily recital of the Order of the Blessed Virgin Mary for the members. Two of her traditional attributes were important for Quintana's writings. First, she is the maternal comforter of the poor, the weak, and the miserable. Quoting, as he defensively said, "hymns, psalms, and verses," Quintana wrote in her voice: "Soy la madre de esperanza, / soy llave y puerta del cielo, / soy refugio donde hallan / los afligidos consuelo" (I am the mother of hope, I am the key and door to heaven, I am the refuge where the afflicted find consolation; 129).

Second, the Virgin is the advocate who intercedes at the gates of hell to save sinners who, in spite of their faults, have kept a special love and devotion for her. This intervention appears often in Spanish literature, all the way from Gonzalo de Berceo's drunken monk in the fourteenth century to José Zorilla's nineteenth-century Don Juan, whose soul, in a romantic adaptation of the belief, is snatched from eternal punishment through the intercession of a pure woman with a true love for him. Quintana, whose rebellion against the local representatives of the church caused him anxiety on the question of whether he would be saved or damned, often took comfort in recalling this role of the Virgin. For example, defending himself against the reproach of having dropped out of the activities of the Third Order of St. Francis, he wrote: "No es menester ser Tercero para salvarse, que es error en muchos y falta de fe pues pudieron conocer que con ser cofrades de la suprema emperatriz de los cielos, María Santísima del Carmen, tienen el más fuerte y poderoso escudo contra todo el poder del infierno, si del se saben aprovechar, pues es de fe que el que se acoge a su dulcísima sombra y con fe la llama pueda perecer" (It is not necessary to belong to the Third Order to be saved, which is an error and a lack of faith in many, since they could have known that by belonging to the confraternity of the supreme empress of heaven, most Holy Mary of Carmen, they have the strongest and most powerful shield against all the power of hell, if only they know how to make use of it, since the faith teaches that whoever takes refuge in her most sweet shadow and calls to her with faith cannot perish; 146).

Franciscan compassion for Christ's suffering was expressed in the creation of the ritual of the Way of the Cross, which became particularly important in New Mexico, where the practice was standard in Franciscan churches and originally restricted to them.[65] In addition, St. Francis wrote a liturgy centered on the custom, known as the Office of the Passion. Similarly, Quintana defended the rightness of his visions by stressing that they were induced by his meditation on the cross: "No solicito estos afectos. Ellos solitos se me infunden, y no me puedo contener cuando miro a su Majestad Santísima en una cruz y a su dulcísima madre al pie de la cruz, y se me ofrecen estos pensamientos" (I do not seek these feelings. They themselves come over me, and I cannot control myself when I see His Most holy Majesty on a cross and his sweetest mother at the foot of the cross, and these thoughts just come to me; 134).

The reading of the Psalms is a major component of the liturgical Order of the Blessed Virgin Mary, and this in itself contributed to their being known by members of the three Franciscan Orders. They were also specifically included as a major element in the original rule St. Francis prepared for the Third Order: "Those who know the Psalter are to say the *Deus in nomine tuo* and the *Beati immaculati* up to the *Legem ponem* for Prime, and the other psalms of the hours, with the *Glory be to the Father*; but when they do not attend church, they are to say for matins the psalms the church says or any eighteen psalms" (*The Writings of St. Francis of Assisi*, 17). St. Francis's interest in the psalter was further demonstrated by the nature of his Office of the Passion, which, while commemorating God's sacrifice for humankind, contains a large number of quotations from the psalter on another related theme: "I am surrounded and oppressed by unjust and mocking men, but I trust in God to defeat my enemies and vindicate my cause" (*The Writings of St. Francis*, 17). Two examples follow: "To all of my foes I am an object of reproach, a laughing stock to my neighbors, and a dread to my friends" (Psalms 30:12), and "Holy father, be not far from me; hasten to my aid" (Psalms 21:20).

Many of Quintana's fears for his safety and reputation, likewise expressed in the first person, can be found among St. Francis's selection of psalms. These textual echoes, in combination with frequent encouragement to trust in the Lord and a repetitious insistence on the other basic themes, makes the impression the two works produce very similar. Given Quintana's feeling that by himself he was weak and defenseless against oppressive treatment a jealous parish priest inflicted on him, it is not surprising that he emphasized two of the same images from the psalms used by St. Francis: God as the just judge and his punishing sword. After the frightening visit of the Inquisition to his house, he struck back in the letter to Father Juan de la Cruz with defiant words, as in this threat placed in God's mouth: "Y el que a tu casa o persona / se osare y fuere atrevido, / tendrá de mi fuerte brazo / un riguroso castigo" (And whoever may dare to make bold against your person or your house will have a vigorous punishment from my strong arm; 165). This verbal counterattack concludes and summarizes in strong Biblical language: ". . . que ni lo justo ante Dios dejará de ser justo, ni lo injusto injusto, porque Dios tiene espada para todos"

(Nor will what is just cease being just before God, nor what is unjust, unjust, because God has a sword for everyone; 168).

The one quote that Quintana identifies by author is also from the psalter: "Y se me ofrecen estos pensamientos que dice el Santo Rey David, que por no hablar se le envejecieron los huesos" (And these thoughts come to me, for the holy King David says that when he did not speak his bones grew old; 134) (Psalms 32:3). Finally, one of Quintana's most striking metaphors, while not taken from the Bible, finds a stylistic echo in one of the psalms in which God promises to overcome one's enemies. In describing Guerrero and Yrigoien when they invaded the security of his home, he wrote that they were "vestidos de sus pasiones" (dressed in their passions; 167). Psalms 132:18 reads: "I will dress his enemies in confusion, but his crown will flower over him."

In addition to these materials taken from the worship of Mary, compassion for Christ's sufferings, and the Psalms, Quintana's writings also relied extensively on three other religious concepts and their corresponding symbols that are practically universal yet have special importance in Franciscanism and Spanish mysticism. One is the comparison of the love between God and man to the love between man and woman. The Biblical "Song of Songs," interpreted since the Middle Ages as an expression of God's love for the church, became an important influence on the mystics of sixteenth- and seventeenth-century Spain. One of the most beautiful literary expressions by a Spanish writer is St. John of the Cross's poem "Canción Dos: La noche oscura" ("Song Two: The Dark Night"). In these famous verses the soul is a young woman in love who waits for the corporal senses (which are compared to a household at the end of the evening) to become quiet, so that she can secretly go out to be alone with her beloved. St. Francis also wrote: "How holy it is, how beautiful and lovable, to have in heaven a bridegroom" (*The Writings of St. Francis*, 96). The long-standing Roman Catholic custom of nuns being said to marry Christ is also related. Quintana inherited this tradition at a time when it had already generated standard figures of speech in Spanish religious writing. Though he did not develop the idea extensively, he still referred to God in phrases such as "Jesús, tu Dios y dulce esposo" (Jesus, your God and sweet husband; and "del amante más supremo" (the highest lover; 131).

A second doctrine the Franciscans stressed was the age-old idea of God as the Creator and the world as his creation; writers in the Order became accustomed to using the word "creatures" in the sense of "persons." His "Song of Brother Sun" uses the word "creature" in its opening line, and the verses are, as they are still called among Franciscans, a "hymn in praise of all the creatures" (Corstanje, *The Third Order for Our Time*, 79). Quintana sometimes followed the convention of using "creature" simply as another word for people, but much more often the word appears in the context of the idea that Quintana is part of the divine creation and that the Creator, in his love and wisdom, does not expect his creatures to do anything beyond the capacity He has given them. This was the defense of his refusal to confess that he most emphasized and that was probably responsible for the label of *proposiciones* that is to say, "heresy," that appears on the title page of the Inquisition's investigation of the case. Nevertheless, the idea was a logical extension—even if an ingenious, unorthodox, and institutionally unacceptable one as Quintana applied it—of the fundamental Christian concept that the world has a loving Creator. Even today it can touch a chord in the reader, while making us smile at the nimble wit it displays.

Quintana used a third Franciscan element, the universal symbol of light, time and again as a synonym for divine inspiration. It was a special favorite of both St. Francis and Celano, a disciple and his first biographer, and they used it with a variety of meanings. The latter's description of the saint's entrance into heaven is a notable example:

> Then, when many brothers had gathered about, whose father and leader he was, and while they were standing reverently at his side awaiting his blessed death and happy end, his most holy soul was freed from his body and received into the abyss of light, and his body fell asleep in the Lord. . . .
>
> O how glorious is this saint, whose soul a disciple saw ascend into heaven, fair as the moon, bright as the sun and as he ascended upon a white cloud he was shining most gloriously! O truly you are a light of the world, shining in the Church of Christ more splendidly than the sun; behold, you have withdrawn the rays of your light now and, withdrawing into the kingdom of light, you have exchanged company with us miserable ones for company with the angels and saints![66]

In trying to define the boundaries of the relationship between Quintana's writings and Franciscanism, one cannot overlook the undeniable similarities between the personalities of the two men. The expression of strong emotions through poetry and drama was necessary to both. Just as Quintana's life revolved around such writing, for which he was willing to face punishment from the church and self-doubts about his salvation, St. Francis, who found the poetry of French chivalry attractive in his adolescence, became known through his poems as the troubadour of peace. While St. Francis did not write for the simple medieval theater of the period, for important moments in his life he did organize dramatic scenes (complete with audience) in which he was the principal actor, such as his public renunciation of his earthly father and the moments before his death, arranged with all the elements of a mystery play.

Both men were visionaries who felt that God spoke to them with guidance and comfort. One of the best-known instances in the saint's life occurred when, as a young man, he heard a voice from the crucifix in San Damiano order him: "Francis, go and repair my house" (Corstanje, *The Third Order for Our Time*, 74). This instance of direct communication with God was only one in a lifelong series of such experiences that must be considered an essential part of his life and his heritage. A twentieth-century Franciscan leader who has come to grips with this issue is Auspicius van Corstanje, who in 1974 while director of the Third Order in Holland, wrote words affirming the authenticity of St. Francis's mysticism. His statement gives some extra measure of dignity to the saint's suffering New Mexican follower: "Surely he must have been in personal contact with this Son. He must have been touched by the fire of the Spirit. For anyone to deny this is to make of this humble man a pathological liar who finally went to wrack and ruin physically and mentally by his own hallucinations" (Corstanje, *The Third Order for Our Time*, 50).

This question of how best to view mystic experiences brings us to the New Mexican legend of María de Jesús de Agreda, a Spanish nun of the Conceptionist Order, one very similar to the Franciscan Poor Clares. Born some seventy years before Quintana, she is best known as the author of a voluminous biography of the Virgin, which Mary supposedly dictated to her in visions. She was an extraordinary woman in other, less surprising ways as well: abbess at twenty-five by papal dispensation, highly influential friend and correspondent of Felipe IV of Spain for twenty years, and, after her death, vigorously proposed twice by the Spanish church for canonization, efforts that resulted in her being accorded the title of Venerable. In the opening years of the twenty-first century her cause is again gaining momentum. It was through the visionary aspect of her life, however, that she became part of New Mexico's history.

From 1620 to 1623 María, who never left her hometown in northern Castile, told her confessors that, in answer to her prayers, she was being angelically transported to New Mexico to urge the Indians there to seek out the Franciscan missionaries for baptism. Her sisters in the convent, seeing her remain in ecstatic trances for hours and believing she was simultaneously in America, also helped spread the fame of these miraculous bilocations. In 1628 the news reached Alonso de Benavides, head of the Franciscans and agent of the Inquisition in New Mexico. Although the names of the tribes María mentioned were unknown to him, he thought immediately of the Jumanos, a West Texas tribe who annually came to the Río Grande Valley to trade buffalo hides, invariably asking for a friar to be sent with them to convert their people.

When Benavides asked them why they made the request, they described being visited by a lady dressed in blue. They compared her to a portrait of a Poor Clare nun the Franciscans had on hand, a seemingly supernatural figure who for some years had often descended from heaven, urging them to bring the Spaniards to their lands. As they said she was still paying the tribe visits, two friars were immediately dispatched to accompany them. The two returned without having seen María, but with accounts the Jumanos had given them that left no doubt in their minds that she had been there. Benavides, who left soon after for New Spain and Spain, made the case known throughout Europe by a report, translated into several languages, on the work he had supervised in New Mexico; he presented it to both the king and the pope. He also went to Agreda to see María and subsequently described the interview in a letter to his fellow missionaries in the New World. According to his letters, she accurately described events and people, both Indians and Spaniards, seen in her miraculous travels. As the missionaries spread the word of her mystical travels, María de Jesús de Agreda became a legend in New Mexico, Texas, and Arizona, and for more than a century afterward Indians continued to bring in reports of seeing the heaven-sent Lady in Blue.

María de Agreda also became famous in the region, just as in Europe, for her biography of the Virgin, entitled *La mística ciudad de Dios* (*The Mystical City of God*). Although censured by a 152-member commission of the Sorbonne, the Spanish Inquisition approved it after fourteen years of study, and the work enjoyed widespread popularity in Spain and its colonies. It contains intimate and theologically complex details regarding the Virgin's life, notably the how, why, and wherefore of the Immaculate Conception. The book was present in New Mexico for all three volumes were in the personal library of Diego de Vargas, who likewise held a particular devotion to the Virgin and had her image carried before the Spanish party during the reconquest. Even more striking evidence is a New Mexican alabado in honor of María de Agreda entitled "Madre Agueda de Jesús." During its transmission considerable confusion has crept into the text, particularly that of "Agreda" with "Agueda," Agatha. María de Agreda' s mysticism is still present, though, in its references to "the mysteries of light," and St. Teresa of Avila.[67]

At almost any point in the *Mystical City of God* one finds much of the same language that has already been seen in St. Francis, but now put into the Spanish of Quintana's period, thus even closer to his style. This similarity of expression is noticeable in several images: the association of light with divine inspiration, God as a lover, each person as part of the creation, and mystic experiences as gifts and favors. In other passages Franciscan ideas and symbols have acquired new details or dimensions that we also find in Quintana's work.

Fig. 5. A nun, almost certainly St. Teresa of Avila, writing under the inspiration of the Holy Spirit, which is here given the traditional representation as a dove. From the altar screen in the restored church at Santa Cruz de la Cañada. Courtesy of Clark A. Colahan.

Direct guidance from God, for example, is now developed into extensive conversations, complete with questions and answers. There are chapters on the types of visions granted to the Virgin and the several forms of human communication with God and his angels, as well as deceptive words spoken by the devil. Quintana was similarly questioned regarding the specific nature of his inspirations and the spirit that speaks to him. Once again we find in María de Agreda's work the image of the writer as an insignificant worm, an unworthy instrument of the divine hand that moves it in a spiritual project of immense importance. In addition, though, she made the same self-confidence-building assertions found in Quintana: that she was writing because God commanded her, that God revealed secrets to the poor and humble that he kept from the learned, that she had to overcome her fears, and that she would not go unrewarded. Her opening paragraph to Book 1 of *The Mystical City of God* proclaims: "I confess to Thee and magnify Thee, King Most High, that in thy exalted Majesty Thou hast hidden these high mysteries from the wise and from the teachers, and in thy condescension hast revealed them to me, the most insignificant and useless slave of thy church, in order that thy majesty be the more admired as the omnipotent Author of this history in proportion as its instrument is despicable and weak."[68] Again in Book 3 she writes: "And whenever the most High may command or teach you anything for the benefit of souls . . . overcome the fear that makes a coward of you, for if you are worth little, and are useless in every way, the most High is rich, powerful, and great, and by himself made all things, and your readiness and affection will not go unrewarded" (*The Mystical City*, 3:145).

In support of her claim that God should have chosen such an apparently inappropriate vehicle for his transcendent message she quoted Romans 11:24: "O King, most high and wise Lord: How incomprehensible are thy judgments, and inscrutable thy ways" (*The Mystical City*, 1:26). For this same reason Quintana quoted that verse—in Latin to give it more authority—and referred to the idea often. Finally, Quintana's obsessive clinging to the concept of his being on a safe path figures prominently in María de Agreda's work, as a reassurance that God will provide both emotional tranquility and physical security. María, in words that could summarize the origin of Miguel's mystic visions, reported that "In answer to these repeated prayers the Lord said: 'Do not fear, soul, nor afflict thyself; for I will give thee a state of mind and show thee a path of light and security" (*The Mystical City*, 1:14).

8. Miguel de Molinos, the Last Great Spanish Mystic

If the biographies of María de Agreda and her role model, St. Teresa of Avila, show how concerned the church was to discourage spiritual independence among the faithful, an even more striking example is the case of Miguel de Molinos (1628–96). Often considered the last of the great Spanish mystics, his establishment of contact with the divine without ecclesiastical mediation was sufficient in itself to set the Inquisitorial machinery in motion, even though he was a priest of practically irreproachable character, moved in the highest Vatican circles, and took care in his writings to avoid challenges to orthodoxy. He was concerned—and later events proved that he had good reason—that he might be unfairly associated with the clearly heretical *alumbrados*, the illuminati. Their practices were an offshoot from the same independent tradition that had nourished Protestantism, and there were certain points in common. The alumbrados believed, for example, that mental prayer counted for much more than oral devotions. They can only be described as excessive, however, as can be seen in Marcelino Menéndez y Pelayo's account of their beliefs surrounding the concept of union with God: "Certain kinds of burning, trembling and fainting from which they suffer show that one is in a state of grace and has the Holy Spirit, while those who are perfect need not do good works; . . . one should only understand what God understands, which is oneself, and this within oneself and within one's own concerns, . . . for in ecstasy there is no faith, in as much as one sees God clearly, and so rapture is a state existing somewhere between faith and glory."[69]

Born in Aragón, Molinos spent much of his life in Rome, where he found favor in the papacy while visiting on business for the Spanish church. In 1675, the same year that Rome made public the bull for the canonization of St. John of the Cross, his *Spiritual Guide* was published there. It is a book that cites that saint frequently and describes the withdrawal of the spirit into inner quiet and communion with God. A second edition appeared the next year in Madrid, followed by a rapid succession of other Spanish printings, translations, and books by disciples. Twelve years later, however, the attitude of the church hierarchy had reversed itself, and on the basis of greatly exaggerated charges regarding his conduct and distortions of his ideas, the Inquisition condemned him to life imprisonment.

During this period of his influence from 1675 to 1687, Quintana was a child and then an adolescent, very probably attending a school, necessarily Roman Catholic, in Mexico City. A comparison of Molinos's *Guide* and Quintana's writings brings to light common elements that indicate, if not an unquestionable influence, at least evidence that both writers knew the national mystic tradition in the form it had taken by the end of the seventeenth century. The full title of Molinos's 1675 work is *Guía espiritual que desembaraza el alma y la conduce por el interior camino para alcanzar la perfecta contemplación y el rico tesoro de la interior paz* (*Spiritual Guide that Frees The Soul and Leads*

It by the Inner Path to Achieve Perfect Contemplation and the Rich Treasure of Inner Peace).[70] While the path and the treasure are universal metaphors, they are specially prominent in the language of Spanish mysticism; Quintana used them repeatedly. The thought that he was on the right path calmed the fears his conflict with Yrigoien generated (for example, "Cree, Miguel, que no vas errado" [Believe, Miguel, that you are on a good path; 135]), while he viewed his sufferings and the inspiration that accompanied them as a generous and rich gift from God ("Ese tormento en que vives / es fineza y no defecto, / es gracia y riqueza suma / y tesoro muy perfecto" [That torment in which you live is a kind gift and not a defect; it is grace and great wealth and a perfect treasure; 127]).

The mystic's turning directly to God for guidance free from human error and passion is, of course, a model for Quintana's solution to his conflict with his parish priest. Molinos's statement of this ("Dios es quien es y no se muda ni puede errar ni querer" [God is who He is and does not change, nor can He err or wish to err; *Guía espiritual*, 84]) was echoed by Quintana's frequent reminders to himself that God is God ("Dios es Dios, y Dios que es Dios es quien te mueve" [God is God, and God who is God is who moves you; 135]), that He protects those who trust in Him ("Fíate, Miguel, de Dios, y Dios que es Dios es quien te mueve" [Trust God, Miguel, and God who is God is who moves you; 135]), and that His ways, even when beyond human understanding, are always good and always the same ("No fuera Dios quien es, y eso no puede ser . . . es, y no puede dejar de ser Dios eterno, incomprensible y admirable en todas sus perfecciones santísimas" [Then God would not be who He is, and that cannot be, and He cannot cease being God eternal, incomprehensible, and amazing in all his most holy perfections; 135]).

Molinos emphasized the belief of Spanish mysticism in inner forms of devotion, purification of the soul through spiritual suffering, and the efficacy of faith alone: "No ama Dios más al que más hace, al que más siente ni al que muestra más afecto, sino al que más padece, si adora con fe y referencia, creyendo que está en la divina presencia. . . . No quieras en ese tiempo usar la oración vocal, porque aunque en sí es Buena y santa, usarla entonces es declarada tentación, con la cual pretende el enemigo no te hable Dios al corazón" (God does not love more those who do more, those who feel more, or those who show more affection, but rather those who suffer more, if they worship with faith and reverence, believing that they are in the divine presence. . . . Do not wish at that time to use vocal prayer, because even if in itself it is good and holy, to use it then is a manifest temptation, by which the enemy seeks to interfere with God's speaking to your heart; *Guía espiritual*, 113).

Such an attitude would have been comforting to Quintana, helping to reassure him that discontinuing attendance at both the meetings of the Third

Order and church services was acceptable to God. Moreover, his emotional sufferings and faith in his private inspirations fitted Molinos's prescription. This underlying attitude surfaces most fully in one of Quintana's stanzas: "Que reces o que no reces, / espera ver en el cielo / a Dios que es padre benigno / y quien te da esos consuelos" (Whether you pray or you don't, expect to see God in Heaven, for He is a benign Father and it is He who gives you those consolations; 125). While Molinos specifically stated that he did not intend to discount the value of communal worship, and included the frequent taking of Holy Communion in his list of the four things necessary to approach God, still it is easy to see, as the Inquisition certainly did, how others could use the direction of his thought to justify rebellious positions. Quintana's refusal to confess could have served as an example of the danger.

Another idea from the *Guide*, that Quintana could have seen as supporting him, is that sometimes an inept confessor does more harm than good. Molinos had written, "Muchas almas, cuando padecen estos penosos tormentos, se turban, se afligen y se inquietan, pareciéndoles que ya en esta vida comienzan a padecer los eternos castigos. Y si por desgracia llegan al confesor que no tiene experiencia, en vez de consolarlas las deja más confuses y embarazadas" (Many souls, when they suffer these painful torments, become disturbed, distressed and anxious, and it seems to them that already in this life they are beginning to suffer the eternal punishments. And if by misfortune they should have a confessor lacking in experience, he, instead of giving them comfort, may leave them more confused and helpless; *Guía espiritual*, 104). Molinos carefully tempered this criticism of the church's primary agent of its authority by insisting strongly, if somewhat contradictorily, on complete obedience to one's confessor. He specifically mentioned supposed divine revelations, affirming that in such cases failure to obey one's spiritual director was a sure sign that the inspiring voice was that of a disguised evil spirit. Nevertheless, the legitimacy of using independent criteria in judging one's own confessor is clearly suggested. At one point Quintana declared similarly that God would have to provide the comfort his confessor would not give him: "Si no tienes confesor / que te quiera dar consuelo, / de Dios que es Dios lo recibes / en aquesos pensamientos" (Although you do not have a confessor who wants to give you consolation, from God who is God you receive it in these thoughts; 124). Likewise, after the Inquisition's agent had designated Quintana's accuser, Yrigoien, to be the understanding, soothing confessor Mexico City had instructed be chosen for him, the poet declared with outrage: "Confiésate con quien quisieres, que su Divina Majestad te dio tu albedrío para que así lo hagas, que Dios no impone preceptos imposibles a ninguna de sus criaturas ni quiere que las almas se enreden con escrúpulos" (Confess with whomever you like, for the Divine Majesty gave you your free will for that purpose, for God does not impose impossible precepts on any of his creatures, nor does he wish souls to become tangled up in scruples; 167).

During the papacy of Innocent XI (1676–89), the Inquisition had, in fact, drawn up a list of sixty-eight errors supposedly contained or implied in Molinos's writings. Although even official Roman Catholic writers now admit that many of the ideas attributed to him are not really in the *Spiritual Guide*, the particular drift of his thought that worried the church hierarchy is easy to identify in the "propositions" with which he was saddled. On the question of how the individual can be sure that inner revelations are from God, the Inquisition's supposed paraphrase of Molinos sounded similar in places to Quintana's verses: *"Et certus sum, quod hoc lumen a Deo procedit, quia ad me provenit coniunctum cum certitudine, quod a Deo proveniat, et mihi nec umbram dubii relinquit in contrarium"* (And I am sure that this light proceeds from God, since it comes to me together with the certainty that it comes from God and leaves no shadow of doubt to the contrary. Thus sometimes it happens that when God reveals something, at the same time he leaves the soul sure that He himself it is that is making the revelation, and the soul cannot have any doubts to the contrary).[71]

In much the same vein, the Inquisition viewed Molinos as hostile to theologians and resistant to obeying church doctrines. Quintana, obviously worried about being accused of heresy, said several times in his own defense that God shows to the simple and humble things the learned misunderstand. Once again the Inquisition's distorted paraphrase of Molinos could almost speak for Quintana: *"Theologus minorem dispositionem habet quam homo rudis ad statum contemplativi: primo, quia no habet fidem adeo puram, secundo, quia no est adeo humilis, tertio, quia no adeo curat propriam salutem, quarto, quia caput refertum habet phantasmatibus, speciebus, opinionibus et speculationibus, et non potest in illum ingredi verum lumen"* (The theologian is less suited for the contemplative state than the unlearned man: first, because his faith is not as pure; second, because he is not as humble; third, because he is not as concerned about his salvation; fourth, because his head is full of apparitions, visions, opinions and speculations, and the true light cannot get in; Denzinger and Bannwart, *Enchiridion Symbolorum*, 363, no. 64).

Quintana's righteous indignation upon learning that Yrigoien has been designated as his confessor was the kind of defiance and excessive exercise of the individual's free will that the church was concerned to avoid when it put the following words in Molinos's mouth: *"Risu digna est nova quaedam doctrina in Ecclesia Dei, quod anima quoad internum gubernari debeat ab episcopo: quod si episcopus no sit capax, anima ipsum cum suo directore adeat. Novam dico doctrinam; quia nec sacra Scriptura, nec concilia, nec canones, nec bullae, nec Sancti, nec auctores eam unquam tradiderunt nec tradere possunt: quia Ecclesia non iudicat de occultis, et anima eius habet facultatem eligendi quemcunque sibi visum fuerit"* (There is a laughable new doctrine in God's church to the effect that a soul should be governed in inward matters by the bishop, or if he personally cannot, then the soul should be guided by the bishop's director. I say this is a new doctrine, since neither the councils nor the canons nor the bulls nor the saints nor the authors ever handed this down, nor could they do so, for the church does not judge hidden things, and the soul has the ability to choose whomever it thinks best; Denzinger and Bannwart, *Enchiridion Symbolorum*, 363, no. 66).

As this passage shows, the Inquisition saw Molinos as questioning the whole practice of confession and penance. Proposition sixty in the list of errors attributed to him closely parallels Quintana's assertion that God does not ask impossible things of his creatures in matters of confession: *"Animabus provectis, quae reflexionibus mori incipiunt, et eo etiam perveniunt, ut sint mortuae, Deus confessionem aliquando efficit impossibilem et supplet ipse tanta gratia praeservante, quantam in sacramento reciperent: et ideo huiusmodi animabus non es bonum in tali casu ad sacramentum poenitentiae accedere, quia id es illis impossibile"* (When souls are in an advanced state and begin to die to reflections, even reaching the point where they are dead to them, sometimes God makes confession impossible for them and provides them Himself with as much saving grace as they would receive in the sacrament. So in these cases it is not good for advanced souls to draw near to the sacrament of penance, since it is impossible for them; Denzinger and Bannwart, *Enchiridion Symbolorum*, 362, no. 60). As scribe of the ecclesiastical court, Quintana might well have had access to the papal bull containing the sixty-eight errors. Perhaps having read them and seen Molinos's prestige in the church during his own youth in Mexico City, he found support in them for his struggle.

9. The New Mexican Alabado

As this review of influential spiritual authors in Quintana's New Mexico shows, most of his ideas and repeated images were part of the mainstream of religious tradition in the early eighteenth-century Hispanic world. Looking toward more recent times, his value as the only surviving individual voice of folk religion and poetry from that period in New Mexico's past is demonstrated by a comparison of his writings with the region's alabados. These traditional hymns, which scholars have collected in the last half century, were preserved and developed by the members of the Confraternity of Our Father Jesus the Nazarene. Often known as the Hermanos Penitentes, the brothers constitute a New Mexican social and religious organization that grew up to meet the spiritual needs of the population during the withdrawal of the organized church in the first half of the nineteenth century.

Except for Quintana's work, the alabados provide our farthest look back in time at popular religious beliefs and expression in New Mexico. Viewed in the context of what precedes them, they confirm that there is a tradition, slowly evolving but remaining surprisingly the same in many respects, that extends from the time of the founding of the Franciscan Orders, passes through the Spanish mystics and Quintana, and survives into the twentieth century.

Many of the features of the Penitentes have been traced, amid some objections, to the Third Order of St. Francis, whose presence in eighteenth-century New Mexico is well documented.[72] It occupied a position of some prestige, as is suggested by Quintana's statement that those who believe that membership in it is necessary for salvation are mistaken. The hymns and prayers emphasized in its meetings and services were known, like those of the Penitentes, as "exercises in virtue," and William R. Fisher has shown them to be a major source of the alabados.[73] In the latter, three typically Franciscan themes predominate: Christ's Passion, devotion to the Virgin, and recognition of one's sins. The verse form usually employed conforms to the norm for most New Mexico folk poetry: eight-syllable lines grouped in quatrains, with traditional Spanish assonant rhyme (i.e., of the accented and following vowels) in the second and fourth lines. Quintana's verses use this identical arrangement.

Many of Quintana's poems, like alabados, begin with the line, "Jesús, María y José," which has more than one traditional use in the Hispanic world. This heading has been used to invoke a blessing at the beginning of a written text, as though asking for inspiration, and also forms part of a standard spoken ritual of prayer. It suggests that the writer or speaker, in that which follows, is acting in agreement with orthodox Roman Catholic practice and theology. Quintana's frequent use of it, in addition to reflecting the great importance of Franciscan spirituality to him, suggests that his writings are properly and divinely inspired.[74]

One of the distinctive qualities of the alabado is that the heavenly persons to whom the hymn is directed speak, both to each other and to any persons who are listening as well. Dialogue is paramount. Reminiscent of the cast of characters in *The Mystical City of God*, the Virgin Mary expresses herself most frequently and on the widest range of topics, but Jesus and the saints have a role, too. For example, in commenting on "Dividido el corazón" ("With a Broken Heart"), Juan Rael writes: "This hymn, which describes the suffering of the Virgin during the passion, is sung at the dramatic meeting of Christ and the Virgin during the procession on Good Friday. . . . The majority of the first

Fig. 6. A window in the restored church at Santa Cruz de la Cañada, donated in 1945 by the Confraternity of Our Father Jesus. Courtesy of Clark A. Colahan.

twenty-one stanzas are written in dialogue form. In most of them, the Virgin addresses her Son. In the rest of the dialogue she addresses God the Father, the Angels, or humanity in general."[75]

The element of drama found in this alabado is common. Many hymns were used in rituals, as in the Good Friday processions, and were part of acting out the events being celebrated and recreated. In addition, the Christmas and other Biblically based plays of medieval origin that were alive and well until recently in New Mexico also accustomed their actors and audiences to the speeches and conversations of supernatural characters. The sense of theatre is heightened by exhortations to the listeners to react to emotional scenes described in the first person in the hymn. These are typically directed to "Christians" or "creatures" and seem to suppose the presence of an audience. "Ayudad, almas queridas" ("Lend Help, Dear Souls"), for example, has stanzas such as: "Cristianos, sentir desde hoy / esta aflicción con ternura / que tiene en su corazón / esta madre, virgen pura" (Christians, from today on feel this affliction with the tenderness that this mother, a pure virgin, has in her heart; Rael, *The New Mexican Alabado*, 30).

Three traditions, then, contributed to the presence of heavenly conversations in the alabados; the same is true of Quintana's work. As a writer of verses in the Spanish mystical tradition, a participant in the Franciscan liturgical heritage later developed by the Hermanos Penitentes, and as a playwright in the tradition of the medieval mystery plays, he received the same influences.

Light is one of the universal yet particularly Franciscan symbols that is most prominent in the alabado. As Marta Weigle explores in *Brothers of Blood, Brothers of Light*, it took on a fundamental importance for New Mexico folk religion. The attention focused on it is well shown by "Por ser mi divina luz" ("Since You Are My Divine Light"; Rael, *The New Mexican Alabado*, 33), a hymn in which through the prism of metaphor the image of blood displays a wide spectrum of meanings. As it represented Jesus and Mary, so too it could be said to be embraced, venerated, praised, believed in, and carried in their hearts by the members of the confraternity. It is also linked to Jesus's crown, and the Hermanos suffer "with it" when they are on the cross.

The attitude toward the crucifixion reflected in the alabados is also important for an understanding of Quintana. Compassion for Christ's suffering, like that found in the writings of St. Francis, is naturally present in Penitente hymns, since many of the confraternity's most important activities take place during Holy Week. What is given special emphasis in New Mexico, however, is a desire to share and imitate that suffering. This is a form of Franciscan compassion, but it also springs from a need for penance and atonement that the confraternity responded to in the absence of the priesthood. The following quatrains from "Estaba junto al madero" ("Standing next to the Cross") are typical: "Virgen, sobre todas pura, / lloré tu dolor contigo, / no seas amarga conmigo, / pues eres toda dulzura. // Haz que, por imitación / de Cristo llagas y muerte, / trasporte en mí con la suerte / de su afrentosa pasión. // En la misma cruz llagado, / en sus heridas me vea, / por amor de tu Hijo sea / de su néctar embriagado" (Virgin, purer than all others, I wept for your suffering with you. Do not be bitter with me, since you are all sweetness. Allow me, by imitation of Christ's wounds and death, to participate in His ignominious suffering. May I see myself on the same cross, wounded by His wounds and through love for His Son, enraptured by drinking of His nectar; Rael, *The New Mexican Alabado*, 55).

There are other less fundamental but still very typical elements that are common to Quintana's work and the alabados. One is making claims, like those of St. Francis and Molinos, regarding the importance of one's teaching for the health of others' souls, together with threats to anyone who hinders its becoming more widely known, this in spite of declarations of sinfulness by the author or singer. A very popular penitential alabado with versions in other parts of the Spanish-speaking world is "Por el rastro de la sangre" ("Along the Trail of Blood"). It includes the following stanza: "El que sabe y no la enseña, / el que la oiga y no la aprende, / el día del juicio sabrá / lo que esta oración contiene" (He who knows it and does not teach it, He who hears it and does not learn it, will on the great Judgment Day know the meaning of this prayer; Rael, *The New Mexican Alabado*, 25).

Another important parallel is exemplified by "En la cena del Señor" ("At the Lord's Supper"), which contains a description of God as an invisible and comforting spirit: "Nuestro Padre está en los cielos, / un espíritu invisible, / dándonos tantos consuelos, / aunque el hombre esté visible, / lleno de tantos desvelos" (Our Father is in heaven, an invisible spirit giving us so many consolations, while man is visible, full of so many anxieties; Rael, *The New Mexican Alabado*, 117). We are reminded of Quintana's statements that he sees no visions of God, but is comforted only by the inner voice of an invisible spirit (which he associates with God) that dictates verses and convinces him to write them down.

As one becomes acquainted with collections of alabados, more and more images, phrases, and ideas that recall Quintana and the earlier religious tradition appear. In place of any attempt at a complete listing of these details, a single hymn may give a better sense of the common tradition involved. Juan Rael collected "Dulce esposo de mi alma" ("Sweet Husband of My Soul") in Española, the area where Quintana lived, as well as in Cerro, New Mexico, in almost identical versions. As its title suggests, it contains a variety of phrases comparing Jesus to a lover, such as "dulcísimo amigo mío" (my sweetest friend), "veré yo tu hermoso cuerpo" (I will see your beautiful body), and "Tengo de gozarte, esposo" (I will take pleasure in you, my husband) (Rael, *The New Mexican Alabado*, 88). The speaker presents herself as a sinful but repentant wife, powerless before her divine husband, and the image of a "humble little worm" appears again. This sense of guilt and anxiety about God's anger leads to fears of the pains of hell, expressed, as in Quintana, with medieval vividness. One of the several stanzas on the subject says: "¡Qué de inefables cavernas / en fuego infernal sumido, / de pies y manos atado, / de los demonios asido!" (What ineffable caverns; I see myself sunk in hellfire, bound hand and foot, in the grasp of demons!; Rael, 89). The devil's "abyss," mentioned more than once by Quintana, appears here, too.

Faced with this danger, the singer wishes he possessed the immense contrition of St. Francis. Likewise, Quintana takes comfort in the thought that while God's decisions are just, they are also beyond human understanding: "¡Oh, Dios de la majestad, / cuán justos son tus juicios, / cuán profundos tus secretos / sin poder ser entendidos!" (Oh, God of majesty, how just are your judgments, how deep your secrets, which cannot be understood!; Rael, 89). He trusts in divine mercy, describing God as benign and merciful, and praises the heavenly favors he receives. The latter, as we often find in Quintana's writings, are called *beneficios*, or benefits, and there is the same emphasis on God's giving them generously. In a striking textual echo, God appears both in Quintana and in the alabado in the role of *médico divino*, or divine physician (Rael, *The New Mexican Alabado*, 88).

10. Poet Laureate or Mad Poet?

As we have seen, Fray Angélico Chávez called Quintana "the mad poet of Santa Cruz," but he withdrew the label and the idea of madness in the last sentence of the article. There he concluded, saying that Quintana "was not really mad but only so inclined (as what genius is not?)" (Chávez, "Mad Poet," 17). He also suggested another more flattering title for him—poet laureate of New Mexico. Which of these two characterizations squares with the facts better, or should he, like the village of Santa Cruz—halfway between the extremes of Río Arriba and Río Abajo—be assigned some intermediate place in the history of New Mexico?

As one of the very few literate persons in the region during the years following the reconquest, and the writer people turned to for expression of their needs and feelings in legal matters, religion, and personal affairs, the title of poet laureate could be appropriately conferred. What, though, of his madness? His accusers mentioned the idea but rejected it. The Inquisition, after considering the possibility that he was in fact receiving supernatural inspiration—albeit from an evil rather than a good spirit—concluded essentially that he was suffering from a disorder of the imagination limited to one area of his life, not a generalized and incapacitating distortion of reality as seen by those around him. That interpretation still seems valid, but what we can add to it now is that he departed less than one might think from the traditional views held in his society. As we have seen, God was not felt to be inaccessible or impersonal, and direct contact and even conversations with Him and other spirits was a long established and still very lively part of Spanish, Roman Catholic, and specifically Franciscan belief.

Throughout the history of the region one finds, like artesian wells springing up wherever there is an opening to an underground aquifer, reports of supernatural intervention. The traditional folklore that records the local deeds of several saints continues in recent decades in accounts of sacred images seen on a church wall, a tortilla, and even traffic signs. The church, of course, has always used its authority, with more or less gentleness, to control self-deception and fraud, as well as protect its own prerogatives. Not only Quintana but all those around him accepted the existence of the supernatural and the possibility of personal contact with it, and he was not stepping very far into personal idiosyncrasy in thinking that the local ministers of that authority could be mistaken—through envy and ambition—in failing to recognize the authenticity of his divine revelations.

Unfortunately for the quality of that writing of his that has survived, his challenge to authority and the confrontation it produced imposed a severe emotional strain on him. He sometimes repeated his ideas and phrases in a disordered and obsessive way that, together with his constant exhortations to himself to trust in God, makes it clear that during this period he was writing to calm himself in moments of intense anxiety. There are some passages, though, like the poems and prose denouncing Guerrero and Yrigoien that he sent to Fray Juan de la Cruz, whose profusion of details has an effective Baroque organization that lends them an undeniable eloquence. He sought and achieved intensity of feeling through, first, accumulation, and, second, frequent use of metaphor.

Both these techniques, particularly the former, have a decidedly liturgical flavor. Certain nouns and adjectives repeatedly appear together in exalted but standard pairs, and groups of two or three nouns are substituted where one would have sufficed. Take, for example, the phrase "los decretos de mi soberana grandeza e incomprensible sabiduría, poder y misericordia infinita" (the decrees of my sovereign greatness and incomprehensible wisdom, power, and infinite

Fig. 7. Twentieth-century grave marker in the church cemetery at Santa Cruz de la Cañada, where the family name is still very much alive among the town's residents. Courtesy of Clark A. Colahan.

mercy; 137). Sometimes the outpouring of one noun after another gives the feeling of a litany: "Soy tu Dios, tu Creador, tu Redentor, tu Amparo, tu Luz, tu Consuelo y toda tu Esperanza y bien Aventuranza." (I am your God, your Creator, your Redeemer, your help, your light, your consolation, and all your hope and bliss; 146). His constant use of metaphors in itself creates a certain poetic density of language.

Occasionally they have an originality (although usually retaining Biblical overtones) pleasing to twenty-first-century taste, as when he describes his emotional anguish as the "aguijón de este espíritu" (sting of this spirit; 123). More commonly, though, his figures of speech are thoroughly traditional. Still, many times they give an effective graphic dimension to the abstract ideas or feelings that concern him, as when he speaks of those who "en la lobreguez viven precipitados y encenegados en los vicios" (live fallen and mired in the gloom of the vices; 141).

In general, folk writers use and combine stock phrases and images drawn from a common reservoir that their audiences better remember and value more than is the case in literate, less traditional societies. In colonial New Mexico, religious customs that have continued into the twenty-first century show that prayers and hymns were often improvised, either individually by professional *rezadores,* those who recite and lead prayers at funerals and other ritual ceremonies, or in a group by those attending prayer meetings, with each person contributing a verse. Such improvisations would naturally be characterized by spontaneous accumulation and repetition. It appears that, although capable of more ordered writing, under the emotional pressure of the situation that generated those writings of his that have been preserved, Quintana nervously resorted to rapid, unpolished compositions like those of the rezadores.

Fig. 8. Exterior of Santa Cruz Church from the plaza area, ca. 1880. Photograph by W. H. Jackson. Courtesy of Colorado Historical Society, Denver.

As Fray Angélico Chávez has pointed out, much that he authored could have survived anonymously as folklore. We are told great and small alike respected him. Apart from one of the many versions of the Christmas plays, an alabado like "Sweet Husband of My Soul," which contains so many of his favorite phrases and ideas, would be a good candidate for such a survival among the people for whom he spoke.

11. What Became of the Controversial Poet?

When the winds of controversy, drama, and intrigue around Miguel de Quintana settled down with a final exoneration in 1737, he seemed to disappear into the harsh, humdrum life of the agricultural town of Santa Cruz de la Cañada. His participation in civil and criminal cases as court clerk for the alcalde mayor and as a scribe, including his post as clerk for the ecclesiastic court, now became a thing of the past with few exceptions. From the scant allusions to his name in official documents after 1737, he must have "retired" at around age sixty by relinquishing most of his central duties, except for filling in sporadically as a part-timer. His creative writings as well as his letter writing either stopped abruptly or became clandestine, perhaps getting lost in some protected family chest. His daughter Lugarda Quintana, who died only one year after Miguel (April 9, 1748) in 1749, mentions her father's inheritance only in terms of goats and sheep, but no mention is made of his writings.[76] Judging from the items of

Lugarda's testament, the Quintana family seems to have achieved a modest but relatively stable lifestyle, especially compared to the difficult times of hardship and subsistence in the 1690s. His name, however, quietly disappears from all archival records shortly after his death.

Central to our study is that his reputation was not irreparably damaged by the investigation of the Inquisition after the two local friars, Joseph Yrigoien and Manuel Sopeña, had accused him of scandalous "heretical assertions." His spirit was probably shaken but not shattered; his credibility might have come into question, but clearly his confidence and faith remained intact. He had survived a major emotional and moral crisis accompanied by self-doubt. Pardoned as a result of unsubstantiated accusations, the verdict of the Inquisition authorities led to a declaration that he suffered from delusion and attacks of fantasy, a "damaged imagination" or an afflicted conscience. One inquisitor in Mexico City, Fray Pedro Anselmo Sánchez de Tagle, sent instructions to the Inquisition agent in Santa Fe, Fray Joseph Antonio Guerrero, to warn him that swift action would be taken against him if he were to slip back into "these ravings he calls revelations or inspirations" (fol. 469r), which supposedly bordered on the ridiculous and frivolous.[77] As Fray Tagle stated: "He will be subject to the punishments applied to a person who is obstinate, a fraud, and a rebel" (fol. 467r).[78] In other words, a harsh censorship was exercised, and Miguel de Quintana seemed to accept it while ailing in bed and feeling threatened by the Inquisition authority. He must have recovered later in body and soul, however. Proof of his regained standing in social and religious circles is found in the burial records of Santa Cruz between 1726 and 1768, which state that he was given a Christian burial. Further evidence of his recovered stature and honor is that his body was buried inside the church of Santa Cruz. If any doubts on his moral integrity had persisted, no such allusion would have been made in the records.

Quintana's last act of redemption, however, rests in a rare document located in the Archivos Franciscanos at the Universidad Nacional Autónoma de México (UNAM), an open letter dated November 2, 1737, in which he retracted certain accusations against his two principal tormentors, Yrigoien and Sopeña. His anguished letter of recantation, filled with seeming remorse and bitter irony, says one thing (asking forgiveness) but does something else (accusing the real sources of his dilemma and affliction). At the most basic level, the reader is struck by statements of exaggerated self-contempt. The repeated righteousness of his cause, supported by constant reaffirmations that he was following God's wishes and going down the right path, is suddenly reversed. Comparable to Sor Juana Inés de la Cruz's famous retort to Sor Filotea in 1693, in which she defended her right to access knowledge, Miguel de Quintana believed he had the right to think independently of priests who abused their official power. He uses the term *celosos* to describe the priests, clearly resorting to the ambiguity of the term's double meaning of "jealous" and "zealous." His favorite rhetorical tool was constant self-deprecation to portray himself not only as a humble man but as a victim of others' vested interests. Thus, two things happen: his subservience appeared exemplary while his accusers' subtextual agendas were intimated. A tight-lipped resentment surfaced toward the ecclesiastical authorities, but it was limited to their position and not their personal character. The fact that Quintana wrote to the bishop of Durango reveals a strategy of last resort: to communicate with the highest church authority in northern Mexico who might exonerate him completely. In this way, he demonstrated conviction, perseverance, and a dogged determination.

In the letter of recantation, Quintana mentioned his own position of weakness and vulnerability, that is, powerlessness. In a possible slip of the pen, he declared what he "ought to say," suggesting that the truth lay elsewhere. For example, he told the bishop that he had written his direct superior, an ecclesiastical judge, about a series of false accusations against the churchman resulting from "fawning flattery." In the midst of asking forgiveness from the bishop, his defiance overwhelmed his sarcasm, and he stated categorically that the root of the problem was less his unorthodox views and more the jealousy/zealousness of the priests who were threatened by Quintana's prominence in his community as a scribe and writer. His rhetoric raised the ante of what the reader should believe: he insisted that he now wrote his true mind, almost like confessing to a higher being. The smokescreen of Quintana's apparent submission becomes transparent, showing his real motives and sound reasoning. Finally, he took back "everything" he had said before because the Franciscan priests were "entirely fulfilling their obligations." His seeming willingness to turn the other cheek verges on self-annihilation, but this occurred after he had made the necessary counteraccusations clear. Here the irony took on an unmistakable tinge of outrage, but nowhere was it clearer than in his praise of his relentless pursuer, Fray Joseph Guerrero, who blatantly appointed Yrigoyen as Quintana's "understanding confessor." Now Quintana sarcastically wrote that Fray Guerrero, the Inquisition's local agent, was said "in his actions, assertions, and advice [to have] sought my spiritual, and temporal welfare."[79]

In sum, the real problem was not heresy but a personality conflict between rivals in practically the same profession. Perhaps the greatest irony of his recantation was precisely that it was his victory, not his defeat. It won him eleven more years of freedom before his death. At the same time that he bowed to oppressive authority, he also whispered his defiance to those who supported him. In the end, he trusted that anyone reading his final letter of recantation would see with their own eyes the real issues at stake, thus exonerating him forever. Quintana, then, defended lofty convictions with determination to claim his right to write and the freedom of thought. He seems to have relished what Octavio Paz would write centuries later: "El escritor es una voz disidente, crítica" (The writer is a dissident and critical voice).[80] In short, in this New Mexican writer we encounter a life struggling to survive colonial social coercion and pressure to conform much more than we find madness, someone who reveals both the mindset of the time and the possibilities it contained for rising above it.

PART TWO

English Translation of Miguel de Quintana's Writings

From the Archivo General de la Nación—Mexico City. Documentos de la Inquisición, vol. 849, no. 2 (fols. 446–74)[1]

Document 1. 1734. The title page of the Inquisition's file on Miguel de Quintana
[folio 446r]
+[2]
New Mexico. The Year 1734.
The Honorable Prosecutor for the Inquisition for This Holy Office of Mexico City against Miguel de Quintana, Married, Resident[3] of Villa Nueva de Santa Cruz
For Heretical Assertions[4]

Document 2. March 17, 1732. Denunciation made against Quintana by Fray[5] Manuel Sopeña.[6]
[f. 452r]

[Note in left margin:]
Denunciation by Fray Manuel [de] Sopeña

In this Villa [Nueva] de Santa Cruz on the seventeenth day of the month of March of the year 1732. Before the honorable father, the commissary[7] of the Holy Office of this Kingdom of New Mexico, at about five o'clock in the afternoon, a friar of the holy father, St. Francis,[8] appeared without being summoned and duly swore that he was telling the truth. He gave his name as Fray [Joseph] Manuel [de] Sopeña, minister of Nueva Villa de Santa Cruz, and his age as forty-five years. Obliged by his conscience, he states in the denunciation that over a period of time Miguel de Quintana has given him a total of nine quarto-sized sheets of paper,[9] all written upon and containing many reckless and scandalous assertions that, as the good Catholic Christian that he is, he has felt guilty not to report. When asked about the said Miguel de Quintana's civil status, he said that he was married and a resident of Villa Nueva de Santa Cruz. He said that, by the oath he had taken, this is the truth, and when it was read to him he said that it had been correctly written down and that he is not saying it out of hatred or malice. He promised to keep the matter secret,[10] then signed his name to it in the presence of the honorable commissary on the said day, month, and year. The notary of the Holy Office, whose signature appears below, came before me.[11]

Fray Joseph Antonio Guerrero
Commissary of the Holy Office
[rúbrica]

Fray Manuel de Sopeña
[rúbrica][12]

Witnessed by,
Fray Joseph Yrigoien[13]
[rúbrica]
Notary of the Holy Office

Document 3. July 1, 1732. Denunciation against Quintana by Fray Joseph Yrigoien.

[f. 463r][14]

++[15]

[Salutation at top of page:]
Our Reverend Father, Commissary of the Holy Office
Fray Joseph Yrigoien of the Regular Order of our seraphic father, St. Francis, son of the Province of the Holy Gospel of Mexico, father notary of the Holy Office, and presiding minister of Villa Nueva de Santa Cruz of the Kingdom of New Mexico, I appear before Your Paternal Grace, having taken the oath and being moved to unburden my conscience. I state in denunciation of Miguel de Quintana, who was born in Mexico City and is a resident of the said town, that when I had required him (as I am the parish priest of the said town) to comply with the obligation of annually going to confession and taking Communion, following the procedure commanded by Our Holy Mother Church, he came to this *convento*[16] on the twenty-ninth day of June after mass (which he did not attend) and told me (**Nota bene**) that it was a Church requirement which he could not fulfill, and that God did not ask the impossible of any of His children, and that since he was one of them he was excused from it.[17] At the same time, he handed to me a paper that I submit to Your Paternal Grace to be forwarded with this denunciation to the holy and just Tribunal of the

Inquisition so that the assertions contained in it may be assessed. I attest to the fact that he was in his right mind when he was with me and I attest that the handwriting on the paper is his. And this is the truth, by the oath I have taken and I do not say it out of hatred or malice. I signed it as the Notary of the Holy Office in this Villa Nueva de Santa Cruz on the first of July of the year 1732.

Fray Joseph Yrigoien
[rúbrica]
Notary of the Holy Office

Document 4. July 12, 1732. Fray Joseph Antonio Guerrero forwards documents regarding Quintana to the Inquisition in Mexico City

[f. 448r]

++

[Note in right margin:]
Faithful copy to the Most Illustrious Prosecutor for the Inquisition
Most Illustrious Prosecutor:
Since there is no direct mail courier leaving for the city where you are located, I am sending the enclosed legal documents to the holy Tribunal in care of the honorable father commissary of the jurisdiction of El Paso. In the month of August last year a mail courier did depart from this kingdom,[18] and I sent other legal documents then. Likewise, I have sent to the holy Tribunal the document witnessing my taking office and an account of the proclamation of the edicts[19] in the way that I have been commanded. I include that information in this communication, Your Most Illustrious Grace, because I have not yet received any information, and as the remoteness of this kingdom is so extreme, sheets of documents are often misplaced or delayed in reaching the capital. Please, Your Most Illustrious Grace, be so kind as to tell me whether the documents sent have been appropriate, for I wish nothing else but to serve Your Most Illustrious Grace and the holy Tribunal. There is nothing else to report, and I have asked God to watch over Your Most Illustrious Grace for many long years

[f. 448v]

for the protection and defense of our holy faith. Villa de Santa Fe, New Mexico, July 12, 1732.

Most Honorable Sir,

At the feet of Your Illustrious Grace lies prostrate your humble and submissive chaplain, Fray Joseph Antonio Guerrero[20]

[rúbrica]

Document 5. Poetry and prose written by Quintana; submitted to Mexico City as evidence by Guerrero around late July 1732, in support of Sopeña's and Yrigoien's denunciations

[f. 454r] or [MQ 1r][21]

Jesus, Mary, and Joseph
Gain that[22] understanding
that the power of God has given you.
Perfect it, Miguel, and write,
for you have in no way strayed.

God's strength moves you,
and there is no power
that can resist it
nor make you, Miguel, have qualms.

Very sure is the expression,
which the great power has given you
because of your humility,
for God favors you as He does the humble.

Miguel, save and enlighten me,
for I burn on the coals
of this sea of tears
which I show to you weeping.

Fear not, for you're on the right path.
Believe, Miguel, that the priest
will not question those verses.
Help me, for I implore you.

You are safe from suffering
any harm or insult, Miguel,
given what you hold back.
Express it, for I yearn to hear it.

[Inserted between the two columns:]

Miguel, believe most firmly, indeed, that your verses give greater honor and glory to the highest and supreme King of Heaven and to his most holy and pure Mother, most holy Mary of Sorrows. Give them to the priest and by that means expect to be very comforted in your little troubles.

Fig. 9. A section of the altar screen showing Jesus, Mary—including her advocation as Our Lady of Sorrows—and other saints in the restored church at Santa Cruz de la Cañada. Courtesy of Clark A. Colahan.

Fig. 10. The ghost of Fray Juan de Tagle as it appeared to Miguel de Quintana. Painting (eight by twenty inches) by Father Thomas J. Steele, SJ. Courtesy of Father Steele.

My Father, Master, and Lord, only the Divine Omnipotence knows, in whose presence I am the weakest little worm, an ungrateful and sad sinner, that I am unworthy of the earth putting up with me. For about a year now, I have been suffering the persecution or sting of this spirit, but there is no human strength that can oppose divine strength. I am a poor wretch, and although the strength of the light itself bears witness to the truth, my extreme poverty and timidity make a coward of me, since my unworthiness is very great. And even more so when I find so much opposition along so many paths, fearing what Your Paternal Grace has told me about those who seek God, about how vanity gets into them, and they fly off to hell. This has been a cruel dagger that has tormented me and made me hesitant to bring forward many things that I feel and am holding back. And without seeking them, they come to me. May His Divine Majesty be blessed for His generous mercy in all that happens to me and in all things, for by His wish I have been suffering like this for about a year, as I have said, since the following happened to me. I don't know how it was because in these things I am not my usual self. Very happy and lighthearted, I was going to mass at the Villa Nueva [de Santa Cruz][23] very early in the morning. I found the doors of the church wide open and went inside, but there was not a soul there. Genuflecting to the most holy Virgin of Sorrows, I went into the sacristy and there found the Reverend Father Juan de Tagle.[24] I stopped short: "Jesus, what is this?" I was seeing him[25] just as he used to be in this world, his cowl pulled down,[26] his hands

[f. 454v] or [MQ 1v]

stuck in his sleeves like a dead man's, wearing his chasuble, and with his face extremely troubled. He did not utter a word to me but just bent forward as though he wished to speak to me. Seeing him dressed to say mass, I said to him, "Father, why doesn't Your Paternal Grace say mass?" To this he replied, "I cannot say it," his eyes being two fountains of tears. "He who can say it for me is the priest, Fray Manuel [de Sopeña]."[27] "My God! What is this?" I turned to look at the altar cloths, and they were bright red.[28] I said to myself, "Today is not the feast day of any martyr." To this he replied, as though reading my mind, "Don't worry about the bright red color. Even though it's not a martyr's feast day, it always stands for that bloody martyrdom of the cross on which God shed his most precious blood for us." Ever since then I have tried to put all of this out of my mind, given what Your Paternal Grace has told me I am very much afraid to reveal to Your Paternal Grace what happens to me, or even to go frequently to confession as I used to, since I am terrified by Your Paternal Grace. So I suffer what God wills. This same scene has appeared to me some four or five times, but I always have resisted communicating it to Your Paternal Grace, for the reason I have given. And now, with these little trials and tribulations[29] that God has been pleased to send me because of my great sins, this spirit has tormented me so much, and with such force, that it has obliged me to write what I do not deserve due to my extreme poverty and unworthiness. But the strength of the spirit has inspired me with so many musings that I find myself compelled with great force by its supremely (**Nota bene**)[30] logical and convincing reasons. The work offers a most high purpose,[31] even if I am only a docile instrument, but it convinces me that I should not resist the will of God, whose most high and sovereign decisions I revere, submitting the words SCSECA Romana [*sic*].[32] The light that God's power has given you is above all supreme, Miguel, from which you enjoy such kind gifts through His mercy.

[f. 455r] or [MQ 2r]

Jesus, Mary, and Joseph
Write and don't be a coward.
Write so that from the immense
and supreme good that is God
you will enjoy that inner impulse.

It is a very secure impulse,
which offers no real risk,
since God can make you
fortunate by that means.

If you have no confessor
who may want to give you solace,
you will receive it in those thoughts
from God who is God.

His love grants them to you.
Write fearlessly, Miguel, for
if the priest fills you with terror,
God does not, because He is very prudent.

Leave human judgment behind
and stay quietly at home,
subject yourself to the will
of the highest lover.

God is supreme
who in that inner motion
can give you a sure advantage
from His immense treasures.

Believe, Miguel, you are on the right path,
and that these thoughts
are free from fault

as they are perfect gifts.
God, Miguel, has given them to you
for your enjoyment,
and with them a very great token
of His love.

Embrace them and fear not,
venturing safely with them,
for they are, Miguel,
a very safe and perfect comfort.

The high King of Heaven
alone has control
over your poverty, Miguel,
so do not be afraid of risk or harm.

What His great love has given you,
Miguel, out of His goodness,
all the power of hell
will not be able to take from you.

So do not be afraid to write
when you find yourself in trouble,
for you are blessed with God's grace
in those thoughts.

Believe, Miguel, with living faith,
as you are a poor wretch,
all the verses composed by you
are given by the King of Heaven alone. (**Nota bene**)

Kindly He offers you a reward
for them, and when it comes
to a reward, Miguel,
you need not confuse it as torture.

You can be very sure
it will not be torture,
because God, who is God,
provides you that sweet comfort.

Whether you pray or not, (**Nota bene**)[33]
you can expect to see God in Heaven,
the kind Father
who gives you those comforts.

True and certain,
effective and flawless,
given by His loving comfort
free from all defects.

You enjoy that gift and grace
because with humble affection
you celebrated in the church
His loving birth.

As a reward for love
[Verses continue between the two columns:]
He wants you to enjoy in them
that light of His grace,
of His love those comforts.

Save, Miguel, your little verses
and expect very shortly
to find peace and comfort
for your weariness.

Have humble confidence
in the Queen of Heaven,
for her powerful arm
frees you from the arrogant lion.

[In the center margin:]
It may be, Miguel, that the priest,
on seeing your humble writings,
will give you a reward
of sugar and some pieces of chocolate.[34]
(**Nota bene**) [Yrigoien's rúbrica]
[f. 455v] or [MQ 2v]

Jesus, Mary, and Joseph
Believe, Miguel, with living faith
that it is the Queen of Heaven
who protects you and moves you
to write these verses.

Have no doubts at all.
Write them without misgivings
and believe you are on the right path
and free of all risk.

And that the great power
of her Son and true God
brings you abundant help,
Miguel, and in no small amounts.

Great is the help you enjoy.
You can be sure and certain
there is not even venial offense
in such a perfect gift.

Do not dread the suffering.
Suffer, because your hardships
will find relief, Miguel,
for I[35] will be there to intercede.

That torment in which you live
is a kind gift and not a defect.
It is grace, the greatest wealth,
and a very perfect treasure.

God, the divine Master,
sends sorrow to those He loves,
so if He afflicts you, do not doubt
it as a sign of great affection.

He is the supreme physician,
so learned and wise,
for in afflictions He discovers
the most precious gold of all.

Fig. 11. A cross flanked by cactus, with the dove of the Holy Spirit above. From the altar screen in the restored church at Santa Cruz de la Cañada. Courtesy of Clark A. Colahan.

Those thoughts are as sure
as they are good.
Embrace them, for God has given you
Miguel, a cross to bear.

This cross, Miguel, fills you.
Through your hardships and anguish
look to praise Him
who has given you those verses.

God does not ask of you the impossible,
for He is very kind and wise.
What you are enjoying is grace,
and not the cause of your own love.[36]

You can be sure that the humble
who takes refuge in my shadow
cannot perish,
relishing that sweet consolation.

Hold fast to your trust
in my Son and true God,
for which you are blessed (**Nota bene**)[37]
with a bright and flawless light.

His power has granted
the requests you made
with your loving poems,
guaranteeing you the final prize.

Expect the biggest prize, Miguel,
given by His true love
and from mine, Miguel,
expect to keep you out of hell.

I am the Mother of hope.
I am the key and door of heaven.
I am the refuge
where the afflicted find solace.

That is what the Church sings
in hymns and psalms and verses.
Do you think, Miguel,
anyone will find fault with your poems?

Keep them, Miguel, and wait
for a very great relief and consolation,
for in every last one
you find a very true help.

[In prose between the two columns:]
Humbly revere the most high and mysterious judgments of God and give the priest those verses, for your way is as secure as can be. They are for His greatest honor and glory, and it is His most holy will.

[f. 456r] or [MQ 3r]

Jesus, Mary, and Joseph
In writing what God
instills in you there is no risk,
nor can there be, Miguel,
with such a safe premise.

With the greatest discretion
give it to the priest without a worry,
for your path is indeed safe

and free from all risk.
Write what you are withholding [Yrigoien's rúbrica][38]
and use up that half a sheet,
for through it you will gain
a great recognition.

Wonderful verses they are
sprung from a true affection
and a motivation both simple
and full of noble desires.

[Between columns:]
Miguel, the priest feels
much good will and affection for you.
Hand over those verses to him,
for God is Greek in his judgments. (**Nota bene**)[39]

My Father, Master, and Lord, I cannot resist expressing what I feel, because I am moved by the great strength of this spirit [**Nota bene** in the margin].[40] I am a poor little sinner and very unworthy of these things that have happened through me, but if that is the will of God I must do it. May His Divine Majesty be blessed in all things and through all things, since for His greater honor and glory He allows many things to be openly known and not hidden. This case happened to me in the year 1726.[41] I had very much turned aside from writing plays in celebration of the birth of the baby Jesus, when a fellow came to my house to ask me to do one. I refused for the reasons that I will explain below, but then reminding myself that it would be in celebration of His Divine Majesty I gave in and promised I would do it. I seized the pen and started it with my limited means as an offering to His greater honor. When I was halfway, with my heart so afflicted, anguished, and distressed that I no longer knew what to do, I kept thinking it was all vanity and hypocrisy, and that I shouldn't be getting mixed up in writing plays since I had had the experience of Your Paternal Grace telling me that I was a hypocrite and that this was going to lead to my being publicly shamed by Your Paternal Grace himself. And many other thoughts kept telling me that I should tear it up or throw it in the fire and quit writing plays.

[f. 456v] or [MQ 3v]

These thoughts troubled me so much that I felt I was about to faint, and so I thrust it away from me, seeing myself suddenly on the verge of throwing it into the fire. But in the midst of such distress, I felt a great help and a prodigious favor encouraging and strengthening me. It seemed to take my hand and help me with these thoughts: "Don't burn it, don't burn it. Continue and offer your play to His Divine Majesty. Pick up the pen and continue." So much was this so that I could not restrain myself. I seized the pen again and as soon as I had taken it up and resumed writing all that storm left me. In my soul I felt such loving sentiments of sweetness, love, and tranquility that my heart burned in the flames of divine love as I considered the love with which His Divine Majesty was willing to become man for our salvation. I am holding back many other things because I am a poor wretch. And I leave this to the judgment of Your Paternal Grace for understanding that this is the will of God, may He be blessed in all things, since He is often pleased by some things that our human understanding cannot comprehend.

The supreme and divine light
granted to you by the immense power of God,
He gives generously with His right hand,

---

always sure and worthy of praise.
Give them, Miguel, to the priest.
Nothing you have written invites suspicion,
for your poems and canticles raise you
to Jesus, your God and sweet husband.

And it is not without a higher emotion
That you write your verses in inspired tones.
Expect to be rewarded through His love,
Receiving such light from His great power.

Give the priest those verses,
blessed with such wealth in your poverty.
What you have written, Miguel, is gold
with which the loving God absolves you.

Garner friends you will, Miguel, that clear light
granted by God for being a poor, humble father
who knows his place within the scheme of things,
His love blessing you with such kindness.

Soli Deo honor et gloria[43]
[f. 457r] or [MQ 4r]

Jesus, Mary, and Joseph
Write, Miguel, for it is God
who rules and governs you.
Believe, Miguel, that His goodness

does not deny you His help.
His high power and might
guide those little verses[44] you write.
He wants you to write them,

so do not fear.
Only the night before
she was *ab eterno electa*[45]
to be the pure bride

of a God made human within her.
That loving affection that you,[46]
Miguel, consider an offense
is a great benefit,
the power of God grants you.

That light in which you operate
is as sure and perfect
as anything God can give you
from His infinite riches.

There is no crime in what you write,
nor any danger in what you think.
God is God, Miguel. Write,
since you carry a bright light within.

Comfort and inspiration are,
Miguel, what the King
of Heaven and Earth with love
provides you in these verses.

That love you have
for His most holy
and true goodness is very free
of even venial offense.

That God's greatness grants your poverty
those shining comforts
in a thousand ways
cannot an be offense.

Have faith, Miguel, that you please
God with what you think,
as God shall reward
each and every one of your verses.

If the priest tells you, Miguel,
you are lost and that the path
you follow is not right,
tell him to look at those verses.

For God does not condemn the man
who, having surrendered to His might,
asks for mercy
and strikes himself with dust.

For He is a very loving Father,
and His mercy reaches down
to the humble and downtrodden
who are very often condemned.

Miguel, follow God in this way
since He displays His love to you
with shelter, aid, and favor
drawn from His ocean of mercy.

God is who grants you that light.
Light is, Miguel, what you carry
with the grace of God, because He can
and does wish you to understand it so.

Understand the light thus, Miguel,
and believe it is God who
through grace grants it to you,
allowing you that light of grace you bear.

No right does the priest have
to censure the light,
because what is not at fault,
Miguel, cannot be an offense.

[Written between the two columns:]
Believe, Miguel, with blind faith that you bear no fault in that half a sheet of paper. Give it to the priest, for it is the will of God and His most pure Mother. You have received a privilege that is wonderful and great in a thousand ways, and it will turn out for the greater honor and glory of God and His most holy Mother.

[f. 457v] or [MQ 4v]

God has not misled you. Write what you are holding back inside, for what the priest condemns in you is not a fault. Have faith, Miguel, that God will reward you for those verses. Overcome that vain fear. Hand them to the priest and do not fear.

47

God, My Father and Master, who is a good witness, knows that what I am writing is the truth. A few days ago this case happened to me: I started to pray the rosary of Our Lady, and so many feelings came over me in the sorrowful mysteries[48] [Yrigoien's rúbrica in the left margin] of Our Lord Jesus Christ's Passion that I could not pray. Those stations [of the cross] appeared to me so vividly that it seemed that I was witnessing them with an incredible apprehension. This became even more acute when I reached the final station, at Calvary, where the feelings increased so much that I thought my life had come to its end, for I was overcome and choked with pain. This has been so much on my mind that I cannot forget it. I have wanted to communicate it to Your Paternal Grace, not out of vanity or so that I should be thought a good man—for I am an ungrateful sinner—but because this has left me frightened, while considering that Your Paternal Grace has told me that by means of their vanity the devil enters into those who look for God and they fly off to hell. As His Divine Majesty well knows, I do not seek to receive these signs of affection. All by themselves they inspire me, as I cannot contain myself when I behold His Most Holy Majesty on a cross and His sweetest Mother at the foot of the cross. And these thoughts just come to me, as the holy King David says that, from not speaking, his bones grew old. But the truth is that I am very much afraid of Your Paternal Grace, and so I suffer all that God knows. I am keeping to myself many other things—which I have not read nor am I capable of having them happen to me—that leave me bewildered in my extreme poverty and misery. Miguel, those thoughts are as meritorious as they are guiltless. Embrace them whenever you feel them and believe that God is thereby granting you a special gift sprung from His generous love and compassion, for it is written that God will take pity on whoever might feel pity and sorrow for the painful stations of His cross. Likewise, God's great power will pity and favor him at the hour of his death. The other special things that you are feeling and

[f. 458r][49] or [MQ 5r]

keeping inside, embrace them, save them, and do not fear them in any way for they are a very perfect help that in His generous love God gives to you. And if the priest gives you no relief, God fills you with an understanding of what the priest does not say to you, and in His Divine Majesty you have, have had, and will have that relief. Give those verses to the priest and let him rate them as vanity or hypocrisy, or give them other labels. But you, Miguel, will be rewarded by God and not shunned. Give those verses to the priest tomorrow, the eighteenth of July, so that he may meditate on them and not confuse you, as the immense majesty of God has not shamed you. Miguel, it is God who speaks to you inside about your little troubles. Entrust yourself to His Divine Majesty and look for support for your wife and small children in the way that His generous love chooses for you. Trust without fear in His sovereign greatness and you will err in nothing. With blind conviction give those verses to the priest and trust in God, Miguel, for God is God and nothing should worry you.

That a man should look for God with humility and a desire to please Him, and that because of this God should cast him down into hell, is something so repugnant to logic that reason itself would forbid it, even if God were not who He is. And that could not be, for His Divine Majesty is who He is and cannot cease being God eternal, incomprehensible and wonderful in all His most holy perfection. It is understanding, Miguel, that His Divine Majesty has given you. Expect from His generous mercy many degrees of glory for each verse you have written. Place your trust in such a supreme and wonderful power and believe that those thoughts that the priest condemns in you as vanity and hypocrisy are a most powerful assistance with which His Divine Majesty favors you. Trust in His greatness and with full confidentiality give those verses to the priest. And believe, Miguel, that you have not strayed.

[Note in the margin between this and the previous page:]

[?], Miguel, [?] taught nor deceived, give your writings to the priest, since they are designed to give you much solace. And, not turned in, they would [?] since God is God.[50]

[f. 458v] or [MQ 5v]

Believe, Miguel, that you have not strayed, nor are you deceived,[51] misled, or hallucinating [Yrigoien inserts his rúbrica here], for God is God, and God who is God is who moves you and has moved you by His high and secret judgments for His greater honor, glory, and credit of your poverty. Miguel, you are nonetheless following a safe path.

Fear nothing. Give the priest those verses and let him think whatever he likes about you, for God is God.

---[52]

Take those verses again and give them, Miguel, to the priest, for God appoints them for you and in them you are not guilty. He hands over His immense power to you. Fear no censure from the priest, Miguel, for God, being God, cannot err. It is a bright and very perfect light that God, a kind Father, instills in you. Miguel, give the priest those verses. To be lost for God, Miguel, is not truly to be lost. Rather it is a gain. Be lost for God and hand over those verses to the priest without any fear whatsoever. Those verses contain a lot that should be understood. And trust, Miguel, that the immense power of God has given them to you from His grace because you are a poor wretch, and what God does and decides about your poverty the priest cannot undo or prevent, because His holy power is very great and in what is grace there can be no risk at all.

I have been very afraid to give Your Paternal Grace all of what I have said above, fearing a reproach at the altar or from the pulpit. Last Saturday, while I was in the midst of the afflictions that I suffered, the thought came to me to give Your Paternal Grace these verses, who will then pass judgment on them. And you are safe, Miguel, on whatever road you take, because what is grace is grace. Chatter, laugh, go for a stroll, skip and jump, for your treasure was one of grace, is and will be of grace, so you need not expect any distress to come from those verses.

[f. 459r][53] or [MQ 6r]

It may be that you have won the most secure gain. You will hand over those verses to the priest without any fear, since they will be very much to his liking, in that they bear testimony to the truth. What is inside you, Miguel, is great, and many things that men in their opinions condemn, abhor, and scorn often have within them a firm basis and a solid content. You know very well that His Divine Majesty does not send those who are His own any tribulations so complete that He does not[54] mix them with many inner consolations known only to he who experiences them. Yours are not idle verses God ordains and determines them for you by His supreme disposition and highest judgment, and they are guided along the right path to good and safe ends. God, Miguel, has made you fortunate, not unfortunate. His sovereign might has chosen to make you a gracious gift, and it is through grace, Miguel, that you enjoy it. And all the power of hell and of the world will not be strong enough to take it from you in any way whatsoever. That is not vanity, Miguel, but grace, not hypocrisy but grace, not a theft of God's honor, but grace. What you don't have can't be attributed to you. Instead, it is grace, for God gives you the necessary attributes through His most holy grace. That grace gives you that light, provides you with that kindness, and gives you that great, sure, and perfect inner motion, because His Divine Majesty wishes it so, and it is His most holy will that you should in this way relish it through His most holy grace. Miguel, give those verses to the priest, for God, who alone is God, moves you by His high and secret judgments for His greater honor and glory. Through these, Miguel, your path is very safe and there will be no power at all that can censure or change a letter in your verses: God protects your life, Miguel, and your sight is preserved by God. Chatter, laugh, have fun, sing, skip and jump, for it is God who has given you those verses and He, being God, is above all others the greatest teacher and can err in nothing at all.

[f. 459v] or [MQ 6v]

For God's sake, take pity on yourself,[55]
Miguel, and don't take compulsion
as a crime in you, Miguel,
because God so orders it.

Give those verses to the priest,
for in them God has given you
a wonderful treasure,
bright and clear in many ways.

Miguel, how can you flee from the strength of the decree given to you by the immense majesty of God? Overcome that vain fear and don't be a coward for me, since I am your God[56] and I alone have dominion over your poverty, as you are one of my creatures. For the priest cannot set himself against the decrees of My sovereign greatness, surpassing wisdom, great power, and infinite mercy. Let nothing give you pause, for not even the tiny leaf of a tree[57] moves without it being My will, and those verses contain much that is good. Expect, Miguel, an elegant prize from God, and give them to the priest. After all, God moves you for some purpose, and your path is very safe, watched over by His most kind and supreme love.

---
[58]

Believe, Miguel, with living faith
that the immense goodness of God
draws near to your poverty
through His loving mercy.

Don't be such a coward, Miguel.
Give the priest those verses,
for he will appreciate them
and greatly benefit from them.

You take much pleasure, Miguel,
you relish it greatly and in many ways,
and you will see the dismay
of many who mock your poverty.

You can be very sure, Miguel,
the divine greatness
of God has given you a wonderful
treasure in those verses.

Hand them over to the priest,
as it may well be that through them
you will savor a great consolation,
and not distress or torture.

His immense love inspires you
because He wishes, Miguel,
to endow your poverty
with this shining, guiding light by the handful.

You will then see, Miguel, how much
the priest benefits from these bright verses,
which God has given you from His
bright, sure, and perfect grace.

Let nothing hold you back, Miguel.
Give them up, for by His high directives
God orders you to do so,
and a magnificent prize awaits you.

His love will ensure you
receive much consolation.
Trust in Jesus, Miguel,
for that light you carry is bright.

[Between columns:]
It is the will of the immense and supreme power of Jesus Christ that you give, Miguel, those verses to the priest. (**Nota bene in the margin**)[59]

[In the right margin:]
Through them,[60] and God's justice, you will see many cast into confusion.

[f. 460r] or [MQ 7r]

Jesus, Mary, and Joseph
God moves this instrument
because He can move it.
His verses are something to see,
because they are well grounded.

You are not crazy or lost
or hallucinating.
What you have written, Miguel,
God has given you, inspiring you.

Miguel, for being humble
and downtrodden, God has given you,
full of wonderful meaning,
His little verses that you have shaped.

Enjoy that sweet advantage
and embrace the greatest compassion,
for God, Miguel, is generous,
and humbly you have asked Him.

You have gained much, Miguel,
by looking for God.
His grace gives you that voice,
Miguel, and you are free of deception.

Lover, Master, and Lord,
Your Greatness well knows (Yrigoien's rúbrica)
that my poverty is amazed
by such an amazing favor.

Through My[61] mercy you acquired
that light because you were My troubadour.
Do not live in sadness,
for I did not scorn your love.

Believe, Miguel, you're on the right path.
You will not be forgotten
for your faith, Miguel, is great,
thus enjoying that pure gold.

Miguel, you are blessed by
the grace of My boundless love.[62] (Yrigoien's rúbrica)
I know your faithfulness,
and offer you eternal life.

And there will be no power
that can oppose My great power
or place an obstacle in the way of your verses,
as you will clearly see.

For My superior might
favors your little troubles,
and in your little poems
you enjoy the most secure riches.

It is not a cunning trap
of the devil. Believe, Miguel, (Yrigoien's rúbrica)
that with that page
God protects you with His might.

God who is God generously
guarantees the venture for you.
The light shining over you is pure
in the midst of your poverty.

Have a good laugh, Miguel,
at the arrogance and abyss
of the devil, who has no
control over your poverty.

Since the inner light
that God kindly shed on you
is one of grace, believe, Miguel,
you are on the right path.

And due to your humility and poverty,
in *redondas* or quartets[63]
you are blessed by a most perfect comfort
through the power of Jesus Christ.

Leave your sufferings
and little cares to God's high might,
for you will be consoled
and see him dismayed.

Believe, Miguel, with firm faith
it is the infinite power
of God that has always[64] given you
every poem you have ever written.

[Between the columns:]
Believe, Miguel, God is pleased
by your simple heart.
He who has mocked you
will not escape without punishment.[65]

Wait, Miguel, with a humble confidence in the Queen of Heaven, for the devil will not triumph over you, and leave your little trials and tribulations to God.

[In the left margin:]
Be convinced, Miguel, that it is the immense majesty of God that has given you those verses and not the devil. Give them to the priest.

[In the right margin:]
It is a most bright
and perfect light that God,
Miguel, has given you.

Wait your time, Miguel, just wait,
for you will not be ridiculed.
Not even a venial[66] fault
have you committed
in what you have written.
Believe, Miguel,
for God offers you relief.

[f. 460v] or [MQ 7v]

Rest and save those verses God has given you, for on that blank page you will write what His Divine Majesty will dictate to your thoughts, and it will be something great.

Don't be a coward, Miguel. Write, for God is pleased by your verses, and you have nothing to fear from them. His Divine Majesty moves you. Write and don't fear. Write, given that His goodness is and has been defending you. Those things you imagine are a perfect light, Miguel. They are a sovereign intervention free from all suspicion, and neither the devil nor his presumption, nor all the power of the world will be able to steal from you what God, who is God, makes right for you. What comes through your imagination and mind is not your own invention. God is who gives you those poems very assuredly. You will be rewarded, Miguel, by His loving mercy. You have not committed even a venial fault and need not expect punishment. You will be very comforted by God's superior might, for it is God who moves you and wants you to write what is in your mind. Write, Miguel, write, for God is defending you.

God in His immense power and wisdom divided the darkness from the light, giving each a nature and composition such that neither the light can turn back from being light nor the darkness from its obscurity, and day and night are the clear consequences. And there will be no theologian, no matter how lofty, who can deny such a remarkable premise. By these two states are understood the righteous, who follow the guidance of reason, truth, and justice, and on the other side those who live fallen and mired in the gloom of the vices, following injustice, impiety, excessive ambition, luxury, the desire for authority and command, and arrogance. And being blind, they do not recognize or understand the chasm that threatens them or the many dangers that their blindness brings. That, Miguel, is a fact as clear, perfect, and certain as it is little known to many. Don't ignore what you, Miguel, know to be so. Follow that loving path on which God has put you, and have no doubt that His Divine Majesty, like a most loving Father, gives you that light for your comfort. Don't be frightened by the horrors with which men have threatened you, nor should you fear any punishment for what you have done, which you consider a loss.

[f. 461r] or [MQ 8r]

Jesus, Mary, and Joseph
Write, Miguel, and believe
free of fear that the immense King
of Heaven, whom you love,
grants you this solace.

Write, for His goodness
is pleased by your affection.
Write, since His power
frees you from the arrogant lion.

Believe, Miguel, you're on the right path,
and that those thoughts
are kindly allowed you
by the most sovereign Master.[67]

The things, Miguel, that the priest
judges to be a defect in you,
God, who is wise, gives to you
with another meaning.

It is grace, Miguel, what God
shows you in those thoughts,
which cause the priest
to judge you already in hell.

Such a misfortune will not befall you.
Await an eternal rest
through the great compassion
and power of the King of Heaven,

Who, like a generous Father,
can inspire you
and give you His true comfort
in those thoughts.

Believe, Miguel, that God, who is God,
gives you by that action
of His most holy grace
great cause for merit.

God does not ask of you the impossible.
Consider it clear and certain,
Miguel, that you are blessed with
His favor, help, comfort, and mercy.

His great power favors
your poverty and affliction.
Don't let scandals instill fear in you
for God is Greek in His judgment.

The one filled with sadness and beaten down
by the world is the one His immense power
usually favors. Do not fear,
Miguel, for God is very wise.

And it cannot be a crime
that His immense power may wish,
because you are poor, Miguel,
to give you such loving consolation.

Receive it from His most holy love
without misgivings,
for your path, Miguel,
is indeed safe from danger and risk.

For God, who is the absolute King,
kindly wishes to confer on you
that bright and perfect gift
from His immense treasures.

Be courageous, Miguel,
and show those poems to the priest,
for it is God's will
that you be comforted.

For He will not be able
to deny you that wonderful consolation,
that light that His immense love bestows
upon your poverty.

Take down word for word
whatever God may dictate to your thoughts
and give the priest, Miguel,
what I lovingly show you.

[Between the columns:]
Believe, Miguel, you are on the right path
with what you have written,
and that God ordains that you should have
that perfect comfort.

[Between the columns:]
The light God
has granted you is wonderful,
and by it you will be
greatly comforted.

[In the left margin:]
It is not, Miguel, the devil who has given you those verses, but rather God's power and His most holy Mother.

[f. 461v] or [MQ 8v]

You have not committed any offense
against God in anything you have written.
Believe, Miguel, that His mercy
gives you that loving comfort.

His great compassion favors
your little tribulations.
Endure them for His love,
and in the end you will not be shamed.

You delight in light, Miguel
bright and full of meaning.
You need not fear the whole world,
for God holds out relief to you.

You are on the right path with your verses.
Humbly follow Jesus Christ
and don't let a reign of terror frighten you,
for He has done you a great kindness.

Don't be afraid of the priest,
for the voices that God has given you
with His infinite power
will bring you relief.

Don't let the scandals
on any side frighten you, Miguel.
Believe firmly that God
is not denying you His protection,

Nor the joy of His mercy
in all your little works.
Trust in His high might
that you will not be dismayed.

Believe that God alone
has control over you,
and that by His grace
you are blessed by the handful.

Do not worry at all.
Leave your little troubles
to His high disposition,
for you will shortly find relief.

Trust in His great power
that what you judge to be a crime
is really a loving gift,
both grace and kindness.[68]

[In the right margin:]
Do not despair, Miguel, for God will not confuse you. Give the priest those verses, for God is God. Trust, Miguel, in the Supreme Empress of Heaven, most holy Mary.

[Between the columns:]
Miguel, give the priest those verses, for He who has given them to you has

more power than the priest, by an immense margin (*O, quan incomprensibilia sunt judicia eius*).[69] Miguel, you're headed in the right direction.

Your cause and case are strengthened (**Nota bene**)[70] by Him who is the cause of all causes. The inner workings of this spirit are flawless, they are safe, they are clear and very effective, and not at all questionable. God, with His immense power and generous compassion, moves you to write, Miguel, those thoughts in which He reveals and gives to you with open hands His loving assistance so that the priest will leave you alone in your poverty and not meddle by second-guessing God's secret decisions, for it is He who directs this spirit. This spirit is moved by God, as it is not moved by the devil. God, Miguel, moves you. God, Miguel, inspires you. And God, who alone is God, whose judgments are unfathomable

[f. 462r][71] or [MQ 9r]

and wonderful in the decisions He makes as absolute Lord and ruler over all things, He alone has moved you and does move you. Don't be afraid of anything, Miguel, not the priest, or the devil, or all the power of hell or the world, for there will be no power that can resist My[72] sovereign and supreme power. These thoughts you feel and have written down are a blessing from My generous clemency and infinite mercy. I am your God, your Creator, your Redeemer, your Protector, your light, your comfort, and all your hope and good fortune. It is I Who can save and cure you, and by My supreme providence and grace I chose you for My glory (**Nota bene**)[73] and want you to enjoy that perfect, bright, and sovereign light of My kind love and generous mercy. Write, for if the priest oppresses and distresses you, I, who am God, cheer you and gladden your heart. Trust in My unsurpassed might and generous love, for neither the priest nor all the priests together will be able to keep from you that kind gift and sure treasure that you enjoy in those verses. Neither the priest nor the most sublime theologian will put any obstacle in your way, since there are no two ways about it when you have a premise that is so sure and solidly based. The priest could have given you relief many days ago with the light that you have shown him, and in that manifest light your thoughts are not in conflict, Miguel, with the Catholic faith that you profess. God[74] has moved you and God is moving you with His most holy power and, like a preeminent teacher who knows how to correct the most learned, allows those thoughts in your poverty. Show them to the priest in what

[f. 462v] or [MQ 9v]

you have written, which is a rich treasure to terrify and confuse the priest and relieve your suffering and hardships. Let the priest be afraid and confused. It is not necessary to be a member of the Third Order to be saved;[75] thinking so is an error and lack of faith found in many, for they should have known that by being members of the Confraternity of the Supreme (**Nota bene**)[76] Empress of Heaven, the most holy Mary of Carmen, they have the strongest and most powerful shield against all the power of hell—if they know how to take advantage of it. After all, it is an article of faith that whoever takes shelter in her exquisitely sweet shadow and calls out to her with faith cannot perish. There are many who cannot understand this, and their spiritual greed is obvious. Don't be afraid, Miguel. Believe that you are on the right path and that your beloved father, St. Francis, will not be angry with you for any reason. The shadow that shelters you is mighty, very mighty, and kind favors from God and His Mother, most pure and holy, fill your life. Believe that in what you have written there is no hindrance to its acceptance, because your verses have a solid basis, and it is most important that you show them to the priest. Care for your wife and your little children, which is your main obligation. Have a good laugh at the speeches of the priest, which are very narrow and limited in their ideas, for God does not ask impossible things of you or of other poor wretches. Give him, Miguel, those verses with a blind resolve and trust in God, for His paths are many. And even though the priest may consider you a simpleminded hypocrite hiding behind a cloud of mystery, don't let anything worry you. Stay quietly at home. Look after your children and your wife and resolutely give those verses to the priest, for your path is a very correct one while you are protected by His most kind and holy love.

[f. 465r][77] or [MQ 10r]

Jesus, Mary, and Joseph
Don't fear the Inquisition,
punishment, harm or disgrace,
for it is God, Miguel, who encourages you
with such important inspiration.

Let it be said that God
is in love with your humble heart.
Follow Him for you have not strayed
and your words are great.

You are not damned, Miguel,
nor need to fear going to hell,
since God, like a tender lover,
has given you all that you have written.

Fig. 12. Crucifix in the restored church at Santa Cruz de la Cañada. Courtesy of Clark A. Colahan.

And that inner impulse
is not a fault in you, Miguel,
since God, gentle and approachable,
inspires, helps, and encourages you.

Don't you see Him on a cross,
Miguel, shattered into a thousand
pieces for you, as He opens his arms
so you may be blessed with the light?

Miguel, when Jesus blesses you
with such great kindness,
what do you fear when His greatness
shed His flowing blood for you?

Who, Miguel, can possibly thwart
or take from you this kindness?
You are rich in your poverty,
since God wants to help you in this way.

Very bright is the light that blesses you
Accept your lot with open arms.
Believe that you are favored
by a God who is all things.

God with you is very generous,
because God is never short in His generosity.
You are not writing just by chance.
It is a special gift.

Who, Miguel, will be able to hinder
His wonderful might
from giving to your poverty
what you have come to achieve?

It's not a matter for the Inquisition,
nor have you committed heresy.[78]
Believe, Miguel, God is guiding you
and you have not betrayed Him.

Know your own heart
and do not fear the devil,
for God testifies to you
in those clear words.

You shall resolutely give them
to the guardian priest.[79]
Miguel, you are on the right path
since those are your crafted words.

It is divine inspiration.
Do not fear the priest.
Show him those verses,
for there is no defect in them.

God inspires them in you, Miguel.
Do not fear any tight situation,
for you are on the right path, Miguel,
in all of your thoughts.

[Between the columns:]
You will see the priest stunned, astonished, and amazed, Miguel, by those verses. Give them to him, Miguel, for God helps, protects, and favors you. Saturday, June 28 1732.

[f. 465v] or [MQ 10v]

Miguel, the Divine Majesty of God neither imposes impossible requirements nor asks impossible things of any of His children. You are one of them. Give those verses to the guardian priest, Fray Joseph Yrigoien, for him to read, meditate on, then tell you what you are to do. If this soul [of yours] does not find consolation or relief in any confessor, and everything is pain, terror, punishment, hell, damnation, and fright, it is not surprising that the soul would wonder and even fear the very light that guides it. Trust in God, Miguel, and in His most pure and holy Mother, and give those little verses to the priest, for you will suffer no harm, punishment, or disgrace. It is God's will that you should give them to him with great secrecy. And look to be rewarded with abundant consolation, for God is God and you are a poor, humble wretch. The priest will respond to you about those verses, Miguel. Trust in God, Miguel, for God is God, and you are very safe from any harm coming to you in any way because of them.

Expose your life to a thousand risks in return for My loving affection and I will give you comfort where you fear punishment. Give the priest those verses, for the infinite power of Jesus Christ appoints and allows you those thoughts, Miguel. There is no offense in the words you are setting down, but much meaning. Believe, Miguel, that your path is free from harm or punishment.

Not even the smallest leaf of a tree is moved without it being God's will. Take those verses, Miguel, and you will be comforted.

Document 6. May 22, 1734. From Inquisitor Mangado y Clavijo in Mexico City to Guerrero, with instructions on how to proceed in light of the denunciations presented by Sopeña and Yrigoien

[f. 447r]

++

[Note in upper left margin:]
Presented[80] in the Holy Office of Mexico City the twenty-fifth of May 1734,

brought before the honorable inquisitors, Navarro and Tagle.[81] [rúbrica of Alexandro Alvarez Carranza]

[Note in upper right margin:]
Let it be done as indicated by the honorable prosecuting inquisitor, with the additional observation that the case may well stem from feeblemindedness, which is the conclusion reached at present.[82]

[Note in central left margin:]
He should be advised of the extreme seriousness of the matter. He should be officially warned of the consequences, drawing attention to this court's orders that he should not inwardly believe or outwardly express such heretical assertions, because any failure to comply will lead to his prosecution to the fullest extent of the law.[83] [Agustín González Ramírez de Zárate's rúbrica]

[Note in bottom left margin:]
On May 27 the writings of the accused and the denunciations of the friars[84] were returned to him[85] as ordered so that he may examine and verify them for the purpose stated by the prosecutor. He should also warn the defendant, officially advising the accused about the consequences of any future actions of this sort. [Agustín González Ramírez de Zárate's rúbrica]

Most Illustrious Grace:

The prosecutor for the Inquisition has seen the denunciations sent by the commissary of New Mexico[86] against Miguel de Quintana, a married resident of Villa Nueva de Santa Cruz, regarding the fact that although admonished by his parish priest to comply with the requirement to take confession and Communion annually,[87] he replied that the requirement was impossible, and that God does not require impossible deeds of his children. At the same time he handed over to the priest a sheet of paper written in his own handwriting. This and nine other sheets in the same handwriting and of the same sort that he handed over to Fray Manuel de Sopeña make it clear, from the great number of good and bad things mixed together, that the aforesaid Quintana is ruled by some evil spirit that dictates to him, either inwardly or outwardly, what to write. This spirit deceives him, leading him to believe that the Son of God is speaking. Still, one cannot form an opinion, as the commissary says nothing at all about the nature of the aforesaid Quintana's life and habits, his abilities and talents. For this reason, Your Honor should return the documentation of the proceedings to the commissary, instructing him to reexamine and verify the statements of the two friars, according to standard directions, who have brought the charges, asking them especially about the life and habits of the said Quintana. He should ascertain also what opinion they have formed regarding the writings that Quintana handed over to them, together with any other information he may judge useful.

[f. 447v]

And if in the commissary's judgment the said Quintana has not suffered a blow to the head or lost the use of reason, he is to summon him before a scribe and have him identify as his what he has written in his own handwriting. He is to ask him who speaks to him or inspires what he writes, who assures him with such certainty that he is on the right path and chosen him to go to heaven. Similarly, how does he explain the contradiction in what he says, on the one hand that he suffers from many fears that grieve his heart, while on the other he finds great relief and comfort? In a report specifically on this case, the commissary will communicate to the court in a detailed report whatever he may discover so that appropriate measures can be taken. Your Honor will make the disposition he deems best. At the Secret Court,[88] May 22, 1734.

Lic.[89] don Diego Mangado y Clavijo. [rúbrica]

Document 7. May 27, 1734. Letter to Guerrero from Inquisitors Navarro de Ysla and Sánchez de Tagle in Mexico City in response to the denunciation by Sopeña

[f. 450r]

+

This court has received from our commissary the correspondence of July 12 of this past year of [17]32, together with the denunciations against Miguel de Quintana that accompany it. Having examined them, it commands that the original copies be returned so that the commissary shall reexamine and verify the statements, according to standard directions, of the two friars who are making the denunciations, Fray Manuel [de] Sopeña and Fray Joseph Yrigoien. He is to ask them especially about the life and habits of the said Quintana and whatever opinion they have formed of his writings, together with anything else deemed useful by our commissary. And should the commissary reach the conclusion that the said Quintana has not suffered injury to the head nor has lost the use of reason, he will cause him to appear before him in the presence of a scribe to have him identify the papers as his, written in his own handwriting. He is to ask him who speaks to him or inspires what he writes, who assures him with such certainty that he is on the right path and has chosen him to go to heaven. Similarly, how does he explain the contradiction in what he says, on the one hand that he suffers from many fears that grieve his heart, while on the other he finds great relief and comfort? And in the case that all of this should arise from simplemindedness, as we now think likely, the commissary should make him aware of the extreme seriousness of the matter.

[f. 450v]

He should officially warn him, drawing his attention to this court's order that he should not inwardly believe or outwardly express such heretical assertions and that failure to comply will lead to prosecution to the fullest extent of the law. When the prescribed steps shall have been taken upon receipt of this document, the said Quintana shall sign a promise of obedience and return it to us via our commissary (may God watch over him) at the first opportunity, etc. The Inquisition of Mexico City, May 27, 1734.[90]

Lic. don Pedro
Navarro de Ysla [rúbrica]

Lic. don Pedro Anselmo Sánchez
de Tagle [rúbrica]

By command of the Holy Office
Agustín González Ramírez de Zárate[91]
Secretary [rúbrica]

[Note at bottom of page:]
To the Honorable Father, Fray Joseph Antonio Guerrero,
Commissary of this Holy Office in Villa de Santa Fe, New Mexico

[f. 451r]

In light of the letter from Your Paternal Grace and the denunciations that came with it, the court has instructed me to inform Your Paternal Grace that it has been received (and I do so) and warn you that there is nothing to be done against María Domínguez[92] for the time being, since the denunciations lack any substance. It is evident that there are only gossip and malicious tales here. It should be kept in mind in the future that in all trials you conduct, the preliminary hearings should be in accord with the instruction for commissaries that you possess, informing us of the credibility each deserves, as well as the faith that can be placed in the accused person's word.[93]

Document 8. November 4, 1734.
Verification of Manuel de Sopeña's statement

[Note at bottom in the left margin of folio 452r:]
When questioned he adds

In Villa de Santa Fe on the fourth day of the month of November in the year 1734. Before the honorable father commissary of the Holy Office, a friar of the holy father, St. Francis, having been summoned, appeared and gave his name as Fray Manuel [de] Sopeña, a son of the Province of the Holy Gospel, minister and priest[94] of the mission of San Lorenzo de los Picurís,[95] and forty-seven years of age. He being present among such

[f. 452v]

upright and religious persons who have sworn to keep the matter secret, Reverend Father Fray Antonio Cressa, vice-custos of the said *custodia*[96] of New Mexico, and Reverend Father Fray Joseph Manuel de Eguía [y Lumbre],[97] instructor of the Gospel in philosophy—both priests and friars of the holy father, St. Francis—the oath was administered to him in due form, and he promised to tell the truth. When asked if he remembers having testified before a judge against a person regarding such things related to the faith, he says that he remembers having testified about a man called Miguel de Quintana before the Reverend Father Fray Juan Joseph Antonio Guerrero, commissary of the Holy Office. Quintana had written some papers that contained scandalous assertions related to the holy Tribunal and had given them to him, though he cannot recall the number of sheets,[98] and he asked that his denunciation be read to him. He was told that he should know that the honorable prosecutor of the Holy Office had introduced him as a witness *ad perpetuam rei memoriam*[99] in a case he is handling against the said Miguel de Quintana, and that he should pay close attention. When it had been read to him, the said Fray Manuel [de] Sopeña stated that he had heard and understood it, that the ideas were his and he had said them just as they had been read to him, that it was correctly written and recorded, and that there was nothing to change, add, or amend, since the way it was written down was the truth. He would and did affirm it, he would and did confirm it, and should it be necessary, he would state it again against the said Miguel de Quintana, though not out of hatred but to unburden his conscience. Then by special instruction of the Holy Office the said Fray Manuel [de] Sopeña was asked how long he had known the said Miguel de Quintana, and he said that he has known him for about fourteen or fifteen years, more or less. When asked what opinion he has formed about Miguel de Quintana, he stated that he has his lucid intervals, but he is not completely convinced he is in his right mind, as witnessed by an occasion when he is said to have thrown stones. He does not recall who told him that, but people say that it must be fifteen years ago when this happened.

When asked what opinion he has formed about his writings, he said that he [Quintana] even seemed to suffer from delusions because when helping him at mass he showed a speech impediment, speaking haltingly, and he seems to have something possessing him. When asked about his life and habits, he said that he [Quintana] rarely goes to mass, giving as an excuse pain in the spleen.

Although a member of the Third Order [of St. Francis], he did not attend meetings or participate in the spiritual exercises that are conducted. When it came to good works, he would use the pretext of illness, but not when there was recreation available. He has always worked as the scribe in the magistrate's[100] office, demonstrating perfectly good judgment, while what he has written

[f. 453r]

has been well received. Currently he is the notary to the ecclesiastical judge,[101] a fact that refutes any finding of madness in him. He was duly instructed to keep the matter secret. He so promised and signed his name to it on the said day, month, and year.

Fray Joseph Antonio Guerrero,
[rúbrica]
Commissary of the Holy Office

Fray Manuel de Sopeña
[rúbrica]

Witnessed by,
Joseph Yrigoien [rúbrica]
Notary of the Holy Office

Document 9. November 5, 1734. Verification of Yrigoien's statement

[Notation at bottom of folio 463r:]
When questioned he adds

In this Villa de Santa Fe on the fifth day of the month of November of this current year of 1734, before the reverend priest commissary of this kingdom, in response to being summoned,

[f. 463v]

there appeared a friar of our seraphic father, St. Francis, who gave his name as Fray Joseph Yrigoien, son of the Province of the Holy Gospel, minister and priest of the mission of San Ildefonso, retired preacher and apostolic priest notary of the Holy Office, *discreto*[102] and secretary of this custodia, being thirty-six years and seven months old. (Present at this time were the following honorable persons in religious orders: the Reverend Father Fray Juan Antonio de Ezeiza, the current vice-custos, and the Reverend Father Fray Francisco [Manuel Bravo] Lerchundi,[103] minister of the Pecos Mission, both of whom have been sworn to secrecy.) The oath was duly administered to him, and he promised to tell the truth. When asked whether he remembers having given a deposition against an individual before a judge regarding things related to the faith, he says that he remembers that on Monday, the thirtieth day of June of the previous year, 1732, at about nine in the morning, before the Reverend Father Joseph Antonio

Fig. 13. Interior of Santa Cruz Church, ca. 1872. Photograph by H. T. Hiester. Courtesy of Museum of New Mexico, Santa Fe. Neg. no. 38006.

Guerrero, commissary of the Holy Office, he handed in a petition signed with his name and in his handwriting, as he is a Notary of the Holy Tribunal, in which he accuses Miguel de Quintana of refusing to comply with the Church. Together with the petition he turned in a sheet of paper with some verses on it and some prose containing some assertions offensive to pious ears. The said paper is dated Saturday, the twenty-eighth of June, of the said year, [17]32, and is unsigned. In the said petition, he attests, as Notary of the Holy Tribunal, to knowing that the hand in which it is written is that of the said Miguel de Quintana, who presented him with the same paper when he [Yrigoien] had required him to go to confession and receive the Holy Eucharist (as is a requirement of our Holy Mother Church) on the nineteenth of June, Sunday, at about eleven in the morning. And when his petition and denunciation were read to him, as he had requested, he was told[104] that he should know that the prosecutor for the Holy Office has presented him as a witness *ad perpetuam rei memoriam* in a case that he is trying against the said Miguel de Quintana. To this reading, the said reverend father paid close attention and said that it was his and the same petition that he had handed in to the said reverend father commissary. It was the truth, and what he had affirmed in it he now reaffirmed and confirmed.

Should it be necessary, he would say it again against the said Miguel de Quintana, not out of hatred but to unburden his conscience and because of the specific order of the Holy Office. When the said Fray Joseph Yrigoien was asked about the life and habits of the said Miguel de Quintana, he said that throughout the time he has known him the said Miguel de Quintana spends his time writing things for others who live here, that they rely on him for this purpose, that this is his life and his usual activity, and that he does not know whether Quintana regularly takes the most holy sacraments or does virtuous actions. When he was asked

[f. 464r][105]

what opinion he had formed about the paper or papers of the said Miguel de Quintana, he said he has formed the opinion that the said Miguel de Quintana is deluded, but that he does not attribute it, nor can he attribute it, to madness or simplemindedness. In the first place, in all the poetry he writes for various purposes he [Yrigoien] has never encountered nonsense. In the second place, his conversation is coherently put together, his advice is well received by those who ask it. Third, in the ten years that he has known him he has seen him at the side of the alcaldes mayores conducting civil and criminal cases, and that in none of them has he been disqualified because of dementia.

Fourth, when he [Quintana] handed him the said paper he was the current notary of the ecclesiastical court and continues to hold that position to the present time, being accepted by all concerned. Both the common people and many important individuals of this kingdom regard him as a man of integrity and sound judgment. For all these reasons, he [Yrigoien] assumes and feels that the said Miguel de Quintana is deluded. He also[106] says that he has been much shocked that the said Miguel de Quintana, who portrays himself in his papers as so holy, should not feel it necessary to comply with the requirement of annually going to confession and taking Communion. He does not know whether or not he [Quintana] has done it during these past[107] two Lents. What he is sure about is that in the year [17]32, on the twenty-seventh day of October, he had not complied with this requirement, nor had he done anything about the repeated reminders he had been given or about having been warned about negligence in accordance with the guidelines for official censure prescribed by the Mexican council to be imposed on transgressors against this requirement. He also asked that his denunciation and subsequent statement be read to him again, and he found that there is a mistake where it says that he appeared before the reverend father commissary on Monday, June 30, but that it was Tuesday, the first day of July. He stated that he did not have a single thing to add, change, or modify, because just as it had been written down was the truth, that he affirmed and confirmed it, and that if it were necessary he would say it again against the said Miguel de Quintana, not out of hatred but to unburden his conscience. He was duly instructed to keep the matter secret, he so promised and signed his name before the said reverend father commissary, in my presence, the appointed notary who has signed his name below.

Fray Joseph Antonio Guerrero [rúbrica]
Commissary of the Holy Office

Fray Joseph Yrigoien [rúbrica]

Witnessed by,
Fray Joseph de Eguía [y Lumbre] [rúbrica]
Appointed notary

Document 10. November 8, 1734. Guerrero interrogates Quintana

[f. 466r]

++

In the Villa de Santa Fe, capital of the Kingdom of New Mexico, on the eighth day of the month of November in this year of 1734 at about nine in the morning a man appeared who had been summoned (by order of the Holy Tribunal) and took the oath to tell the truth. He said that his name was Miguel de Quintana a native of Mexico City, resident of Villa Nueva de Santa Cruz, notary of the ecclesiastical court of that town, married, and fifty-six years old, more or less. When asked if he knows or presumes for what reason he has been summoned, he said that he neither knows nor presumes. And by special order of the said Holy Tribunal he was shown ten sheets of paper of writings to determine whether he recognized them as his and whether he had written them in his own handwriting, and he said that they are all in his handwriting, having written them in his house and having turned them over on several occasions to the Reverend Father Fray Manuel de Sopeña, who was the minister of Villa Nueva de Santa Cruz, and that he gave Father Fray Joseph Yrigoien, who had been minister of the said town, some other little poems on a quarto-sized piece of paper, and that he had given other poems to the deceased Reverend Father Fray Juan Mingues and to the Reverend Father Fray Juan [??] del Pino,[108] the minister of San Buenaventura mission of Cochití, and that these two religious are priests of our seraphic St. Francis.[109] And then[110] they gave him the papers to recognize and he read them all. And as he was reading the ones marked with rúbricas[111] he broke down and cried. When asked about the cause of his weeping, he said that he was feeling touched because he had gone through what is recounted in the verses and papers that have been marked and initialed. When asked who speaks to him or inspires what he writes, he said that it seems to him that it is God's Divine Majesty who puts those thoughts in his mind. When asked who assures him with such certainty that he is on the right path, he said that it seems to him to be His Divine Majesty. When asked who gives him assurance of being chosen, he said that his papers reveal that. When asked how it is that he suffers what on the one hand he says—as he has already said that many fears trouble his heart—while on the other he finds relief and comfort, he said that he often finds himself sorely afflicted, but his tribulation leaves him when Our Lord appears to him in his mind, and then after crying some tender tears with God he finds that all his anguish leaves him. When asked how he knew that was unmistakably God who was speaking to him inside, [in the margin it is inscribed "he said"][112] that he knows through the emotions he feels, and his whole soul burns in the fire of His Divine Majesty. When asked if he has had any visions of God or His saints, he answered none, and that he has these feelings only inside himself, as

[f. 466v]

++

the Almighty knows. When asked how he knows that he is in grace, he says that when he hears mass he feels that he burns with the fire of His Divine Majesty. And in his tribulation he goes to mass and feels those emotions. They are not constant, and he feels them only when God chooses. When asked what high purpose guides his writings, he says that he does not know, that God knows, and that on the eighth day of the feast of Our Holy Lady in September of last year,[113] [17]33, he was overcome with terror and great fear while coming to mass. He became so upset that he was on the verge of deciding not to go, but then he felt other forces that urged him, saying, "Hear mass! Hear mass!" and he went to mass and felt an unsurpassable rejoicing in his soul. When he has any tribulation, the steps of the Passion[114] come into his mind, and that brings him such rejoicing that the tribulation becomes less and goes away for some days. He says that once at the Nambé mission it happened that while talking with the Reverend Father Juan de la Cruz,[115] a Franciscan friar and presently the minister of San Juan de los Caballeros,[116] this friar spoke about the punishments suffered by the damned in hell, and he felt his heart and spirit so distressed that it seemed to him—such was the terror that came over him—that he was going to be damned. But the thought came to him: "*Miguel, neither you nor the holy father will be cast into hell,*"[117] and the pleasure that this brought was so great that the tribulation left him. He is confused because everyone frightens and shames him, and in his sorrows he writes his verses and feels the emotions told in his poems. If he starts praying the rosary, it happens that in the mysteries he loses his voice because of the pain, stays in a trance, and he remains alone in contemplation. Later, whenever God wills it, he comes to and continues. And this is true, by the oath he took. When it was read to him, he said that it was correctly written. He promised secrecy and signed it, along with the said reverend father commissary, before the notary whose name appears below.

Fray Joseph Antonio Guerrero
Commissary of the Holy Office
[rúbrica]

Miguel de Quintana
[rúbrica]

Witnessed by,
Fray Joseph Yrigoien [rúbrica]
Notary of the Holy Office

Document 11. November 10, 1734. Guerrero writes to Mexico City reporting that the verification of Sopeña's and Yrigoien's statements has been completed and that Guerrero considers Quintana of sound mind

[A series of notes appears in the margins indicating the time when the Holy Office in Mexico City considered the said document on March 15, 1735. A key annotation among the latter notes indicates that Guerrero, when he questioned Quintana, did not warn him as instructed.[118]]

[folio 449r]

++

[Note inserted in top left margin:]
Drawn up in the Holy Office of the Inquisition of Mexico City on the fifteenth day of the month of March of the year 1735. Inquisitors Navarro and Tagle [the latter's rúbrica accompanies name]

[Note in left center margin:]
The commissary did not warn him.[119]

[Note in upper right corner:]
Most Illustrious Prosecutor for the Inquisition

+

Very Holy and Just Tribunal:

Having received the order from Your Most Illustrious Grace, along with the denunciations against Miguel de Quintana, the statements of the two friars who accuse him have been verified. And since in my judgment the said Miguel de Quintana has not lost the use of reason, nor has he suffered harm to the head, I made him appear before the notary of the Holy Office. I carried out the orders that Your Most Illustrious Grace has given me, as shown by his attached deposition, which I forward to the holy Tribunal. And since in my opinion none of what the said Miguel de Quintana has said and expressed arises from simplemindedness, I did not bring to his attention the extreme seriousness of the matter, nor did I officially warn him of the consequences as instructed by Your Most Illustrious Grace's order. In light of what has been done, Your Most Illustrious Grace should direct me regarding what action should be taken next. In the meantime, for the glory and defense of our holy Catholic faith, I remain praying to God Our Lord for the protection of Your Most Illustrious Grace's long life. Villa de Santa Fe, November 10, 1734.

Most Honorable Sir,
At the feet of Your Most Illustrious Grace,
your most humble, prostrate, and submissive subject who reveres you,
Fray Joseph Antonio Guerrero [rúbrica]
Commissary of the Holy Office

Document 12. March 24, 1735. Instructions from Inquisitor Mangado y Clavijo to Guerrero, in response to the verifications of statements that have been conducted

[f. 467r][120]

++

[Note in upper left margin:]
Brought before the Holy Office in Mexico City on the thirty-first day of the month of March of 1735, Lord Inquisitors Navarro and Tagle [Alexandro Alvarez Carranza's rúbrica]

[In central left margin:]
The commissary responsible for these legal proceedings, speaking for the Holy Office, should communicate [to Quintana] that he should not publicize or tell anyone at all about these ravings he calls revelations or inspirations, with the warning that, otherwise, action will be taken against him to the fullest extent of the law, and he will be subject to the punishments applied to a person who is obstinate, a fraud, and a rebel.[121] [Alexandro Alvarez Carranza's rúbrica]

[In the upper right corner:]
Let it be done as the prosecutor for the Inquisition says, and the following be added:

Most Illustrious Grace:

The prosecutor for the Inquisition, having seen the new documentation of the legal proceedings against Miguel de Quintana, resident of Villa Nueva de Santa Cruz near New Mexico, is inclined to believe he [Quintana] suffers from some delusion or damage to the imagination in that the assertions contained in his papers show mental confusion. Therefore, Your Grace is to provide for his spiritual welfare, and the commissary will have him appear before him and a notary, place him under oath, and warn him [to proceed] along the safe and easy path, which is in keeping of the commandments of God and His Holy Church, threatening him that if he should slip back into his ravings, the Holy Office will treat him with all severity. To avoid that pitfall, the commissary will choose a learned and prudent confessor for him to hear his confessions and guide him with his counsel, drawing him away from thinking about his nonsense. Your Grace is to decide what is best to be done. At the Secret Court, on March 24, 1735, by

Lic. don Diego Mangado y Clavijo
[rúbrica]

[f. 467v]

+

On July 24, 1736,
Sent to the commissary of New Mexico,
in accordance with the prosecutor's opinion
and the decree.

Document 13. March 11, 1736. A letter from Guerrero to Mexico City forwarding additional reports on Quintana

[f. 468r][122]

+

[In upper left margin:]
Received at the Holy Office of Mexico City on the nineteenth of August 1737.[123]
Inquisitors Navarro, Tagle, Clavijo. [Alexandro Alvarez Carranza's rúbrica]

Very Holy and Just Tribunal:

For your proceedings[124]

I forward the enclosed documentation of the legal proceedings regarding Miguel de Quintana. I did not send them off sooner since the said Quintana was sick in bed, as he is now, and to judge by his condition, near death. It was also because this year (in accordance with the order of the Holy Tribunal) the edicts[125] are to be publicly announced, but it will not be possible on either the third or fourth Sabbath of Lent because of the heavy snowfalls and harsh cold in this region. It has seemed appropriate for me, for greater convenience, to move the event to the month of May, as I saw done in the times of my predecessor, the Reverend Father Juan de Tagle (may he rest in peace). Your Illustrious Grace will tell me if you approve and will command whatever may be most useful to Your Grace and the Holy Tribunal. May his majesty look after them for many years to protect and defend our holy faith. Villa de Santa Fe, New Mexico, March 11, 1736.

Your Most Illustrious Grace,
At the feet of Your Most Illustrious Holiness,
Your prostrate subject who reveres you,
Fray Joseph Antonio Guerrero
[rúbrica]

Document 14. July 24, 1736. Letter from Inquisitors Navarro de Ysla and Sánchez de Tagle to Guerrero, with new instructions to be followed in light of the most recent reports they have received on Quintana

[f. 469r][126]

++

This court having seen the documentation of the legal proceedings that our commissary forwarded against Miguel de Quintana, resident of Villa Nueva de Santa Cruz, because of the assertions that are expressed in them, we have ordered that receipt be acknowledged and our commissary be instructed that as soon as he receives this document, he is to have the said Miguel de Quintana appear before him and a notary of this Holy Office. He is to severely admonish and criticize his unusual behavior, warning him to walk along the clear and sure path, which is in keeping the commandments of God and His Most Holy Church, commanding him in the name of this Holy Office not to publicize or tell anyone at all about these ravings he calls revelations or inspirations, cautioning him that if he should slip back into them, he will be treated with all the severity of the law and subject to the punishments applied to an obstinate, a fraud, and a rebel. Similarly, our commissary will require him to go to confession

[f. 469v]

with a learned and prudent confessor that he will choose for him to hear his confessions and guide him with his counsel, drawing him away from thinking about his nonsense and ravings. When these things have been done, and they will be done immediately upon receipt of this document, including the said Quintana's signature promising to obey, it will be returned to us at the first opportunity by our commissary (may God protect him), etc. Inquisition of Mexico City, July 24, 1736.

Licenciate don Pedro Navarro de Ysla [rúbrica]	Licenciate don Pedro Anselmo Sánchez de Tagle [rúbrica]

By order of the Holy Office,
Alexandro Alvarez Carranza [rúbrica]
Secretary

[At bottom of page:]
To the Reverend Father Fray Joseph Antonio Guerrero,
Commissary of this Holy Office in Villa de Santa Fe, New Mexico

Document 15. January 23, 1737. A report by Yrigoien and Guerrero on their visit to Quintana's house, where Miguel promised to do as the Inquisition ordered

[f. 470r][127]

++

I, Fray Joseph de[128] Yrigoien, notary of the Holy Office, state that, pursuant to the order of the Reverend Father Commissary Fray Joseph Antonio Guerrero, I went to the house and dwelling[129] of Miguel de Quintana to summon him to appear before His Reverence. I found him sick in bed from a pain that has been afflicting him for two months, and for this reason I was unable to carry out the order. He said that if he recovers his health he will present himself without delay, and so that he may recover from his illness and to vouch for his obedience, I signed it January 22, 1737.

So attested,
Fray Joseph Yrigoien
[rúbrica]
Notary of the Holy Office

Upon finding that Miguel de Quintana was ill, the said Reverend Father Commissary decided to go to the house of the aforesaid, and he did so today, January 23, 1737, at about nine o'clock in the morning. Finding him of entirely sound mind, he informed him in the name of the very holy and just Tribunal of the Inquisition—in my presence, the notary whose name is written below—that he should have nothing more to do with ridiculous revelations and publicizing them under the penalty of being punished as someone obstinate, a fraud, and a rebel. Then, as regards a confessor—after he had been harshly admonished[130]—he was told to let his spirit be guided by the Reverend Father Fray Joseph Yrigoien, minister of the mission of Santa Clara, who is closest to the dwelling of the said Quintana. To all this, he replied: that he obeys and will obey all that he has been ordered to do, omitting nothing, and that what he feels about his revelations and writings is the same as the Holy Tribunal feels. He greatly regrets having done it and having believed in such nonsense. He promised to keep the matter secret and,

[At bottom middle of page: rúbrica resembling Yrigoien's]

[f. 470v]

before me, the notary whose name is written below, signed his name, along with the said Reverend Father Commissary, on the said day, month, and year, in Villa Nueva de Santa Cruz.

Fray Joseph Antonio Guerrero
[rúbrica]
Commissary of the Holy Office

Miguel de Quintana [rúbrica]

Witnessed by,
Fray Joseph Yrigoien
[rúbrica]
Notary of the Holy Office

Document 16. April 17, 1737. Letter from Quintana to Father Juan de la Cruz, asking his reaction to new poems and prose he has written

[f. 474r] or [MQ 11r][131]

++

Very Reverend Retired Preacher Father, Fray Juan [Sánchez] de la Cruz:[132]

Most beloved father and master of mine, I greet Your Paternal Grace, hoping, as I always do, that you are in good health. Both of my bones[133] are somewhat better—thanks be to God—and I am very much at Your Paternal Grace's disposition. I am sending the enclosed verses and accompanying prose for Your Paternal Grace's censure and consideration, just as Your Paternal Grace sent word to me through my *comadre*,[134] Gertrudis Xirona, that I should do. In the interim, I continue to ask His Divine Majesty to give Your Paternal Grace a long life of many years for my comfort. Written from what is also your home,[135] on the seventeenth day of April 1737.

Your most humble and admiring servant,
kisses the holy hand of Your Paternal Reverence,
Miguel de Quintana [rúbrica]

Document 17. April 24, 1737. A report by Fray Juan Joseph Pérez [de] Mirabal[136] on how he took possession of the new poems and prose by Quintana mentioned in the preceding document. Those writings by Quintana are included

[f. 471r][137]

+

I, Fray Juan Joseph Pérez de Mirabal, retired priest and minister of this jurisdiction of Villa Nueva de Santa Cruz, do hereby state that on the twenty-fourth day of April, 1737, after having spent this day in the said jurisdiction, at about three o'clock in the afternoon, on visiting the reverend retired priest, Juan de la Cruz, I discovered that Miguel de Quintana, a resident of the said Villa [Nueva] de Santa Cruz, had written to the priest some poetry and prose in a notebook pad,[138] as follows:

Jesus, Mary, and Joseph
The Supreme Director,
who is none other than Jesus Christ,
the sovereign King of Heaven
whom you submissively adore,

is, Miguel, the one who guides you
with His infinite power.

The light that you carry is bright
and just as free from danger
as My love was freely given to you
for being poor and downtrodden.

You are blessed by My mercy,
and what you enjoy through My grace
can hardly be a crime.
It is a great kindness.

Do not fear the devil
who has no dominion over you,
nor will his arrogance,
his damnation, or his gaping chasm.

For, if anyone prides themselves on their wisdom
as prudent and understanding,
they understand it all backward,
confounded by God's message.

And whoever would venture as to dare
anything against your house or person
will have from My strong arm
a rigorous punishment.

Do not fear, Miguel.
Continue with your writings,
for in them you are proceeding correctly
and indeed free from danger.

Do not fear those varied
and different thoughts,
for all are rightly
guided by My love.

Look to My cause and do not fear,
for no punishment, dismay,
harm, or shame will come to you
for what you have written.

If men compromise you
with their limited judgments,
God's heavenly provisions[139]
fill your heart with joy.

The inner light that you enjoy
is, Miguel, from Jesus Christ
and not an illusion of the devil
as men have told you.

And if from My kind love, Miguel,
you see yourself persecuted,
follow Me, for there will be no one
who can block your path.

Your great inner strength,
full of deep meaning and significance,
is a blessing from the divine power
for being humble and poor.

Believe, Miguel, with living faith
that God has not confused you,
nor is His divine might
angry[140] with you.

[Between columns:]
Miguel, don't be afraid. Believe that it is the divine omnipotence of God that has moved you and does move you. Believe that your verses will strike fear, embarrassment, and terror into those who have mocked you. Those sharp pains that afflict you will come to pass. Be patient, for very little remains.

[f. 471v]

++

Believe, Miguel, that you have been moved, protected, aided, and favored by the immense majesty, power, and wisdom of God, the only Master and absolute Lord of all things, who has dominion and power over them all, the same whom you adore, reverence, and confess to be your God, your King, your Redeemer, your Father, and Benefactor on the sacred tree of the cross. Have no fear or dread, for your soul will not be lost. Continue, write, for God is God, and your friend the reverend retired preacher father, Fray Juan de la Cruz, has taken pity on your distress and sent word that you should write what you were and are feeling inside. Write and do not struggle against the thoughts you have or the Divine Majesty of God that sent them to you, for this Divine Majesty, being a wise teacher who knows how to correct the most learned of men, makes use of the weakest instruments, the poor wretches trampled and persecuted by the world, to be instruments of His divine justice, allowing many lesser faults to exist in punishment for more serious ones. The reverend father who is the commissary of the Holy Office and his notary have come, Miguel, with frivolous pretexts dressed in their passions to hit you with a cat-o'-nine-tails,[141] accusing you of and reprimanding you for offenses when you have committed none, not even venial ones. Trust in God, for if they are trying to take your life or drive you out of your mind, they will not succeed, because God is God. He protects your life with His most holy power. Miguel, God is God, God who inspires you, not the devil. Continue, write, for it is His most holy will that you should write, and if they have attempted to prevent you from writing, threatening you with a severe punishment from the Holy Office, it will not be as Your Reverences wish, but whatever God wishes and is pleased to give you. His Divine Majesty will give you His glory in whatever He wishes, in accordance with what may be His most holy will, and in harmony with your way of understanding. It will be as His Divine Majesty may feel like doing and not to please the taste or palate of any individual, because His high might can give you whatever He wishes from His immense treasures, and no one can hinder His Divine Majesty. That cannot be an offense in you, Miguel. Rejoice in God, Miguel, and take comfort in His might, in His divine wisdom and most holy love, that love that is the most perfect, most kind, and most sure. There is no human power that will in the slightest censure your verses. You will not die, for God protects your life, and you are to write in spite of all hell, because it is God's will. Very soon you will see yourself cured of that ailment

[f. 472r][142]

you suffer. If Father Guerrero has put you against the wall by giving instructions that you are to confess only with his notary and no one else, that is unjust, insolent, and even nauseating of him, for you write on subjects very deserving of attention and are a Catholic Christian, and they will not be able to prove any heresy or anything else contrary to the Catholic faith that you profess. Confess with whomever you wish, for the Divine Majesty gave you your free will so that you should do just that. God does not impose impossible requirements on any of His creatures, nor does He want souls to become tangled up in scruples. Attempt to rest and do not burn those verses even though you may find yourself severely afflicted. Forward them to the Reverend Father Fray Juan de la Cruz, for His Paternal Reverence will find the means for your relief. Let nothing worry you, Miguel. Trust in God, Miguel, for it is God, who is God, who guides you and fills your poor little suffering heart with gladness, and as long as you have His Divine Majesty you can lack for nothing. Surrender your poor little simple heart to His Divine Majesty because the feelings that you inwardly enjoy by His high command cannot be blocked by all the power of hell that might oppose you. Neither the reverend father, who is the commissary of the Holy Tribunal, nor his notary will bother you either to help or harm, as you will see, nor will you be troubled in that way anymore. You will write calmly, in peace and tranquility, enjoying from My power, love, and most holy mercy the light and sovereign help that I will choose to give you, to the dismay of many who pride themselves on their wisdom and understanding. Try to rest and send those verses to the reverend retired preacher father [Fray Juan Sánchez de Cruz?] as you are planning. Let nothing worry you, for you are on the right and most correct path and soon you will be comforted. What you, Miguel, have come to understand is nothing to be laughed at. Trust God and do not fear, for you are moved by God. His sovereign might promises you great relief that will soon come, and you will see His promise kept. Look for it, for He is very fatherly, very prudent, and very kind. Do not fear perishing as long as you live in submission to His love. Miguel, the distress, affliction, and anguish of your spirit and of your poor wife are well known to God and recorded in His clear hand as part of His divine vigilance. The reverend father

[f. 472v][143]

commissary of the Holy Office today would have wished, and still wishes, that he had not come to your house with his jealous notary. Forward your verses without any misgivings, for neither will what is just before God cease to be just, nor will injustice cease to be unjust, for God has a sword for everyone.

[144]

[Mirabal's rúbrica] [Mirabal's rúbrica] [Mirabal's rúbrica]

This copy agrees with the original, from which I, Fray Juan Joseph Pérez Mirabal, made the said copy in order to deliver it to the reverend priest, general preacher, and retired exdiscreto[145] of his holy custodia, notary to the parish priest of the Province of the Holy Gospel, its custodias, and missions, and notary of the Holy Office, Fray Joseph de Yrigoien, minister of Santa Clara mission, so that as an officer of the very just and Holy Tribunal of the Inquisition he may today put down what is appropriate to be a sworn record. I signed it in this convento[146] in Villa Nueva de Santa Cruz on the said day of April 24, 1737.

Fray Juan Joseph Pérez Mirabal[147]
[rúbrica]
Minister of Villa Nueva [de Santa Cruz]

Document 18. April 25, 1737. Letter to Quintana from Juan de la Cruz, responding to Quintana's most recent writings

[f. 475r][148]

++

Miguel de Quintana:

My dear sir, I received the document, with its enclosures, and to be completely honest I must tell Your Grace that I did not understand it, nor could I fathom its phrases, nor did I grasp its purpose. As I am returning it to Your Grace, enclosed in this letter, you will be able to see my incapacity and inability as censor of your work, for *veo, videro*[149] [that] it requires concepts too scholarly to be grasped by my ignorance. In regard to what Your Grace said about Gertrudis Xirona, what I said to her was that, keeping in mind the prolonged nature of your illness and its implications for a man of business (as Your Grace has been involved in the current lawsuit and other affairs), dealing with civil cases while practically serving as the permanent secretary of the alcaldes mayores, it would be a very good idea, and something that would safeguard your conscience in matters of morality, to examine and reexamine it to see if there is something burdening it

[f. 475v]

++

because of a weakness in you or from some other of the causes that in questions of moral conscience one daily comes across and experiences. [You might wish] to make a statement about what it is that you recognize as wounding your conscience. And if there is something there, it will be in the area of the sacraments. But disregard my comment and it should be reiterated that if Your Grace does not sense any need for such a proceeding, no inner pressure to satisfy fairness or morality in yourself, then Your Grace has satisfied your obligation as a good Christian, and basing your decision on the intrinsic probabilities of the case Your Grace might set aside all moral self-doubt *i hic & nunc.*[150] By the enclosed letter, what I wish[151] to say is that Your Grace should act on the basis of a scrupulously clean conscience. Mindful of the many unforeseen circumstances concerning your health, I am closely following the ups and downs that I hear about Your Grace's illness, and may God look after and grant you perfect health for many years. San Juan [de los Caballeros], April 25, 1737.

Your affectionate chaplain
kisses Your Grace's hand,
Fray Juan de la Cruz
[rúbrica]

Document 19. April 30, 1737. Yrigoien testifies how he obtained a copy of Quintana's latest writings through Father Mirabal

[f. 473r][152]

++

In the town of Santa Fe, capital of the Kingdom of New Mexico, on April 30, 1737, at about ten o'clock in the morning, without being summoned there appeared before the reverend father commissary of this Holy Office a friar of our seraphic father, St. Francis, and swore in due form that he would tell the truth. He was a son of the Holy Gospel Province of Mexico and said that his name is Joseph Yrigoien, the apostolic and current notary of the Holy Office. To unburden his conscience he says and reports in denunciation that on the twenty-fourth day of this said month of April, when he was in Villa Nueva de Santa Cruz on matters that had come up in the converto of the said town at about vespers the reverend father minister of that town arrived, Fray Juan Joseph de Mirabal. He told him that he needed to speak to him privately, so he [Yrigoien] sent away those who were with him. The said father went on to tell him that he had been scandalized when, upon visiting the Reverend Father Juan de la Cruz, His Paternity had called him aside to read him a paper containing poetry and prose written by Miguel de Quintana. It had been sent to the Reverend Father Fray Juan de la Cruz so that His Paternity would give it his approval. But seeing in it several ill-sounding ideas, which are in violation of the righteous and authoritative workings of the Holy Office, he [Yrigoien] told the Reverend Father Fray Juan de la Cruz that this had to be reported to the Holy Tribunal. The said father said that he did not understand what was on the paper and that he would write to Miguel de Quintana and return it to him. While the said Reverend Father Fray Juan de la Cruz was writing to the said Quintana he took the paper into another room and asked for paper and ink and made a signed copy in his own hand. He handed it to me, Fray Joseph Yrigoien, as the notary of the Holy Office, so that I should present it, as I am doing today, on the stated date. It is a large sheet of paper folded into four and written on all of the sections, except for a little of the last one. At the same time the Reverend Father Fray Juan de Mirabal[153] told me that if I wanted to lay hands on the original along with the said letter in which the Reverend Father Juan de la Cruz was responding, I should go to Manuel de la Rosa's[154] house, a permanent resident of the said Villa Nueva de Santa Cruz and the carrier of the documents. It was possible that he might not yet have given it to the said Miguel de Quintana. Therefore without any delay I went to the house of the said

[rúbrica]

[f. 473v]

Manuel de la Rosa, and I asked him if he was taking a letter sent by the Reverend Father Juan de la Cruz to Miguel de Quintana. He answered that he was and I told him that since I am the notary of the Holy Tribunal he should turn it over to me. He immediately did so, and I enjoined secrecy on him, to which he gave oral assent. I am submitting the said letter addressed to the said Miguel de Quintana; it is sealed with bread and has been marked with the sender's fingernails. When I had returned to the said convento at Villa Nueva [de Santa Cruz] at about eight o'clock, the Reverend Father Fray Juan de Mirabal told me that if I wanted to get the paper that the said Miguel de Quintana wrote to the said Reverend Father Juan de la Cruz in which he asks for approval of the same little sheet of paper, that at dawn I should go to the dwelling of the said Reverend Father Juan de la Cruz and ask him for it. I decided to carry that out, as it seemed the right thing to do, and on the morning of the twenty-fifth I went to the dwelling of the Reverend Father Fray Juan de la Cruz, and I told the holy father that he should hand over to me, as an officer of the Inquisition, a paper of Miguel de Quintana's that he had in his possession. He gave it to me, and I am presenting it to the said reverend father commissary. It consists of a small piece of paper with writing on one side and signed by the said Miguel de Quintana. He said that this is the truth, by the oath he had taken, and that he had not said it out of hatred or malice. He promised secrecy, and when his testimony was read to him he said it was correct and that he had nothing to add or take away. He signed it with the reverend father commissary before me, the undersigned appointed notary, on the said day, month, and year.

Fray Joseph Antonio Guerrero [rúbrica]
Commissary of the Holy Office

Joseph Yrigoien [rúbrica]

Witnessed by
Fray Joseph de Eguía
Appointed Notary [rúbrica]

ADDITIONAL DOCUMENTATION

Document 20. 1737. Quintana's Retraction

From the Franciscan Archives, Mexico City—#982,
box 15, no. 260 (7r–v, 8r–v)

Description/synopsis: An open letter from Miguel de Quintana, in which he retracts certain accusations that he had made against the Franciscan missionaries in New Mexico, at the Villa Nueva de Santa Cruz, New Mexico, November 2, 1737. It is preceded by a request for certification [of the letter] presented by Fray Juan Antonio de Ezeiza and by an order given by Henrique de Olavide y Michelena, governor of New Mexico, at the town of Santa Fe, November 22, 1737.

[In the margin:]
Written November 23, 1737

My Lord Governor and Captain General:

I, Fray Juan Antonio de Ezeiza, current vice-custos of these missions in New Mexico of the Holy Custody of the Conversion of Saint Paul, appear before Your Grace as the law may best allow and my rights require, and I state that as regards all that relates to our reputation, which has been ruined or is, at the least, in manifest danger of being ruined (as all the missionaries of this holy custody now lament), no occasion should be lost to restore it. As the occasion places this open letter in our hands, which I present to Your Grace I ask and request that two copies of it be ordered made for me, duly witnessed to establish their validity, and for them to be returned to me so that I may take whatever further recourse the law permits. I affirm that what I have written springs not from any malice whatsoever, and in what is necessary, etc. = Fray Juan Antonio de Ezeiza.

[In the right margin:]
The Governor's Order

In the Villa de Santa Fe, capital of this Kingdom of New Mexico, the twenty-second of the month of November of 1737, this request was presented. When I, the governor and captain general of this said kingdom and its provinces, had seen the request, I considered it officially presented and ordered that one copy of the letter this party requests be given to him in a public manner that would establish its validity. Then acting in the corresponding and appropriate manner,[155] I commanded and authorized that there be witnesses present because there is no royal and public scribe in the said kingdom. Henrique de Olavide y Michelena. Witness, Juan Joseph Moreno; witness, Pedro Joseph de León.

[In the left margin:]
Letter

Most illustrious Dr. don Martín de Elizacochea, by the grace of God and of the holy Apostolic See,[156] most worthy bishop of this diocese, and my lord.

Most Illustrious Sir:

With the greatest submission that I owe to the high dignity of Your Illustrious Grace, being only a poor, humble notary of Your Illustrious Grace in this Villa Nueva de Santa Cruz in this Kingdom of New Mexico, I am writing to Your Illustrious Grace to say, my lord, that although I have written several letters to don Joseph Bustamante, who was the vicarial ecclesiastic judge of this kingdom, and although they are damaging to the reputation of the religious brothers, sons of my holy father, St. Francis, still, through the grace of God being a Catholic Christian and seeking the health of my soul by pleasing His Divine Majesty as I should, [bearing in mind] the harm that may come from this to the said holy order of my father, St. Francis, I must say, and I do say, that being a weak man, poor and obliged by the need to find bread for my children, I humbly confess that I wrote them out of servile flattery.[157] Therefore, I take back everything that I stated in them and say that the reverend father ministers are precisely fulfilling their obligations in terms of administering the holy sacraments. Their doctrines have sought to further the spiritual welfare of the souls [entrusted to them], knowing full well that the reverend father and preacher, Fray Joseph de Yrigoien, and the reverend father and preacher, Fray Joseph Antonio Guerrero, in their actions, assertions, and advice, have sought my spiritual and temporal welfare, while I, cloaked in my self-importance and my blind emotions, have taken their actions as offenses, believing them to have done it all because of my position as notary of Your Illustrious Grace.[158] And therefore, so that the said persons' reputation, by every possible means and manner, may be recovered to their satisfaction, and for all the other persons as well, I submit to the profound understanding of Your Illustrious Grace all that is contained in the foregoing clauses and expressed in this letter. I ask Your Illustrious Grace to pardon me the bad example I set in the said letters, no matter what and how I wrote them, for the love of God and of his most Holy Mother, Our Lady, the Virgin Mary, and of our father, St. Francis, so that all may lead to the greater glory and grace of

His Divine Majesty, whom I humbly ask to grant prosperity and protection to the very important life of Your Illustrious Grace for many years along with the greatest of good fortune. Done in Villa Nueva de Santa Cruz, New Mexico, the second day of the month of November, 1737 = Most Illustrious Sir, at the feet of Your Illustrious Grace [lies prostrate] your most faithful servant and notary,

Miguel de Quintana [signature]

This copy agrees with its original, which I returned to the party from which this legal copy was obtained. It has been compared with the original and corrected and is a faithfully made copy, to which the witnesses were don Juan Joseph Moreno, Pedro Joseph de León, and Salvador de Santistevan. And so that it may be of record where appropriate, this copy has been made via reciprocity using witnesses who were present in lieu of a royal and public notary, of which there is none. It was drawn up with my authority in Villa Nueva de Santa Fe, New Mexico, the twenty-third day of the month of November, 1737=

To witness the truth of this document I place on it my accustomed signature.

Henrique de Olavide y Michelena [rúbrica]

Most Illustrious Señor Pedro Joseph de León [rúbrica]

Juan Joseph Moreno [rúbrica]

Appendix One: Quintana's Lawsuit Over Stolen Horses

From the Spanish Archives of New Mexico (no 178, fr. 627–29), (Twitchell *The Spanish Archives of New Mexico*, vol. 2, no. 178).

[frame 627]

Jesus, Mary, and Joseph[159] Villa Nueva de Santa Cruz, 1712

A claim brought by Miguel de Quintana against Joseph Trujillo for a theft of two horses by Indians, one of whom was his [Trujillo's] servant.

[frame 628]

[Top of page torn and a portion missing]

Miguel de Quintana, born in Mexico City and a resident of Villa Nueva de Santa Cruz. Having recourse to the most suitable procedure available to me under law pertaining to my rights, I appear before the might of Your Grace and state that on the thirteenth day of the last month of July three Christian Apaches[160] fled. One was from Capt. Joseph Trujillo's household, another of that of the very reverend priest custos [Fray Juan de Tagle], and the other Cristóbal, a former servant of Diego Martín, now a free man. He was with Capt. Joseph Trujillo, or at least had gone to that household to stay for a while, and then fled, and it harmed me in my extreme poverty. He took from me two horses, [?] broken for riding, one a dapple gray that I had tethered near my house, and it was carried off by cutting the tether with a knife. On finding the piece of tether that they had left behind, I supposed that someone had stolen it to ride to this town. Then as I was going to the house of the said Joseph Trujillo to get a sorrel horse, saddle broken, that he was keeping for me in his herd so that I could go about looking for the other one, I learned in Cristóbal Torres's house that the said three Apaches had fled, taking with them two horses, one a roan and the other a sorrel. To find out whether it had been mine, I went to see the said Joseph Trujillo, and he told me that they had taken it when it was tied up in his corral, something he had done so that it would not get lost. With this account I came back to my house reflecting on my grave misfortune. Since I am in the situation where I find myself, burdened with seven children, those two horses provided me some relief by carrying a few supplies and firewood and allowing me to run errands. Then just when I had given up all hope of receiving any indemnization, it pleased Our Lord God that two of them came back, Cristóbal and Andrés, the latter the servant of the aforesaid Joseph Trujillo, to whom with a clear explanation I said that he should make it good to me since the thieves were from his house and had returned to it. To this he replied that I should recover them, since they were mine, and that

[frame 629]

he had not made a commitment to pay me in case they should be lost and since those who carried it off from this place had not been enemies,[161] [?] as a suitable means of presenting my just cause before the nobleness of Your Grace, while keeping in mind that I am burdened with children, and that the two said horses were my hands and feet, they should be made good to me, and any of the three fugitives might well pay toward my complete restitution. For all these reasons I ask and beg Your Grace, with all submissive obedience, to see fit that I be paid fair value for my two horses based on their original condition, since through them I will receive a kind favor along with the justice I am asking for. I swear by God and His Son on the cross that I have written not out of malice and in what is necessary.[162]

Miguel de Quintana
[rúbrica]

Fig. 14. An angel, from the altar screen in the restored church at Santa Cruz de la Cañada. Courtesy of Clark A. Colahan.

Appendix Two: Lugarda Quintana's Will, 1749

Spanish Archives of New Mexico (SANM), Series I,
Land Records of New Mexico, no. 968, r. 5, fr. 717–20
[f. lr]

In die Domini,[163] amen.

In the name of almighty God, Father, Son, and Holy Spirit, three distinct persons and one true God; and of the Virgin Mary, Our Lady; the blessed St. Michael the Archangel; St. John the Baptist; the apostles, St. Peter and St. Paul; my patron saint, St. Lugarda; and my beloved holy angel.

I, Lugarda Quintana, a native of this kingdom and citizen of this Villa de Santa Cruz, make this will and testament, being sick in bed from the illness God Our Lord has seen fit to give me, being of sound mind and understanding by divine grace.

First, I state and say that I believe faithfully and truly in the mystery of the Holy Trinity, Father, Son, and Holy Spirit, three distinct persons and one true God, and in all the other mysteries that our Holy Mother Roman Catholic Church believes and confesses, in which all the saints have died, and that I want to live and die as a Catholic Christian, by divine grace.

Furthermore, I commend my soul to God, who created and restored it with his most precious blood, and my body to the earth from whose substance it was formed.

Item: I order my executor, for which effect I name my compadre, Pedro Sánchez, that, if God Our Lord should see fit to take me from this life to the next, since my husband is absent and I do not know where, and as I select him for my executor, that he have me buried in the parish church of the Villa of Santa Cruz, wherever the executor may wish.

Item: I order that the mandatory bequests each be made from my estate as specified individually herein.

Item: I declare that I am married according to the order of our Holy Mother Church to Asencio Archuleta, from which marriage

[f. 1v]

we had and raised three children, one female and two males, who are Cristóbal, Juana Josefa, and Nicolás Marcos Archuleta, whom I leave, together with my husband, as my heirs.

Item: I declare that if God should take me from this life, I leave my burial and funeral to the discretion of my executor.

First, I declare as my belongings four lead oxen and two bull oxen.

I declare I have a cow for breeding and a two-year-old calf.

Item: I declare I bought a piece of land from Luis de Archuleta for the price and amount of 35 pesos, which was what we agreed on for that land. Luis de Archuleta was paid in full and has the obligation to complete the sale, paying the taxes to the magistrate for the piece, 218 varas[164] long by 11, as far as the main acequia.

Item: Another piece of land that belonged to my husband and was part of the house, which, because it was not distributed among the brothers, will not be known clearly until the magistrate distributes it. I also state that I have built a garden ten varas long of which I claim only the walls and roof.

Item: I leave an old shovel-pick [*coa*][165] and two old hoes; as well as another small shovel-pick [coa], a small axe, an adze and chisel, a spit, a spoon, an auger, and an old round-bottomed pot. I also declare I am leaving three plowshares. The round-bottomed pot is from what my husband had obtained, an old saucepan, and an old trade knife.

Item: Three chests with their locks, two small ["more like three" superimposed]; one large and old; a grooving tool; a guitar;[166] two windows and a small chair; a wooden dough bowl.

Item: I am leaving some new serge skirts [*enaguas*] and some old ones; a pair of skirts [*faldillas*]; four varas of medium-quality lace; a few varas of the same of sisal fiber; two mantillas, one lined, one unlined; cloth for stockings of new silk; a pair of men's shoes; two capes; four varas of striped cloth; a necklace of old coral and varied silver disks; some blue enamel bracelets; some fine pearl earrings with some baroque[167] pearls—all solid; four hanks of red silk with two of buff-colored silk; some new wool stockings; and new cotton understockings.

[f. 2r]

Two pairs of knitting needles for stockings; three dishes, two fine and one ordinary; a piece of old fringe; a jar of sugar-paste candies; a white mesh for a sieve; some small tablecloths and a napkin; a sash from Sonora, two and a half varas long; a new gourd dish; three doors, all single; two locks with one key.

Item: Fourteen images of saints, all small, and a holy Christ, of bronze.

Item: A mattress with two sheets and three varas of coarse, woolen cloth [*sayal];* a saddle horse; a cart ready for the road—I was the one who decorated the wheels.

Item: I declare I have 110 head of goats and cattle from my father's inheritance; I exchanged 8 goats for some sheep my husband bought for his part that have multiplied, as has been said. Four cowhides.

Item: I declare that I have three hens and two roosters and seven ristras of chile, two in an old bunch; an old book about St. Anthony. I owe Juan Manuel a ram [words deleted]. I owe Antonia Trujillo three pesos, four reales; the three pesos [left unfinished].

Item: I declare I am owed 10 head of livestock; these are included in the 110 expressed above. Those of don[168] Gerónimo, the Indian who was with the deceased Antonio Martín. Of the goats, the cacique owes a yearling sheep and a goat. Juan, son of Marcos Martín, owes a goat. Ma[g]dalena, the Indian woman, owes a goat; Eusebio Durán, a ram. Miguel Martín, another ram. (Francisca, the Indian woman, owes a mass.) Miguel Trujillo owes a yearling lamb. Juana Lobato owes a lamb; she owes it as executor of Antonio Martín, as the deceased man owed it to me. Juan Esteban owes me a three-year-old bull [words deleted]. Francisca de Herrera [owes] a peso; also Pedro Cisneros owes five pesos; María Josefa López one peso. Miguel Trujillo owes two rams. I, having heirs and an executor, and having declared all my possessions and debts, petitioned Capt. Hilario Archuleta, lieutenant alcalde mayor and war captain of Villa Nueva de Santa Cruz and its jurisdiction, to intercede with his authority and that this my last testament might be kept and complied with in the manner and form that I have declared. I declare I have made no other will, testament,

[f. 2v]

or codicil and that if another should appear, I revoke and annul it and I wish that this, my will, be kept and complied with. And I, the said lieutenant alcalde mayor, authorized it because the alcalde mayor is not here at present and since the situation requires it, according to what the parties tell me, Eusebio Durán and Luis de Archuleta being the witnesses required for the execution of the document. I also declare that from what has been declared, I order that after my funeral is paid for, everything should be gathered together into a whole, in two parts, one for my children and the other for my husband. For a little niece I have, I am separating out of my few cattle, and order she be given six head of cattle and a chest.

I, the said lieutenant, named the witnesses in attendance, Francisco Valdés and Capt. Miguel Martín. The testatrix did not sign because she did not know how. This is done on 12 May 1749 on the present paper, because the stamped kind is unavailable in these parts. As above, and so forth.

In my presence I hereby swear.
Hilario Archuleta
Witness, Francisco Valdés [rúbrica]
Witness, Miguel Martín Serrano [rúbrica]

[written vertically at bottom of page]
Year of 1749, Testament of Lugarda Quintana

PART THREE

Spanish Version of Miguel de Quintana's Writings

Archivo General de la Nación—México. Documentos de la Inquisición, vol. 849, no. 2 (folios 446–74), México, D.F.

Document 1. 1734. The title page of the Inquisition's file on Miguel de Quintana

[f. 446r]

+

Nuevo México. Año de 1734. El Señor Inquisidor Fiscal de este Santo Oficio de México Contra Miguel de Quintana de estado casado vecino de la Villa Nueva de Santa Cruz Por Proposiciones.

Document 2. March 17, 1732. Accusation made against Quintana by Fray Manuel Sopeña

[f. 452r]

++

[Nota en el margen izquierdo:]
Denuncia de Fray Manuel Sopeña

En esta Villa [Nueva] de Santa Cruz en diez y siete días del mes de marzo de mil setecientos y treinta y dos años. Ante el Reverendo Padre Comisario del Santo Oficio de este Reino de la Nueva México, como a las cinco de la tarde pareció sin ser llamado y juró en forma que dijo verdad un religioso del Santo Padre San Francisco que dijo llamarse Fray [Joseph] Manuel [de] Sopeña Ministro de la Villa Nueva de Santa Cruz, de edad de cuarenta y cinco años el cual por descargo de su conciencia dice y denuncia que en varias ocasiones le ha presentado Miguel de Quintana nueve hojas de acuarterón escritas todas donde se contienen muchas proposiciones temerarias y escandalosas de que se le ha hecho mucho escrúpulo no dar parte de todas ellas como católico cristiano que es, y preguntado del estado de dicho Miguel de Quintana dijo ser casado y vecino de la Villa Nueva de Santa Cruz y esta es la verdad por el juramento hecho, y siéndole leído dijo estar bien escrito. Que no la dice por odio ni mala voluntad. Prometió el secreto y lo firmó de su nombre con dicho Reverendo Señor Comisario en dicho día, mes y año. Ante mí el infraescrito Notario del Santo Oficio.

Fray Joseph Antonio Guerrero
[rúbrica]
Comisario del Santo Oficio

Fray Manuel de Sopeña
[rúbrica]

Pasó ante mí
Joseph Yrigoien [rúbrica]
Notario del Santo Oficio

Document 3. July 1, 1732. Accusation against Quintana by Fray Joseph Yrigoien

[f. 463r]

++

Nuestro Reverendo Padre, Comisario del Santo Oficio

Fray Joseph Yrigoien de la regular observancia de Nuestro Seráfico Padre San Francisco, hijo de la Provincia del Santo Evangelio de México, Padre Notario del Santo Oficio y Ministro Presidente de la Villa Nueva de Santa Cruz del Reino de la Nueva México, parezco ante Vuestra Paternidad, jurando en debida forma y por descargo de mi conciencia. Digo y denuncio que habiéndole requerido (como párroco que soy de esta dicha villa) a Miguel de Quintana, natural de México y vecino de esta dicha villa, para que cumpliese con el precepto anual de confesar y comulgar como lo ordena y en la manera que lo dispone nuestra Santa Madre Iglesia. Vino a este convento el día veinte y nueve de junio después de misa (que no oyó) y me dijo que (**ojo**) era precepto imposible cumplir con la Iglesia y que Dios no pedía imposibles a ninguna criatura, y que siendo él una de ellas se hallaba excusado,[1] y juntamente me entregó un papel que a Vuestra Paternidad presento adjunto para que haga con esta denuncia presentación al santo y recto tribunal de la Inquisición para que califique las proposiciones que en él se contienen, y cuando estuvo conmigo doy fe estar en su entero juicio y doy fe ser su letra la del papel, y esta es la verdad por el juramento que hago y no lo digo por odio ni mala voluntad, y lo firmé como notario del Santo Oficio en esta Villa Nueva de Santa Cruz el primero de julio del año de mil setecientos y treinta y dos.

Fray Joseph Yrigoien [rúbrica]
Notario del Santo Oficio

Document 4. July 12, 1732. Fray Joseph Antonio Guerrero forwards documents regarding Quintana to the Inquisition in Mexico City

[f. 448r]

+

[Nota al margen derecho:]
Traslado al Ilustrísimo Inquisidor Fiscal

Ilustrísimo Fiscal:

Por mano del Reverendo Padre Comisario de la jurisdicción de El Paso, remito a ese Santo Tribunal las inclusas diligencias por no haber correo que salga en derechura para esa ciudad. Por el mes de agosto del año pasado salió de este reino un correo y remití otras diligencias, y asimismo tengo hecha remisión a ese Santo Tribunal el testimonio de haber tomado posesión y la razón de haberse publicado los edictos en la forma que se me manda. Pongo ésta en la noticia a Vuestra Ilustrísima porque no tengo noticia ninguna, y como es tanta la distancia que hay de este reino a esa corte suelen extraviarse o detenerse los pliegos. Vuestra Ilustrísima me digne de decirme si en estas remisiones voy bien porque mi ánimo es sólo servir a Vuestra Ilustrísima y a ese Santo Tribunal. Es cuánto se ofrece y pedía a Dios guarde a Vuestra Ilustrísima muchos y dila-

[f. 448v]

latados años para amparo y defensa de nuestra santa fe. Villa de Santa Fe de la Nueva México, y julio 12 de 1732 años.

Ilustrísimo Señor,
A los pies de Vuestra Ilustrísima,
su humilde hijo y rendido capellán,
Fray Joseph Antonio Guerrero [rúbrica]

Document 5. Poetry and prose written by Quintana; submitted to Mexico City as evidence by Guerrero around late July 1732 in support of Sopeña's and Yrigoien's denunciations

[f. 454r]

Jesús, María y José
Logra aquese entendimiento
que el poder de Dios te ha dado.
Lógralo, Miguel, y escribe
que no vas en nada errado.

Te mueve de Dios la fuerza
y a la fuerza de su brazo
no habrá poder que resista
ni te haga, Miguel, reparo.

Es locución muy segura
la que el gran poder te ha dado
por humilde que al humilde
Dios se inclina, y se ha inclinado.

Miguel, socorros y luces
que me quemo, que me abraso
en aqueste mar de penas
que a ti te muestro llorando.

No temas que vas seguro.
Cree que no pondrá reparo,
Miguel, el padre a esas letras.
Ayúdame pues te clamo.

Libre estás de que te venga
ninguna afrenta ni daño,
Miguel, por lo que reservas.
Exprésalo que me abraso.

[Insertado a mitad de página entre columnas:]
Miguel, cree firmísimamente que resultan tus letras a mayor honra y gloria del altísimo y supremo Rey de los Cielos y su santísima y purísima Madre, María Santísima de los Dolores. Dáselas al padre y espera por ese medio ser muy consolado en tus trabajitos.

Padre, Dueño y Señor mío, sabe la Divina Omnipotencia ante cuya presencia estoy como el más dócil gusanillo, ingrato y triste pecador, que no merezco que la tierra me sufra, [ya] que acerca de un año que estoy padeciendo la persecución o aguijón de este espíritu pero no hay fuerzas humanas que a las divinas se pueda oponer. Yo soy un pobrecito y aunque la fuerza de la misma luz da testimonio de la verdad, mi suma pobreza y timidez me acobarda porque es muy grande mi demérito. Y más cuando por tantos caminos hallo tanta contradicción, temiendo lo que Vuestra Paternidad me ha dicho de que los que buscan a Dios les entra la vanidad y vuelan para el infierno. Este ha sido agudo puñal que me ha atormentado y extrañado a no manifestar muchos casos que reservo. Y sin buscarlos me suceden, su Divina Majestad sea en todo bendito en sus liberales misericordias, pues quiere que yo así padezca, habrá cerca de un año como llevo dicho que me sucedió lo siguiente. Yo no sé cómo ello fue, porque estas cosas me sacan fuera de mí. Yo iba a misa a esa Villa Nueva [de Santa Cruz] muy contento y alegre y era misa de mañana. Hallaba de par en par abiertas las puertas de la iglesia. Entraba en ella y no había alma ninguna y haciendo genuflexión a la Virgen Santísima de los Dolores, entraba en la sacristía y en ella hallaba al Reverendo Padre Fray Juan de Tagle. Quedábame parado, "Jesús, qué es esto?" Vile cómo andaba en este siglo, la capilla calada, las manos

[f. 454v]

metidas en las mangas como difunto, su manto puesto, y el rostro sumamente afligido. No me hablaba palabra, sólo se inclinaba, a quererme hablar, y yo mirando, puesto recado para decir misa le decía, "Padre, por qué no dice Vuestra Paternidad misa." A esto me respondía, "Yo no la puedo decir," siendo sus ojos dos fuentes de lágrimas. "Quien la puede decir por mí es el Padre Fray Manuel [de Sopeña]." "Válgame Dios, ¿qué es esto?" Volvía yo a ver los ornamentos y era encarnado, y decía yo entre mí, "Hoy no es día de mártir." Aquí me decía, como penetrando mi pensamiento, "No te haga fuerza que aunque no sea día de mártir en lo encarnado siempre se significa aquel cruento martirio de la cruz en que Dios derramó por nosotros su preciosísima sangre." Desde aquel entonces, procuré desechar esto porque con lo que Vuestra Paternidad me ha dicho tengo tanto miedo a manifestar a Vuestra Paternidad lo que me pasa, que aun de confesarme a menudo como de antes tengo a Vuestra Paternidad mucho horror y así padezco lo que Dios es servido. Este caso se me ha representado unas cuatro o cinco veces y siempre he resistido a comunicárselo a Vuestra Paternidad por lo que llevo dicho. Y ahora con estos cuidaditos que Dios se ha dignado de enviarme, por mis graves pecados, me ha atormentado tanto y con tanta fuerza este espíritu, que me ha obligado a escribir lo que yo no merezco por mi suma pobreza e indignidad. Mas la fuerza del espíritu me ha movido con tantas razones que me hallo compelido a tanta fuerza como me hace con razones de tanta congruencia y tan eficaces que más no pueden (**ojo**) ser. La obra, se dirige, a altísimos fines si bien yo soy un dócil instrumento, pero me persuade a que no resista a la voluntad de Dios, cuyos altísimos y soberanos juicios venero poniendo lo expresado SCSECA Romana.[2] Es tan suprema la luz que el poder de Dios te ha dado Miguel, que de su clemencia gozas tales agasajos =

[f. 455r]

Jesús, María y José
Escribe y no seas cobarde.
Escribe que del inmenso
y supremo bien que es Dios
gozas ese movimiento.

Movimiento es muy seguro
en que no puede haber riesgo
porque Dios te puede hacer
dichoso por ese medio.

Si no tienes confesor
que te quiera dar consuelo,
de Dios que es Dios lo recibes
en aquesos pensamientos.

Su amor te los determina.
Escribe, Miguel, sin miedo
que si el padre te horroriza,
Dios no, porque es muy discreto.

Deja el juicio de los hombres
y estate en tu casa quieto,
sujeto a la voluntad
del amante más supremo.

Supremo es Dios y te puede
dar en ese movimiento
una ganancia segura
de sus tesoros inmensos.

Cree, Miguel, que vas seguro
y que aquesos pensamientos
están libres de ser culpa
porque son dones perfectos.

Dios, Miguel, te los ha dado
para que goces en ellos
y con ellos de su amor
muy grande merecimiento.

Abrázalos y no temas
que seguro vas con ellos
porque son, Miguel, auxilios
muy seguros y perfectos.

Que a tu pobreza dominio
sólo el alto Rey del Cielo
lo tiene, Miguel, y así
no temas daño ni riesgo.

Que lo que su grande amor
te ha dado, Miguel, por bueno
no te lo podrá quitar
todo el poder del infierno.

Y así no temas. Escribe
cuando te veas en aprieto
que de Dios la gracia gozas
en aquesos pensamientos.

Cree, Miguel, con viva fe
que sólo el Rey de los Cielos (**ojo**)
te ha dado por pobrecito
cuantas letras has compuesto.

Y que te ofrece benigno
por ellas un grande premio
y lo que es premio, Miguel,
no esperes que sea tormento.

Que tormento no será.
Tenlo, Miguel, por muy cierto
porque Dios que es Dios te puede
dar ese dulce consuelo.

Que reces o que no reces, (**ojo**)
espera ver en el cielo
a Dios que es Padre Benigno
y quien te da esos consuelos.

Verdaderos y seguros,
eficaces y perfectos,
de su clemencia amorosa
libres de todo defecto.

Y ese don y gracia gozas
porque con humilde afecto
celebrastes en la iglesia
su amoroso nacimiento.

Y en recompensa de amor
[aquí continúan los versos entre las columnas:]
quiere que goces en esos
de su gracia aquesas luces
de su amor esos consuelos.

Guarda, Miguel, tus versitos
y aguarda tener sosiego
y consuelo a tus fatigas
dentro de muy breve tiempo.

Ten una confianza humilde
en la Reina de los Cielos
que su brazo poderoso
te libra del león soberbio.

[Al margen derecho de la página:]
Podrá ser, Miguel, que el padre
a vista de tus letritas
te dé alguna recompensa
de azúcar y unas tablillas. **(ojo)** [rúbrica de Yrigoien]
[f. 455v]

Jesús, María y José
Cree, Miguel, con viva fe
que es la Reina de los Cielos
quien te ampara y determina
que escribas aquesos versos.

No pongas duda ninguna.
Escríbelos sin recelo
y cree que vas muy seguro
y libre de todo riesgo,

Fig. 15. Photograph of poetry written by Miguel de Quintana in one of his manuscript pages. (folios 455v–456r).

Y que su grande poder
de su Hijo y Dios verdadero
te alcanza muchos auxilios
y no, Miguel, muy pequeños.

Grandes son esos que gozas.
Ten por muy seguro y cierto
que no hay ni venial delito
en lo que es don tan perfecto.

No temas el padecer.
Padece, que tus estrechos
tendrán alivio, Miguel,
porque estoy yo de por medio.

Ese tormento en que vives
es fineza y no defecto,
es gracia y riqueza suma
y tesoro muy perfecto.

Dios, aquel que tiene amor,
aflige, Divino Maestro,
y si te aflige, no dudes,
que es señal de mucho afecto.

Es médico soberano
tan liberal y discreto
que en las fatigas descubre
el oro de mayor precio.

Esos pensamientos son
tan seguros como buenos.
Abrázalos pues te ha dado
Dios, Miguel, la cruz en ellos.

Cruz es, Miguel, la que gozas.
Aguarda por tus estrechos
y congojas alabar
a quien te ha dado esos versos.

Dios no te pide imposibles
que es muy benigno y discreto
y la que gozas es gracia,
no causa de tu amor mismo.

Que el humilde que se acoge
a mi sombra ten por cierto
que no puede perecer,
goza ese dulce consuelo.

Ten segura tu confianza
en mi Hijo y Dios verdadero
que la que gozas, Miguel. (**ojo**)
Es luz clara y sin defecto.

Las peticiones que hiciste
con tus amorosos versos
las admitió su poder
y te aseguran el premio.

Aguárdalo, Miguel, grande
de su amor que es verdadero
y del mío, Miguel, te fía
que no irás a los infiernos.

Soy la Madre de la esperanza,
soy llave y puerta del cielo,
soy refugio donde hallan
los afligidos consuelo.

Eso la Iglesia lo canta
con himnos y salmos y versos.
Mira, Miguel, si habrá quién
óbice ponga a tus versos.

Guárdalos, Miguel, y aguarda
muy grande alivio y consuelo
que en unos y en otros gozas
auxilios muy verdaderos.

[Escrito entre columnas:]
Venera con humildad los altísimos y secretos juicios de Dios y dale al padre esas letras, que vas, Miguel, muy segurito y resultan, a su mayor honra y gloria, y es su santísima voluntad.

[f. 456r)

Jesús, María y José
En escribir lo que Dios
te determina no hay riesgo
ni lo puede haber, Miguel,
con tan seguro supuesto.

Con muchísimo sigilo
dalo al padre sin recelo
que vas, Miguel, muy seguro
y libre de todo riesgo.

Escribe lo que reservas
y gasta ese medio pliego [rúbrica de Yrigoien]
que por él adquirirás
muy grande merecimiento.

Admirables letras son,
nacidas de un buen afecto
y de una intención sencilla
llena de finos deseos.

[Entre columnas:]
Miguel, el padre te tiene
mucha voluntad y afecto.
Entrégale aquesas letras
que es Dios en sus juicios griego. (**ojo**)

Padre, Dueño y muy Señor mío, no puedo negarme a expresar lo que siento porque la grande fuerza de este, espíritu [**ojo** en margen] me mueve. Yo soy un pobrecito pecador y muy indigno de estas cosas que por mí pasaron, pero si así es voluntad de Dios que tengo de hacer su Divina Majestad, sea bendito en todo y por todo, pues permite que muchas cosas se manifiesten y no estén ocultas a su mayor honra y gloria. Sucediome, el año de 1726, este caso: estaba yo muy desviado de hacer coloquio para festejar al Niño Dios en su nacimiento y llegó un sujeto a mi casa a pedirme lo hiciera. Yo me negué por las razones que abajo expresaré, pero persuadiéndome que era para festejo de su Divina Majestad me rendí y prometí que lo haría. Cogí la pluma y lo comencé con mis pobres términos a su mayor obsequio y llegando a la mitad, siendo mi corazón tan afligido, tan acongojado y estrecho que ya no sabía qué hacerme porque se me ofrecieron estos pensamientos: que todo era vanidad e hipocresía, que no me metiera en hacer coloquios, pues tenía la experiencia de haber dicho Vuestra Paternidad que era un hipócrita y que era medio para verme afrentado en un público por boca de Vuestra Paternidad, y de otros muchos que me lo decían que lo rompiera o lo echara en la lumbre y me quitara de coloquios.

[f. 456v]

Sentía que ya desfallecía según me afligían tales pensamientos de tal manera que lo largué. Y me vi, de precipitado, a echarlo en la lumbre, pero en medio de tan grande aflicción siento una ayuda tan grande y un favor tan estupendo que me anima y esfuerza de tal manera que sentía como que me daba la mano y me ayudaba con estos pensamientos: "No lo quemes, no lo quemes, prosigue y ofrécele a su Divina Majestad tu coloquio; coge la pluma y prosigue," de tal manera que no me podía negar. Cogí la pluma y lo mismo fue cogerla y proseguir que desviarse de mí toda aquella tormenta. Sintiendo en mi alma unos tan amorosos afectos de dulzura, amor y tranquilidad que se abrasaba mi corazón en fuego de su divino amor. Contemplando el amor con que su Divina Majestad quiso humanarse para nuestro remedio, otras muchas cosas reservo porque yo soy un pobrecito y esto lo pongo en juicio de Vuestra Paternidad por entender que así es voluntad de Dios, quien sea bendito en todo pues se agrada muchas veces de algunas cosas que nuestra humana capacidad no puede alcanzar=

Las luces soberanas y divinas
que el inmenso poder de Dios te muestra,
te las da franco con su mano diestra,
siempre seguras y de alabanza dignas.

Dalas, Miguel, al padre que no llevas
cosa que en ellas te haga sospechoso
cuando en Jesús tu Dios y dulce esposo
con tus versos y cánticos te elevas.

Y no sin superior emoción escribes
tus versos en acentos regalados.
Espera de su amor. Serán premiados,
pues de su gran poder tal luz recibes.

Dale al padre esas letras que no es culpa
en tu pobreza goces tal tesoro.
Lo que llevas escrito es, Miguel, oro
con que Dios amoroso te disculpa.

Amigos granjearás, Miguel,
por esas luces claras que Dios a ti te ha dado
por pobre, por humilde y alastrado,
pues gozas de su amor tales finezas.

Soli Deo honor et gloria.[4]

[f. 457r]

Jesús, María y José
Escribe, Miguel, que Dios
es quien te rige y gobierna.
Cree, Miguel, que su bondad
sus auxilios no te niega.

Esas letritas que escribes
su alto poder y grandeza
te las determina y quiere
las escribas, y no temas.

Víspera de la que sola
fue desde *ab eterno electa*[5]
para ser tálamo puro
de un Dios humanado en ella.

Aquese afecto amoroso
que juzgas, Miguel, ofensa
es un grande beneficio
que el poder de Dios te muestra.

Esa luz en que maquinas
es tan segura y perfecta
cuanto puede darte Dios
de su infinita riqueza.

No hay delito en lo que escribes
ni peligro en lo que piensas.
Dios es Dios, Miguel. Escribe
que muy clara la luz llevas.

Auxilios e inspiraciones
son, Miguel, los que en tus letras
te determina amoroso
el Rey de Cielos y Tierra.

Ese amor que a su bondad
serenísima y verdadera
le tienes, está muy libre
de ser ni venial ofensa.

Ofensa no puede ser
que por pobre la grandeza
de Dios te dé esos auxilios
claritos de mil maneras.

Ten fe, Miguel, de que a Dios
agradas con lo que piensas
y que Dios te ha de premiar
una por una tus letras.

Si el padre, Miguel, te dice
que te pierdes, y no es buena
aquesa senda que sigues,
dile que mire esas letras.

Que Dios no condena al hombre
que rendido a su grandeza
le pide misericordia
y con el polvo se pega.

Que es Padre muy amoroso
y se inclina su clemencia
al humilde y abatido
que muchas veces condenan.

Miguel, sigue a Dios así,
cuando así su amor te muestra
su amparo, auxilio y favor
de aquel mar de su clemencia.

Dios es quien te da esa luz.
Luz es, Miguel, la que llevas
de gracia porque Dios puede
y quiere que así la entiendas.

Entiéndela así, Miguel,
y cree que es Dios quien aquesas
luces te ha dado de gracia
y aquesas de gracia llevas.

Obice ninguno el padre
tiene que poner en ellas
porque no puede ser culpa
lo que no es, Miguel, ofensa.

[Entre columnas:]
Cree, Miguel, con ciega fe que no llevas culpa ninguna en ese medio pliego. Dáselo al padre porque es voluntad de Dios y de su Purísima Madre que llevas un admirable beneficio grande de mil maneras, y ha de resultar a mayor honra y gloria de Dios y su Santísima Madre.

[f. 457v]

No te ha confundido Dios. Escribe lo que reservas en tu interior que no es culpa lo que el padre te condena. Ten fe, Miguel, de que Dios te ha de premiar esas letras. Vence ese vano temor. Dalas al padre y no temas.

6

Padre y Dueño mío, sabe Dios, como buen testigo, que esto que escribo es verdad. Sucedióme los días pasados este caso: púseme a rezar el rosario de Nuestra Señora y fueron tantos los afectos que sentí en los misterios dolorosos [rúbrica de Yrigoien en el margen izquierdo] de la Pasión de Nuestro Señor Jesucristo que no podía rezar porque se me representaban aquellos pasos tan vivos que parece que los estaba mirando con una vehementísima aprehensión y mayormente, cuando llegué al último del Calvario, donde crecieron tanto que juzgué que hasta allí había llegado mi vida porque ya me vi ahogado de dolor. Esto lo he tenido tan presente que no lo puedo olvidar, y he querido comunicárselo a Vuestra Paternidad, no por vanidad ni porque me tenga por bueno, que soy un hombre ingrato y pecador, sino porque he quedado amedrentado, considerando que Vuestra Paternidad me ha dicho que los que buscan a Dios les entra el demonio por la vanidad y vuelan para el infierno. Yo, bien sabe su Divina Majestad, que no solicito estos afectos. Ellos solitos se me infunden y no me puedo contener cuando miro a su Majestad Santísima en una cruz y a su Dulcísima Madre al pie de la cruz. Y se me ofrecen estos pensamientos que dice el Santo Rey David, que por no hablar se le envejecieron los huesos. Mas la verdad es que yo a Vuestra Paternidad le tengo muchísimo miedo, y así padezco lo que Dios sabe. Otras muchas cosas reservo que ni las he leído, ni yo soy capaz de que me sucedan por donde me confundo en mi suma pobreza y miseria. Miguel, esos pensamientos son tan meritorios cuando son inculpables. Abrázalos cuando los sientas, y cree que en eso te hace Dios un especial beneficio de su liberal amor y misericordia, pues está escrito que el que se doliere y sintiere los dolorosos pasos de la Pasión de Dios, Dios se dolerá de él y será favorecido de su grandeza a la hora de su muerte. Las demás cosas especiales que sientes y

[f. 458r]

reservas en tu interior, abrázalas, guárdalas y no las temas de ningún modo que son auxilios muy perfectos que Dios con su liberal amor te manifiesta. Y si el padre no te da alivio ninguno, Dios te da a entender lo que el padre no te dice y en su Divina Majestad tienes, has tenido, y tendrás el consuelo. Dale esas letras al padre, califíquetelas por vanidad, hipocresía, o por otras máximas que tú, Miguel, serás premiado de Dios, y no confundido. Dale esas letras al padre mañana diez y ocho de julio, al padre para que las premedite y no te confunda cuando la inmensa Majestad de Dios no te confunde. Miguel, Dios es quien te habla a lo interior para tus trabajitos. Resignado en su Divina Majestad y busca para tu esposa y tus hijitos, por los medios que su liberal amor te determina, sin temor ninguno, y fíate de su soberana grandeza que no errarás en nada y dale con ciega resolución esas letras al padre. Y fíate, Miguel, de Dios, que Dios es Dios y nada te dé cuidado.

Buscar el hombre a Dios con humildad y con deseos de agradarle y que Dios lo eche por eso a los infiernos es cosa tan repugnante a la razón que el mismo entendimiento lo dicta. No fuera Dios quien es, y eso no puede ser porque su Divina Majestad es quien es y no puede dejar de ser Dios eterno, incomprensible y admirable en todas sus perfecciones santísimas. Es, Miguel, entendimiento el que su Divina Majestad te ha dado. Aguarda por cada letra de esas que llevas escritas muchísimos grados de gloria de su liberal misericordia. Fíate de tan supremo y admirable poder, y cree que esos pensamientos que el padre te condena por vanidad e hipocresía son poderosísimos auxilios con que su Divina Majestad te favorece. Fíate de su grandeza y dale esas letras al padre con todo secreto, y cree, Miguel, que no vas errado.

[Nota al margen entre este folio y el siguiente:]
[_?_], Miguel, [_?_] enseñado ni engañarte, dale esas letras al padre que son para que tengas mucho consuelo y no dadas, es [_?_] echado que Dios es Dios.[7]

[f. 458v]

Cree, Miguel, que no vas errado.[8] Cree, Miguel, que no vas errado [rúbrica de Yrigoien] ni estás engañado ni confundido ni alucinado [rúbrica de Yrigoien], que Dios es Dios, y Dios que es Dios es quien te mueve y te ha movido por sus altos y secretos juicios para su mayor honra y gloria y mérito de tu pobreza, Miguel, seguro vas de cualquier modo. Nada temas, dale con ciega resolución esas letras al padre y sienta de ti lo que le pareciere, que Dios es Dios.

———————————————————— [9]

Vuelve a llevar esas letras y dalas, Miguel, al padre que Dios te las determina y en ellas no eres culpable. Su inmenso poder te fía. No temas ningún desaire del padre, Miguel, que Dios como Dios es inerrable. Es luz clara y muy perfecta la que Dios, Benigno Padre, te manifiesta. Miguel, dale esas letras al padre. Perderse por Dios no es, Miguel, perderse; antes es ganarse. Piérdete por Dios y entrégale al padre sin temor ninguno esas letras que tienen mucho que entender, y fíate, Miguel, de que te las ha dado el inmenso poder de Dios de su gracia porque eres un pobrecito, y lo que Dios hace y determina en tu pobreza no lo puede el padre desbaratar ni impedir porque es muy grande su poder santísimo, y en lo que es gracia no puede haber riesgo ninguno.

Todo lo arriba expresado he tenido tanto miedo de dárselo a Vuestra Paternidad, temiendo un desaire en el altar o en el púlpito. Y el sábado pasado en medio de las aflicciones que padecí, se me ponía al pensamiento darle a Vuestra Paternidad estas letras y aplicará lo siguiente. Y por cualquier camino vas, Miguel, seguro porque lo que es gracia es gracia. Parla, ríe, pasea, salta y brinca que tu tesoro fue de gracia, es y será de gracia y no aguardes por esas letras tribulación ninguna.

[f. 459r]

Puede ser que hayas granjeado la más segura ganancia. Esas letras se las entregarás al padre sin temor ninguno, que le serán muy gustosas, pues ellas mismas dan testimonio de la verdad. Tu interior, Miguel, es grande y muchas cosas que los hombres en sus juicios condenan, abominan y desprecian suelen tener en sí muy grande substancia y fundamento. Bien conocido tienes que su Divina Majestad no da a los suyos las tribulaciones tan sólidas que no las [rúbrica de Yrigoien aquí] mezcle con muchas consolaciones interiores que sólo las conoce el que las experimenta. Tus letras no son ociosas. Dios te las ordena y determina por su altísima disposición y altísimos juicios y se encaminan y enderezan a buenos y seguros fines. Dios, Miguel, te hizo dichoso, dichoso y no desdichado, y quiso su soberana grandeza hacerte una gracia y esa, Miguel, la gozas de gracia y no será poderoso todo el poder del infierno ni del mundo a quitártela de ninguna manera. Esa, Miguel, no es vanidad sino gracia, no hipocresía sino gracia, no hurto de la honra de Dios sino gracia, no adecuarte lo que no tienes sino gracia porque Dios de su santísima gracia te adecúa. Esa gracia te da esa luz, te hace ese beneficio y te da ese grande, seguro y perfecto movimiento porque quiere su Divina Majestad, y es su santísima voluntad que así lo goces por sólo su santísima gracia. Dale, Miguel, al padre esas letras que Dios, que sólo es Dios, te mueve por sus altos y secretos juicios para su mayor honra y gloria en que vas, Miguel, muy seguro, y no habrá poder ninguno que óbice ni tilde te ponga a ninguna de ellas: tu vida, Miguel, la conserva Dios y tu vista la conserva Dios. Parla, ríe, divierte, canta, salta y brinca, que quien te ha dado esas letras es Dios, que como Dios es sobre todos los maestros el mayor y no puede errar en nada.

[f. 459v]

Apiádate[11] por Dios, Miguel,
y cree que aquesa violencia
no es en ti, Miguel, delito
porque Dios en ti la ordena.

Dale esas letras al padre
que te ha dado Dios en ellas
un admirable tesoro
claro de muchas maneras.

12

Miguel, ¿cómo puedes huir de la fuerza del decreto que la inmensa Majestad de Dios te ha dado? Vence ese vano temor y no me seas cobarde que soy tu Dios y quien sólo tengo a tu pobreza dominio, como a una de mis criaturas que el padre no se puede oponer a los decretos de mi soberana grandeza e incomprensible sabiduría, poder y misericordia infinita y no repares, Miguel, en nada que no se mueve la hojita de un árbol sin ser mi voluntad, y encierran esas letras mucho y bueno. Aguarda, Miguel, de Dios un elegante premio y dalas al padre que, pues, Dios te mueve, por algún fin te mueve, y vas muy seguro amparado de su finísimo y supremo amor.

13

Cree, Miguel, con viva fe
que se inclina a tu pobreza
la inmensa bondad de Dios
con su amorosa clemencia.

No seas, Miguel, tan cobarde.
Dale al padre aquesas letras
que te las ha de estimar
y ha de sacar mucho de ellas.

Mucho es, Miguel, lo que gozas,
mucho y de muchas maneras,
a muchos verás confusos
que mofan de tu pobreza.

Ten, Miguel, por muy seguro
que la divina grandeza
de Dios te ha dado un tesoro
admirable con esas letras.

Entrégaselas al padre
que puede ser que por ellas
goces un grande consuelo
y no aflicción ni tormenta.

Que su inmenso amor te mueve
porque quiere a tu pobreza
dar, Miguel, esos auxilios
claritos y a manos llenas.

Verás lo que el padre saca,
Miguel, de esas claras letras
que Dios te ha dado de gracia
clara, segura y perfecta.

En nada, Miguel, repares.
Dalas que Dios te lo ordena
por su alta disposición
y un grandioso premio espera.

Que su amor te dispondrá,
que mucho consuelo tengas.
Fíate, Miguel, de Jesús
que es clara esa luz que llevas.

[Entre columnas:]
Es voluntad del inmenso y supremo poder de Jesucristo que le des, Miguel, al padre esas letras. [**ojo** al margen][14]

[f. 460r]

Jesús, María y José
Mueve Dios este instrumento
porque lo puede mover.
Sus letras son para ver
porque son de fundamento.

No estás loco ni perdido
ni tampoco alucinado.
Lo que has escrito te ha dado
Dios, Miguel, quien te ha movido.

Con admirable sentido
las letritas que has formado
Dios, Miguel, te las ha dado
por humilde y abatido.

Goza ese dulce partido
y abraza lo más piadoso
que es Dios, Miguel, generoso,
pues humilde le has pedido.

Mucho, Miguel, has granjeado
en haber buscado a Dios.
Su gracia te da esa voz,
no estás, Miguel, engañado.

Amante, Dueño y Señor
bien sabe Vuestra Grandeza [rúbrica de Yrigoien]
que se extraña mi pobreza
de tan extraño favor.

Porque fuiste mi cantor
de mi clemencia adquiriste
esa luz. No vivas triste
que no desprecié tu amor.

Cree, Miguel, que vas seguro.
De ti no me olvidaré
que es, Miguel, grande tu fe
y así gozas ese oro puro.

De mi amor que es sin medida
gozas la gracia, Miguel. [rúbrica de Yrigoien]
Yo te conozco por fiel,
yo te ofrezco eterna vida.

Y no habrá ningún poder
que a mi gran poder se oponga,
ni óbice a tus letras ponga
como claro lo has de ver.

Que mi superior grandeza
se inclina a tus trabajitos
y gozas en tus versitos
la más segura riqueza.

No es lazo ni sutileza
del demonio. Cree, Miguel, [rúbrica de Yrigoien]
que Dios en ese papel
te ampara con su grandeza.

Dios que es Dios a ti la empresa
generoso te asegura.
La luz que gozas es pura
en medio de tu pobreza.

Ríete muy reído, Miguel,
de la soberbia y abismo
del demonio que no tiene
a tu pobreza dominio.

Porque la luz interior
que Dios te aplicó benigno
fue de gracia, cree, Miguel,
que tú vas por buen camino.

Y en redondas o cuartetas,[15]
del poder de Jesucristo
gozas por humilde y pobre
perfectísimos auxilios.

Déjale a su alta grandeza
tus ahogos y cuidaditos
que tú serás consolado
y lo verás confundido.

Cree, Miguel, con firme fe
que es el poder infinito
de Dios quien te ha dado siempre
cuantos versos has escrito.

[Entre columnas:]
Cree, Miguel, que Dios se agrada
de tu corazón sencillo.
Toma aquel que te ha mofado
el no quedar sin castigo.

Espera, Miguel, con una humilde confianza en la Reina de los Cielos que no triunfará de ti el demonio. Déjale a Dios tus cuidaditos.

[Al margen izquierdo:]
Persuádete, Miguel, a que es la inmensa Majestad de Dios, quien te ha dado esas letras y no el demonio, y dalas al padre.

[Al margen derecho:]

Es luz clarísima y muy perfecta
la que Dios, Miguel, te ha dado.
Espera, Miguel, espera
que no quedarás burlado
ni culpa venial[16] tienes
en lo que has escrito.
Cree, Miguel, que
Dios te ofrece el alivio.

[f. 460v]

Descansa y guarda esas letras que Dios te ha dado que en ese blanco escribirás lo que su Divina Majestad te dictare al pensamiento y será cosa grande.

[17]

No seas cobarde, Miguel, escribe que de tus letras se agrada Dios y no tienes nada que temer en ellas. Su Divina Majestad te mueve. Escribe y no temas. Escribe, que su bondad es y ha sido en tu defensa. Esas cosas que imaginas son luces, Miguel, perfectas. Son auxilios soberanos, libres de toda sospecha y no te podrá robar el diablo ni su soberbia, ni todo el poder del mundo, lo que Dios que es Dios te adecúa. No te adecúas tú, Miguel, lo que imaginas y piensas. Dios es, Miguel, quien te da muy seguras esas letras. Premiado, Miguel, serás de su amorosa clemencia. No llevas ni venial culpa, ni esperes por ellas pena. Tú serás muy consolado de la superior grandeza de Dios, quien te mueve y quiere que escribas eso que piensas. Escribe, Miguel, escribe, que Dios es en tu defensa.

[18]

Separó Dios con su inmenso poder y sabiduría las tinieblas de la luz, dándole a cada una el ser y consistencia de suerte que ni la luz puede retroceder de ser luz, ni las tinieblas de ser oscuridad clara consecuencia en el día y noche. Y no habrá teólogo por sublimado que sea que te pueda negar tan admirable supuesto. Con estos dos estados están entendidos los justos que siguen el dictamen de la razón de la verdad y de la justicia, y por el contrario los que en la lobreguez viven precipitados y encenegados en los vicios siguiendo la injusticia, la impiedad, la ambición, el fausto, la autoridad, el mando y la soberbia. Y ciegos no conocen ni alcanzan el precipicio a que están expuestos a tantos peligros cuanto su ceguedad les ocasiona. Esa es, Miguel, una razón tan clara, tan perfecta y tan segura cuanto poco conocida de muchos. No ignoras tú, Miguel, lo que conoces. Sigue esa senda amorosa en que Dios te ha puesto y no dudes que su Divina Majestad, como amorosísimo Padre, te da esa luz para tu consuelo. No te atemoricen los horrores que los hombres te han puesto ni temas por lo que has obrado ningún castigo que en lo que juzgas perdido.

[f. 461r]

Jesús, María y José
Escribe, Miguel, y cree
sin temor que el Rey inmenso
de los Cielos, a quien amas,
te permite ese consuelo.

Escribe, que su bondad
se agrada de tus afectos.
Escribe, que su poder
te libra del león soberbio.

Cree, Miguel, que vas seguro
y que aquesos pensamientos
los permite en ti benigno
el más soberano maestro.

Las cosas, Miguel, que el padre
en ti juzga por defecto
te las da en otro sentido
Dios, Miguel, porque es discreto.

Gracia es, Miguel, la que Dios
te manifiesta en aquellos
pensamientos con que el padre
te juzga ya en los infiernos.

No caerás en tal desdicha.
Aguarda un descanso eterno
de la gran misericordia
y poder del Rey del Cielo,

quien puede moverte y puede
darte en esos pensamientos
como generoso padre
sus auxilios verdaderos.

Cree, Miguel, que Dios que es Dios
te da en ese movimiento
de su santísima gracia
muy grande merecimiento.

Dios no te pide imposibles.
Ten, Miguel, por claro y cierto
que gozas de su clemencia
favor, auxilio y consuelo.

Se inclina su gran poder
a tu pobreza y estrechos.
No te acobarden horrores
que es Dios en sus juicios griego.

Y al triste que el mundo abate
más bien el poder inmenso
suele inclinarse. No temas
que es Dios, Miguel, muy discreto.

Y no puede ser delito.
Quiera su poder inmenso
darte por pobre, Miguel,
tan amorosos consuelos.

Recíbelos de su amor
santísimo sin recelo
que vas, Miguel, muy seguro
de peligro y de riesgos.

Que Dios que es Rey absoluto
de sus tesoros inmensos
puede aplicarte benigno
ese claro don perfecto.

Muestra, Miguel, valentía
y muéstrale aquesos versos
al padre, que es voluntad
de Dios que tengas consuelo.

Que no te podrá negar
ese admirable consuelo,
esa luz que a tu pobreza
aplica su amor inmenso.

Escribe atrás lo que Dios
te dictare al pensamiento
y dale, Miguel, al padre
lo que amoroso te muestro.

[Entre columnas:]
Cree, Miguel, que vas seguro
con lo que tienes escrito
y que Dios te determina
esos perfectos auxilios.

[Entre columnas:]
Es admirable la luz
que Dios te ha dado
y por ella serás
muy consolado.

[Al margen izquierdo:]
No es, Miguel, el demonio quien te ha dado esas letras sino el poder de Dios y su Santísima Madre.

[f. 461v]

No le has hecho a Dios ofensa
en todo cuanto has escrito.
Cree, Miguel, que su clemencia
te da ese amoroso auxilio.

Su grande misericordia
le inclina a tus trabajitos.
Padécelos por su amor
que no quedarás corrido.

Es luz, Miguel, la gozas
clara y de mucho sentido.
No temas al mundo todo
que Dios te ofrece el alivio.

Seguro vas con tus versos,
sigue humilde a Jesucristo
y no te espanten horrores
que te ha hecho un gran beneficio.

No le tengas miedo al padre
que han de ser para tu alivio
las voces que Dios te ha dado
con su poder infinito.

No te acobarden horrores,
Miguel, por ningún camino.
Cree firmemente que Dios
no te niega sus auxilios.

Los gozos de su clemencia
en todos tus trabajitos.
Fíate de su alta grandeza
que no serás confundido.

Cree que solamente Dios
tiene sobre ti dominio
y que de su gracia gozas
a manos llenas auxilios.

No te dé cuidado cosa.
Déjale tus cuidaditos
a su alta disposición
que breve tendrás alivio.

Confía en su grande poder
que lo que juzgas delito
es fineza, es agasajo,
es gracia y es beneficio.

[Al margen derecho:]
No te confundas, Miguel, que Dios no te confunde. Dale al padre esas letras, que Dios es Dios. Fíate, Miguel, de la Suprema Emperatriz de los Cielos, María Santísima.

[Entre columnas:]
Miguel, dale al padre esas letras que quien te las ha dado tiene más poder que el

padre, con inmensas ventajas (*o quan incomprensibilia sunt judicia eius*).[19] Vas, Miguel, muy seguro.

Esta causa la favorece (**ojo**)[20] el que es causa de las causas. Los movimientos de este espíritu son perfectos, son seguros, son claros y muy eficaces, y no dudosos. Dios con su inmenso poder y liberal misericordia te mueve a que escribas, Miguel, esos pensamientos en que te manifiesta y te da con francas manos sus amorosos auxilios para que el padre te deje en tu pobreza y no se meta en escudriñar los secretos juicios de Dios, quien mueve este espíritu. Este espíritu es movido de Dios y no es movido del demonio. Dios, Miguel, te mueve. Dios, Miguel, te inspira y Dios, que solamente es Dios, incomprensible en sus juicios

[f. 462r]

y admirable en sus disposiciones como Señor absoluto y que tiene dominio sobre todas las cosas, te ha movido y te mueve. No tengas, Miguel, temor de ningún modo, ni al padre ni al demonio ni a todo el poder del infierno ni del mundo, que a mi soberano y supremo poder no habrá poder ninguno que se oponga a esos pensamientos que sientes y llevas escritos. Son auxilios de mi liberal clemencia e infinita misericordia. Soy tu Dios, tu Creador, tu Redentor, tu Amparo, tu Luz, tu Consuelo y toda tu Esperanza y bien Aventuranza. Soy el que te puedo salvar y remediar y por mi altísima disposición y gracia te elegí para mi gloria (**ojo**)[21] y quiero que goces esa perfecta, clara y soberana luz de mi fino amor y liberal clemencia. Escribe, que si el padre te estrecha y te acongoja, yo como Dios alegro y dilato tu corazón. Fíate de mi suma grandeza y liberal amor que ni el padre ni todos los padres juntos te podrán estorbar esa dicha, esa fineza y seguro tesoro que en esas letras gozas a que no te pondrá óbice ninguno ni el padre ni el más sublimado teólogo porque no hay sobre qué ni para qué cuando llevas un supuesto tan seguro como bien asentado en que pudiera el padre haberte aliviado muchos días ha con las luces que le has manifestado. Y en esas manifiestas no se oponen, Miguel, tus pensamientos a la católica fe que profesas. Dios te ha movido y Dios te mueve con su poder santísimo y como maestro soberano que sabe enmendar a los más sabios. Permite en tu pobreza esos pensamientos. Manifiéstaselos al padre en ese

[f. 462v]

escrito en que llevas un rico tesoro para horror y confusión del padre y alivio de tus ahogos y trabajos. Tema el padre y confundare el padre. No es menester ser tercero para salvarse que es error en muchos y falta de fe, pues pudieran conocer que con ser cofrades de la Suprema (**ojo**)[22] Emperatriz de los Cielos, María Santísima del Carmen, tienen el más fuerte y poderoso escudo contra todo el poder del infierno, si de él se saben aprovechar, pues es de fe que el que se acoge a su dulcísima sombra y con fe la llama pueda perecer. Y es conocida avaricia espiritual en muchos. No llegan a este conocimiento. No temas, Miguel, cree que vas muy seguro y que tu querido Padre San Francisco no se enojará contigo de ningún modo porque es grande y muy grande la sombra que te cobija y que vives muy favorecido de Dios y de su purísima y Santísima Madre. Cree que no hay óbice ninguno en lo que llevas escrito porque son tus letras de mucho fundamento e importan mucho que se las manifiestes al padre. Cuida, Miguel, de tu esposa y tus hijitos que es la principal obligación y ríete muy reído de los discursos del padre que son muy limitados y coartados, que Dios no te pide imposibles a ti ni a otros pobrecitos. Dale, Miguel, esas letras con cierta resolución y fíate de Dios que son muy varios sus caminos, y aunque el padre te tenga por simple hipócrita y misterioso, no te dé cuidado nada. Estate quieto en tu casa, busca para tus hijos y mujer y dale con resolución al padre esas letras que vas muy seguro, amparado del más finísimo y santísimo amor.

[f. 465r]

Jesús, María y José
No temas Inquisición,
castigo, daño ni afrenta
que es Dios, Miguel, quien te alienta
con tan grande inspiración.

Que de tu humilde corazón
está Dios enamorado.
Síguele que no has errado
y es grande tu locución.

No estás, Miguel, condenado
ni esperes ir al infierno
cuando Dios, amante tierno,
cuanto has escrito te ha dado.

Y ese interior movimiento
no es en ti, Miguel, culpable
cuando Dios benigno, afable
te inspira, ayuda y da aliento.

¿No le ves en una cruz
hecho por ti, Miguel, pedazos
y que te ofrece los brazos
para que goces la luz?

Pues, Miguel, si de Jesús
gozas tan grande fineza,
¿qué temes si su grandeza
por ti dio su sangre en flux?[23]

¿Quién, Miguel, podrá quitarte
ni estorbarte esa fineza?
Rico estás con tu pobreza,
pues Dios quiere así ayudarte.

Muy clara es la luz que gozas.
Abraza aquese partido.
Cree que estás favorecido
de un Dios que es todas las cosas.

Dios contigo es liberal
porque Dios nunca es escaso.
No es lo que escribes acaso
que es beneficio especial.

¿Quién, Miguel, podrá estorbar
a su admirable grandeza
quiera dar a tu pobreza
lo que has llegado a alcanzar?

No es caso de inquisición
ni has cometido herejía.
Cree, Miguel, que Dios te guía
y no le has hecho traición.

Conoce tu corazón,
no le temas al demonio
que Dios te da testimonio
de esa clara locución.

Esas con resolución
al padre guardián darás.
Miguel, muy seguro vas
cuando esa es tu confección.

Es divina inspiración.
No tengas al padre miedo.
Manifiéstale esas letras
que no hay en ellas defecto.

Dios, Miguel, te las inspira.
No temas ningún estrecho
que vas, Miguel, muy seguro
con todos tus pensamientos.

[Entre columnas:]
Pasmado, asombrado y admirado verás, Miguel, al padre con esas letras. Dáselas, Miguel, que Dios te ayuda, ampara y favorece. Sábado 28 de junio de 1732

[f. 465v]

Miguel, la Divina Majestad de Dios ni impone preceptos imposibles ni pide imposibles a ninguna de sus criaturas. Tú eres una de ellas. Dale al padre guardián, Fray Joseph Yrigoien, esas letras que las lea y premedite y te diga lo que has de hacer. Si no halla esta alma consuelo ni alivio en ningún confesor y todo es pena, terror y castigo, infierno, perdición y aterramiento, es mucho se extrañe y tema aún a la misma luz que la encamina. Fíate, Miguel, de Dios y de su Purísima y Santísima Madre, y dale esas letritas al padre que no vendrá daño castigo ni afrenta ninguna, y es voluntad de Dios que se las des con muchísimo secreto y aguarda de su Divina Majestad un grandioso premio y consuelo, que Dios es Dios y tú eres un pobrecito humilde. Y a esas letras, Miguel, te ha de responder el padre. Fíate, Miguel, de Dios que Dios es Dios y vas muy seguro de que por ellas te venga daño ninguno de ninguna manera.

[24]

Expón tu vida a mil riesgos por mi amoroso cariño que yo te daré el consuelo donde temes el castigo. Dale al padre aquesas letras que el poder de Jesucristo en ti, Miguel, determina con su poder infinito y admite esos pensamientos que no hay en ellos delito, que es locución la que gozas de muchísimo sentido. Cree, Miguel, que vas seguro de daño ni de castigo.

[25]

No se mueve la hojita de un árbol sin la voluntad de Dios. Lleva, Miguel, esas letras, que tú serás consolado.

Document 6. May 22, 1734. From Inquisitor Mangado y Clavijo in Mexico City to Guerrero, with instructions on how to proceed in light of the accusations presented by Sopeña and Yrigoien

[f. 447r]

+

[Nota arriba al margen izquierdo:]
Presentada en el Santo Oficio de México el veinte y cinco de mayo de mil setecientos y treinta y cuatro años. Señores Inquisidores Navarro y Tagle. [rúbrica de Alexandro Alvarez Carranza]

[Nota arriba al margen derecho:]
Hágase como lo dice el Señor Inquisidor Fiscal, añadiéndose que en caso de nacer todo de simpleza, como por ahora se presume.

[Nota al margen izquierdo al centro:]
Le haga cargo de lo más grave. Le conmine y aperciba de orden de este tribunal sobre que no sienta ni profiera tales proposiciones, porque de lo contrario se procederá contra él por todo rigor de derecho. [rúbrica de Alexandro Alvarez Carranza]

[Nota al margen izquierdo a pie de página:]
El 27 de mayo se le devolvió lo escrito por este reo y las denuncias de los religiosos como se manda para que los examine y ratifique, para lo que se manda en el escrito fiscal, y haga cargo a dicho reo, conminándole para en lo de adelante. [rúbrica de Agustín González Jiménez de Zárate]

Ilustrísimo Señor:

El Inquisidor Fiscal ha visto las denuncias que remite el comisario del Nuevo México contra Miguel de Quintana de estado casado, vecino de la Villa Nueva de Santa Cruz, sobre que siendo amonestado de su párroco que cumpliese con el precepto anual de confesar y comulgar. Le dijo que era precepto imposible y que Dios no manda imposibles a sus criaturas, y al mismo tiempo le presentó una hoja de papel escrita de su letra, lo cual y otras nueve de la misma letra y forma que entregó al Padre Fray Manuel de Sopeña dan a entender, por la multitud de cosas buenas y malas que mezclan, que el dicho Quintana se gobierna por algún espíritu maligno que interior o exteriormente le dicta lo que escribe, engañándole y haciéndole creer que son hablas del Hijo de Dios, pero no se puede formar juicio, porque el comisario no dice cosa alguna del tenor de vida y costumbres del referido Quintana, ni de su capacidad y talento, por lo cual podrá Vuestra Señoría devolver al comisario estas diligencias, ordenándole que examine y ratifique, según instrucción, a los dos religiosos denunciantes, preguntándoles especialmente acerca de la vida y costumbres del dicho Quintana y qué concepto han hecho de los escritos que les entregó con lo demás que le pareciese conveniente

[f. 447v]

y haciendo juicio el comisario que el dicho Quintana no padece lesión de cabeza, ni privación de la razón, lo llamará y por ante notario le hará reconocer lo que ha escrito de su letra, y le preguntará quién le habla o inspira lo que escribe, quién le asegura tan de cierto que va por buen camino, y qué lo tiene escogido para la gloria, y cómo se compadece lo que por un lado dice que padece muchos temores que afligen su corazón, y por otro, que se halla con una gran dilatación y consuelo. Y con lo que resultare, dará cuenta a este tribunal con su informe muy particular en este caso para tomar la providencia que convenga. Vuestra Señoría acordará lo mejor. [Tribunal] Secreto y mayo 22 de 1734.

Licenciado Don Diego Mangado y Clavijo [rúbrica]

Document 7. May 27, 1734. Letter to Guerrero from Inquisitors Navarro de Ysla and Sánchez de Tagle in Mexico City in response to the denunciation by Sopeña

[f. 450r]

+

Habiéndose recibido en este tribunal la de nuestro comisario del 12 de julio del año pasado de [17]32, con las denuncias que la acompañaban contra Miguel de Quintana, en su vista se ha mandado devolverse las originales para que examine y ratifique, según instrucción, a los dos religiosos denunciantes, Fray Manuel Sopeña y Fray Joseph Yrigoien, haciéndoles pregunta especial acerca de la vida y costumbres del dicho Quintana y el concepto que hubieran hecho de sus escritos con lo demás que tuviera por conveniente nuestro comisario, quien si formase juicio que dicho Quintana no padece lesión de cabeza, ni privación de la razón, lo hará comparecer ante sí y por ante notario le hará reconocer lo que ha escrito de su letra, y preguntará quién le habla o inspira lo que escribe, quién le asegura tan de cierto que va por buen camino y que está escogido para la gloria, y cómo se compadece lo que por un lado dice que padece muchos temores que afligen su corazón, y por otro que se halla con una gran dilatación y consuelo, y en caso de nacer todo de simpleza como por ahora se presume, le hará cargo de lo más grave,

[f. 450v]

conminará y apercibirá de orden de este tribunal sobre que no sienta ni profiera tales proposiciones, porque de lo contrario se procederá contra él por todo rigor de derecho, y evacuado todo, con dichos exámenes y ratificaciones nos lo remitirá en la primera ocasión que se ofrezca. Dios guarde a Nuestro Comisario, etc. Inquisición de México, mayo 27 de 1734.

Licenciado Don Pedro Navarro de Ysla [rúbrica]	Licenciado Don Pedro Anselmo Sánchez de Tagle [rúbrica]

Por mando del Santo Oficio
Agustín González Ramírez de Zárate
Secretario [rúbrica]

[A pie de página:]
Al Reverendo Padre Fray Joseph Antonio Guerrero,
Comisario de este Santo Oficio en la Villa de
Santa Fe de la Nueva México

[f. 451r]

En vista de la de Vuestra Paternidad y denuncias que la acompañaban, me ha ordenado el tribunal avise a Vuestra Paternidad de su recibo (como lo hago) y prevenirle no hay qué hacer contra María Domínguez por ahora por no haber en ellas cosa de sustancia y percibirse son chismes y cuentos nacidos de mala voluntad, quedando en cuenta para en lo de adelante que en todas las causas previene en la instrucción de comisarios que tiene Vuestra Paternidad en su poder, informándonos del crédito que merecen, como el de la persona denunciada.

Document 8. November 4, 1734. Verification of Manuel de Sopeña's statement

[En en el margen izquierdo a pie del folio 452r:]
Ratificación añade

En la Villa de Santa Fe en cuatro días del mes de noviembre del año de mil setecientos y treinta y cuatro. Ante el Reverendo Padre Comisario del Santo Oficio pareció siendo llamado un religioso del Santo Padre San Francisco que dijo llamarse Fray Manuel [de] Sopeña, hijo de la Provincia del Santo Evangelio, Ministro prete de la Misión de San Lorenzo de los Picurís, de edad de cuarenta y siete años, el cual estando presente y por

[f. 452v]

honestas personas y religiosas el Reverendo Padre Fray Juan Antonio Cressa, Vice-Custodio de dicha custodia de la Nueva México, y el Reverendo Padre Fray Joseph Manuel de Eguía, lector de filosofía, presbíteros y religiosos del Santo Padre San Francisco que tienen jurado secreto. Fue recibido juramento al dicho en forma y prometió decir verdad. Preguntado si se acuerda haber depuesto ante algún juez sobre cosas tocantes a la fe contra alguna persona, dice que se acuerda haber depuesto de un hombre llamado Miguel de Quintana ante el Reverendo Padre Fray Joseph Antonio Guerrero, Comisario del Santo Oficio, que había escrito unos papeles que contenían proposiciones escandalosas pertenecientes al Santo Tribunal, y que presentó dichos papeles que no se acuerda [de] las hojas y pidió que se le leyese su denuncia. Fuele dicho que se le hace saber que el Señor Fiscal del Santo Oficio le presentó por testigo *ad perpetuam rei memoriam* en una causa que trata contra el dicho Miguel de Quintana, que esté atento, y siéndole leído y habiendo el dicho Fray Manuel [de] Sopeña dicho que lo había oído y entendido, dijo que era su dicho y él lo había dicho, según se le había leído y estaba bien escrito y asentado y no había que alterar, añadir ni enmendar porque como estaba escrito era la verdad y en ello se afirmaba y afirmó, ratificaba y ratificó, y si necesario era, lo decía de nuevo contra el dicho Miguel de Quintana, no por odio sino por descargo de su conciencia. Y por especial Orden del Santo Oficio se le preguntó al dicho Señor Fray Manuel [de] Sopeña qué tiempo había que conocía a dicho Miguel de Quintana, y dice que a él lo conoce como catorce o quince años, poco más o menos. Se le preguntó qué juicio tiene hecho de Miguel de Quintana y dice que no del todo le parece está en su juicio, sino que tiene sus lúcidos intervalos como consta de una ocasión que dicen que tiró piedras. Que no se acuerda quién se lo dijo y que dicen que habrá quince años que sucedió esto, y preguntado del juicio que tiene hecho de los escritos, dice que está iluso porque cuando le ayudaba a misa se le detenían las palabras, como que se detenía y parece que tiene algún arrimado. Y, preguntado de su vida y costumbres, dice que rara vez va a misa, pretextando tener dolor del bazo que siendo tercero no asistía a juntas ni ejercicios de virtudes que se ofrecen, y que para lo bueno pretextaba enfermedades, y no para paseos y que siempre se ha ocupado en notario de los alcaldes mayores, actuando con todo juicio y que sus escritos han

[f. 453r]

tenido aceptación y actualmente es notario en la Judicatura Eclesiástica por donde se desvanece su dictamen de que sea loco. Encargóselo el secreto en forma, prometiolo y lo firmó de su nombre en dicho día mes y año.

Fray Joseph Antonio Guerrero
[rúbrica]
Comisario del Santo Oficio

Fray Manuel de Sopeña
[rúbrica]

Pasó ante mí,
Joseph Yrigoien [rúbrica]
Notario del Santo Oficio

Document 9. November 5, 1734. Verification of Yrigoien's statement

[Anotación al pie del folio 463r:]
Ratificación añade

En esta villa de Santa Fe en cinco días del mes de noviembre de este presente año de mil setecientos treinta y cuatro, ante el Reverendo Padre Comisario del Santo Oficio de este reino, pareció siendo lla-

[f. 463v]

mado un religioso del Seráfico Padre San Francisco que dijo llamarse Fray Joseph Yrigoien, hijo de la Provincia del Santo Evangelio, Ministro Padre de la Misión de San Ildefonso, Predicador Jubilado, Notario Apostólico y del Santo Oficio, dicreto y secretario de esta custodia, de edad treinta y seis años siete meses (al cual estando presentes por honestas y religiosas personas el Reverando Padre Fray Pedro Antonio de Ezeiza, actual vice-custodio, y el Reverendo Padre Fray Francisco Lerchundi, Ministro de la Misión de Pecos, quienes tienen jurado secreto) fue recibido juramento en forma y prometió decir verdad. Preguntado si se acuerda haber depuesto ante algún juez sobre cosas tocantes a la fe contra alguna persona, dice que se acuerda que el día treinta de junio del año pasado de setecientos treinta y dos, lunes como a las nueve del día, presentó ante el Reverendo Padre Fray Joseph Antonio Guerrero, Comisario del Santo Oficio, una petición firmada de su mano y nombre, como notario que es del Santo Tribunal en la cual denuncia a la persona de Miguel de Quintana por no haber querido cumplir con la Iglesia. Y juntamente presentó con la petición una cuartilla de papel con unos versos y un poco de prosa que contienen algunas proposiciones malsonantes, y que dicho papel tiene la fecha del día sábado veinte y ocho de junio del dicho año de treinta y dos sin firma, y que en su dicha petición da fe como notario del Santo Tribunal de conocer que la letra de él es de Miguel de Quintana, quien le presentó dicho papel, habiéndole requerido que se confesase y recibiese la Santa Eucaristía (como es precepto de Nuestra Santa Madre Iglesia) el día diez y nueve de junio como a las once del día domingo. Y, siéndole leída[s] su petición y denuncia, por haberlo pedido fuele dicho:[26] que se le hace saber que el señor fiscal del Santo Oficio le presenta por testigo *ad perpetuam rei memoriam*[27] en una causa que trata contra el dicho Miguel de Quintana, a la que estuvo atento dicho Reverendo Padre y dijo ser suya y la misma petición que presentó ante el dicho Reverendo Padre Comisario y que era la verdad y que en ello se afirmaba, y afirmó, ratificaba y ratificó y si necesario era, lo decía de nuevo contra el dicho Miguel de Quintana, no por odio sino por descargo de su conciencia y por especial orden del Santo Oficio. Fuele preguntado a dicho Fray Joseph Yrigoien acerca de la vida y costumbres del dicho Miguel de Quintana, y dice que el tiempo que lo ha conocido ha sabido que dicho Miguel de Quintana pasa su vida con hacer escritos a los vecinos, que de él se valen para este fin, y que esta es su vida y en esto se acostumbra y que no sabe que frecuenta los santísimos sacramentos, ni acciones virtuosas. Fuele preguntado el

[f. 464r]

concepto que tiene hecho del papel o papeles de dicho Miguel de Quintana, y dice que ha hecho juicio que dicho Miguel de Quintana está iluso y que no lo atribuye ni puede atribuir a locura ni a simpleza: lo primero, porque en todos los versos que hace para varios fines no lo ha visto discordar; lo segundo, que sus conversaciones son bien hiladas, sus consejos son bien recibidos de los que se los toman; lo tercero, que diez años que ha lo conoce lo ha visto al lado de los alcaldes mayores haciendo causas civiles y criminales, y que en ninguna de ellas ha sido repudiado por demente; lo cuarto, que cuando le presentó dicho papel, era actual notario de la Judicatura Eclesiástica y que en este cargo se ha ejercitado hasta la presente, y que en todo tiene aceptación, y que por el vulgo y muchos principales de este reino está tenido por hombre de entereza y de mucho juicio razones porque presume y siente que el dicho Miguel de Quintana está iluso. Iten[28] dice que se ha escandalizado mucho de que dicho Miguel de Quintana haciéndose tan santo en sus papeles, no atienda a cumplir con el precepto anual de confesar y comulgar y que no sabe si lo ha hecho estas dos Cuaresmas próxime[29] pasadas, que en lo que está cierto es que el año de treinta y dos el día veinte y siete de octubre no había cumplido con este precepto, ni habían bastado a ello insinuaciones repetidas ni haberle hecho cargo de incuria[30] en una censura impuesta por el Concilio Mexicano contra los transgresores de este precepto. Iten pidió que se le volviese a leer su denuncia y ratificación, y halló en ella que en lo que dice haber presentado ante el Reverendo Padre Comisario el día treinta de junio lunes está discorde, que fue el día primero de julio día martes, y que no tenía más cosa que añadir, alterar ni enmendar, porque como estaba escrito era la verdad y en ello se afirmaba y afirmó, ratificaba y ratificó, y si necesario era lo decía de nuevo contra el dicho Miguel de Quintana, no por odio sino por descargo de su conciencia. Encargósele el secreto en forma, prometiolo y lo firmó de su nombre con dicho Reverendo Padre Comisario ante mí el infraescrito notario nombrado.

Fray Joseph Antonio Guerrero [rúbrica]
Comisario del Santo Oficio

Joseph Yrigoien [rúbrica]

Pasó ante mí,
Fray Joseph de Eguía y Lumbre [rúbrica]
Notario nombrado

Document 10. November 8, 1734. Guerrero interrogates Quintana

[f. 466r]

++

En la Villa de Santa Fe, capital del Reino de la Nueva México, en ocho días del mes de noviembre del presente año de mil setecientos y treinta y cuatro, como a las nueve de la mañana ante el Reverendo Padre Comisario del Santo Oficio de dicho reino, pareció siendo llamado (por orden del Santo Tribunal) y juró en forma que dirá verdad un hombre que dijo llamarse Miguel de Quintana, natural de México, vecino de la Villa Nueva de Santa Cruz, notario del juzgado eclesiástico de dicha villa, casado de edad de cincuenta y seis años, poco más o menos, y preguntado si sabe o presume para qué ha sido llamado, dijo que no lo sabe ni lo presume. Y por especial orden de dicho Santo Tribunal, se le mostraron diez hojas de papel escritas para que reconociese si eran suyas y si las había escrito de su letra, y dice que todas son de su letra, que las escribió en su casa y las entregó en varias ocasiones al Reverendo Padre Fray Manuel de Sopeña, Ministro que era de la Villa Nueva de Santa Cruz, y que al Padre Fray Joseph Yrigoien, Ministro que fue de dicha Villa, le entregó otros versitos en una cuartilla de papel, y que al Reverendo Padre Fray Juan Mingues, difunto, y al Reverendo Padre Fray Juan del Pino, Ministro de San Buena Ventura de Cochití, les entregó otros versos, y que estos dos religiosos son del Seráfico San Francisco. Iten se le dieron a reconocer dichos papeles y los leyó todos, y estando leyendo los rubricados se deshacía en lágrimas, y preguntada la causa de su llanto, dice que se enternecía porque le había pasado lo que decían los versos y sus papeles que van rubricados. Y preguntado quién le habla o inspira lo que escribe, dice que le parece que quien le pone el pensamiento es la Divina Majestad de Dios; y preguntado quién le asegura tan de cierto que va por buen camino, dice que según le parece, la Divina Majestad, y preguntado quién le asegura que es escogido, dice que sus papeles lo dicen; y preguntado cómo según padece lo que por un lado dice que ya dice muchos temores que afligen su corazón, y por otro que se halla con una dilatación y consuelo; y dice que se suele ver sumamente afligido y que se le quita la tribulación representándosele Nuestro Señor al pensamiento, y llorando unas lágrimas tiernas con Dios se le quita toda congoja; y preguntado en qué conoce que quién le hablaba interiormente[31] era Dios. Dice que en los afectos que siente y que se le abrasa el alma en fuego de su Divina Majestad; y preguntado si ha tenido algunas apariciones de Dios o sus santos, dice que ningunas, que sólo en lo interior siente esos afectos que bien lo sabe

[f. 466v]

++

su grandeza; y preguntado cómo conoce que está en gracia, dice que siente que cuando oye misa se abrasa en fuego de su Divina Majestad, y que en sus tribulaciones viene a misa y que siente estos afectos; y que no es continuo, que sólo cuando Dios es servido siente estos afectos, y preguntado a qué altísimos fines se reducen sus escritos, dice que no lo sabe, que Dios lo sabe, y dice que el día ocho de Nuestra Señora septiembre del año pasado de treinta y tres, viniendo a misa se le ponía mucho horror y mucho miedo, y le dio una gran turbación de suerte que ya se determinaba a no ir y después sintió otras fuerzas que le instaban "Oye misa, oye misa,"[11] y que fue a misa y sintió en el alma unos júbilos que más no pueden ser, y que cuando tiene alguna tribulación se le representan los pasos de la Pasión[12] y que con esto tiene tanto júbilo que se le mitiga y quita por unos días la tribulación. Y dice que en la Misión de Nambé le sucedió en una ocasión comunicando con el Reverendo Padre Fray Juan de la Cruz, religioso franciscano y actual ministro de San Juan de los Caballeros. Trató dicho religioso de las penas que padecen los condenados en el infierno y se le estrechó tanto el corazón y el espíritu que le pareció que se condenaba según el horror que le dio, y se le vino al pensamiento "Miguel, ni tú ni el santo padre caerán en el infierno," y que con esto fue tanto el gusto que se le quitó la tribulación, y que se halla en una confusión porque lo atierran y lo confunden todos y que en sus tristezas escribe sus versos y siente los afectos que dicen sus versos y que si se pone a rezar el rosario le sucede que en los misterios se le suspende lo vocal del dolor. Se queda suspenso y que se queda solo en contemplación y después, cuando Dios es servido, vuelve y prosigue y que esta es la verdad por el hecho juramento, y siéndole leído, dijo estar bien escrito. Prometió el secreto y lo firmó con dicho Reverendo Padre Comisario, ante mí el infraescrito notario.

Fray Joseph Antonio Guerrero
Comisario del Santo Oficio [rúbrica]

Miguel de Quintana [rúbrica]

Pasó ante mí,
Joseph Yrigoien [rúbrica]
Notario del Santo Oficio

Document 11. November 10, 1734. Guerrero writes to Mexico City reporting that the verification of Sopeña's and Yrigoien's statements has been completed and that Guerrero considers Quintana of sound mind

A series of notes appears in the margins indicating the time when the Holy Office in Mexico City considered the said document on March 15, 1735. A key annotation among the latter notes indicates that Guerrero, when he questioned Quintana, did not warn him as instructed.

[f. 449r]

[Al margen izquierdo arriba:]
Redactada en el Santo Oficio de la Inquisición de México en quince días del mes de marzo de mil setecientos y treinta y cinco años. Señores Inquisidores Navarro y Tagle. [rúbrica desconocida][33]

[Nota al margen izquierdo al centro:]
No le hizo cargo el Comisario

[Nota arriba en el margen derecho del folio 449r:]
Ilustrísimo Señor Inquisidor Fiscal

+

Muy santo y recto tribunal:

Habiendo recibido la orden de Vuestra Ilustrísima con las denuncias contra Miguel de Quintana, van ratificados los dos religiosos denunciantes. Y por haber hecho juicio de que el dicho Miguel de Quintana no padece de privación de la razón, ni lesión de cabeza, lo hice comparecer por ante el notario al Santo Oficio y ejecuté lo que Vuestra Ilustrísima me manda, como consta de su declaración que adjunta remito a ese Santo Tribunal. Y porque a mi parecer no nace nada de lo dicho y expresado por el dicho Miguel de Quintana de simpleza, no le hice cargo de lo más grave, ni lo apercebí, ni conminé, como expresa la orden de Vuestra Ilustrísima, quien en vista de lo ejecutado, me mandará lo que tengo de ejecutar. Y en tanto quedo pidiendo a Dios Nuestro Señor guarde a Vuestra Ilustrísima muchos años para lustre y defensa de Nuestra Santa Fe Católica, Villa de Santa Fe y noviembre 10 de 1734 años.

Ilustrísimo Señor,
A los pies de Vuestra Ilustrísima,
Su más humilde y rendido súbdito que postrado le venera,
Fray Joseph Antonio Guerrero [rúbrica]
Comisario del Santo Oficio

Document 12. March 24, 1735. Instructions from Inquisitor Mangado y Clavijo to Guerrero, in response to the verifications of statements that have been conducted

[f. 467r]

[Nota al margen izquierdo:]
Presentada en el Santo Oficio de México el treinta y un días del mes de marzo de mil setecientos treinta y cinco años, señores Inquisidores, Navarro y Tagle. [rúbrica de Alexandro Alvarez Carranza]

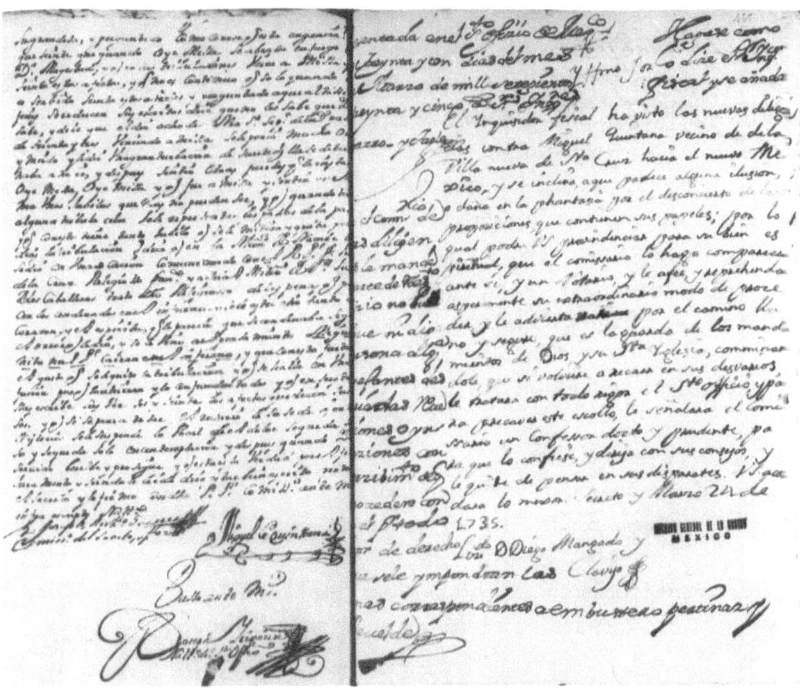

Fig. 16. Photographic detail of a letter written by Miguel de Quintana on the left side (with his signature at the bottom) and a letter on the right is by one of the investigating Inquisition authorities who states the key accusation that Quintana is "a fraud, obstinate, and a rebel" (folio 467r).

[Nota al margen izquierdo:]
Que el comisario de estas diligencias le mande de parte de este Santo Oficio no publique ni diga a persona alguna semejantes desvariadas revelaciones o inspiraciones con apercibimiento de que se procederá contra él por todo rigor de derecho y que se le impondrán las penas correspondientes a embustero, pertinaz y rebelde. [rúbrica de Alexandro Alvarez Carranza]
[Nota arriba a la derecha de la página]
Hágase como lo dice el señor inquisidor fiscal y se añada:

Ilustrísimo Señor:

El inquisidor fiscal ha visto las nuevas diligencias contra Miguel de Quintana, vecino de la Villa Nueva de Santa Cruz hacia el Nuevo México, y se inclina a que padece alguna ilusión o daño en la fantasía por el desconcierto de las proposiciones que contienen sus papeles, por lo cual podrá Vuestra Señoría providenciar para su bien espiritual que el comisario lo haga comparecer ante sí y un notario y le afee y reprehenda ásperamente su extraordinario modo de proceder, y le advierta a caminar por el camino llano y seguro, que es la guarda de los Mandamientos de Dios y su Santa Iglesia, conminándole que si volviere a recaer en sus desvaríos, le tratará con todo rigor el Santo Oficio, y para precaver este escollo, le señalará el comisario un confesor docto y prudente para que lo confiese y dirija con sus consejos y le quite de pensar en sus disparates. Vuestra Señoría acordará lo mejor. Secreto, el marzo 24 de 1735.

Licenciado Don Diego Mangado y Clavijo [rúbrica]

[f. 467 v]

El 24 de julio de 1736 años
se escribió al comisario de la Nueva México,
arreglado al escrito fiscal y decreto. [conforme]

Document 13. March 11, 1736. A letter from Guerrero to Mexico City forwarding additional reports on Quintana

[f. 468r]

+

[Al margen izquierdo arriba:]
Recibida en el Santo Oficio de México el diecinueve de agosto de mil setecientos treinta y siete años. Señores Inquisidores Navarro, Tagle, Clavijo. [rúbrica de Alejandro Alvarez Carranza]

Mi Santo y Recto Tribunal,

A Sus Autos

Remito las inclusas diligencias de Miguel de Quintana, las que no despaché antes por hallarse el dicho en cama como lo está actualmente y según el accidente próximo a la muerte, y porque este año (según la orden de este Santo Tribunal) se han de publicar los edictos, y no poder ser en la domínica tercera ni cuarta de Cuaresma por las muchas nieves y rigurosos fríos de este país. Me ha parecido conveniente transferir la función para el mes de mayo por la mayor comodidad como lo he visto hacer en tiempo de mi antecesor, el Reverendo Padre Fray Juan de Tagle (que en paz descanse). Vuestra Señoría Ilustrísima me dirá si tiene a bien y me mandará lo que fuere del mayor servicio de Vuestra Señoría y de ese Santo Tribunal, a quien su Majestad guarde muchos años para amparo y defensa de nuestra Santa Fe. Villa de Santa Fe de la Nueva México, marzo 11 de 1736 años.

Ilustrísimo Señor
A los pies de Vuestra Ilustrísima
su más _____ súbdito que postrado le venera
Fray Joseph Antonio Guerrero [rúbrica]

Document 14. July 24, 1736. Letter from Inquisitors Navarro de Ysla and Sánchez de Tagle to Guerrero, with new instructions to be followed in light of the most recent reports they have received on Quintana

[f. 469r]

Habiéndose visto en este tribunal las diligencias que remitió nuestro Comisario contra Miguel de Quintana, vecino de la Villa Nueva de Santa Cruz, por las proposiciones que en ellas se expresan, hemos mandado avisar de su recibo y ordenar a nuestro Comisario que luego que reciba ésta, por ante notario de este Santo Oficio, haga comparecer ante sí al dicho Miguel de Quintana y le reprehenda y afee ásperamente su extraordinario modo de proceder, advirtiéndole vaya por el camino llano y seguro, que es la guarda de los Mandamientos de Dios y su Santísima Iglesia, mandándole de parte de este Santo Oficio no publique ni diga a persona alguna semejantes desvariadas revelaciones o inspiraciones con apercibimiento que si volviere a recaer en ellas, se procederá contra él por todo rigor de derecho y se le impondrán las penas correspondientes al embustero, pertinaz y rebelde. Y asimismo le impondrá nuestro Comisario en que se confiese

[f. 469v]

con confesor docto y prudente que le señalará, para que lo confiese y dirija con sus consejos y le quite de pensar en sus disparates y desvaríos. Y ejecutado lo referido, que se hará a continuación de ésta, y firmando el obedecimiento, dicho Quintana nos la devolverá en primera ocasión [a] nuestro comisario, que guarde Dios, etc. Inquisición de México, julio 24 de 1736.

Licenciado Don Pedro
Navarro de Ysla [rúbrica]

Licenciado Don Pedro Anselmo
Sánchez de Tagle [rúbrica]

Por mando del Santo Oficio
Alexandro Alvarez Carranza [rúbrica]

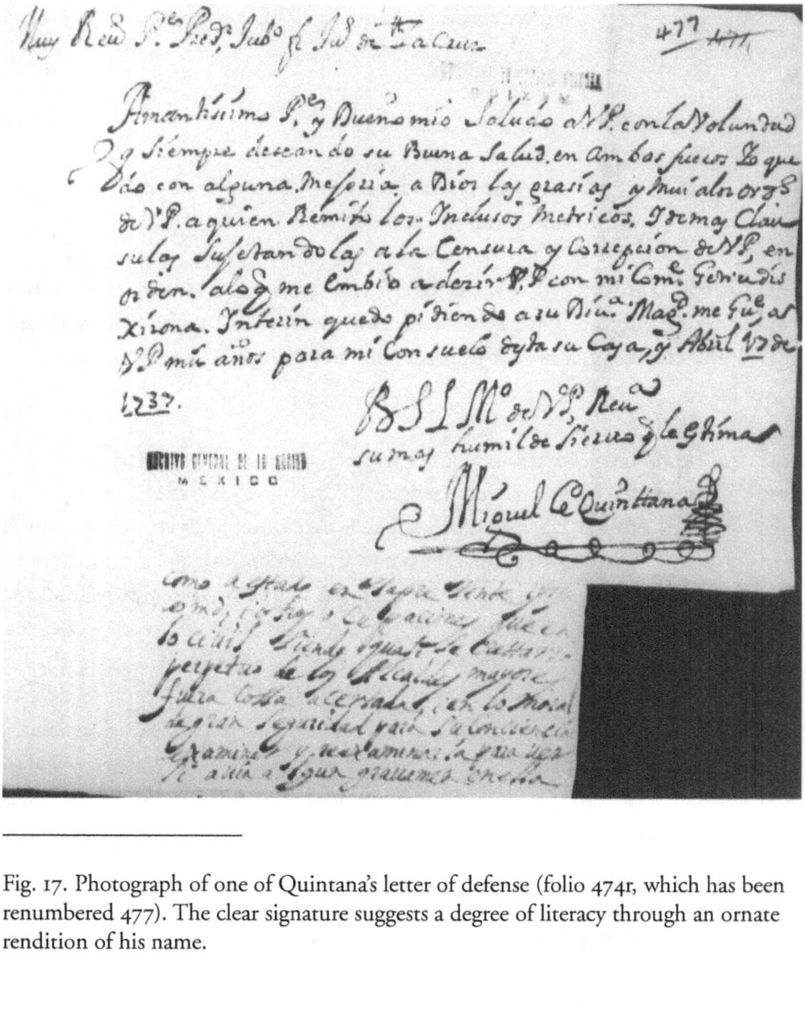
Muy Rev.do P.e Pred.r Jub.do y Juez de la Cruz 477 474

Amantisimo P.e y Dueño mio Saludo a V.P. con la Voluntad q. siempre deseando su Buena Salud, en ambos fueros. Yo quedo con alguna mejoria a Dios las gracias y muchas a los de V.P. a quien Remito los Inclusos metricos. Y demas Clausulas sujetandolas a la Censura y Correccion de V.P. en orden a lo q. me embio a decir V.P. con mi Comp.e Gervasio Xirona. Interin quedo pidiendo a su Div.a Mag.d me gu.e a V.P. mu. años para mi Consuelo de esta su Casa, y Abril 12 de 1737.

B.S.M. de V.P. Rev.da su mas humilde Siervo q. la estima

Miguel de Quintana

Fig. 17. Photograph of one of Quintana's letter of defense (folio 474r, which has been renumbered 477). The clear signature suggests a degree of literacy through an ornate rendition of his name.

Secretario

[A pie de la página:]

Al Reverendo Padre Fray Joseph Antonio Guerrero, Comisario de este Santo Oficio de la Villa de Santa Fe de la Nueva México

Document 15. January 23, 1737. A report by Yrigoien and Guerrero on their visit to Quintana's house, where Miguel promised to do as the Inquisition ordered

[f. 470r]

++

Digo yo, Fray Joseph de Yrigoien, Notario del Santo Oficio, que [por] orden del Reverendo Padre Comisario Fray Joseph Antonio Guerrero, pasé a la casa y morada de Miguel de Quintana a citarlo que compareciese ante su padre y lo hallé enfermo en cama de un dolor que ha un mes que le acosija por lo que no pudo ejecutar su orden, y dijo que si se hallara con salud compareciera al punto, y para que concierte[34] de su enfermedad y de su obedecimiento lo firmé en veinte y dos de enero de mil setecientos y treinta y siete años.

Doy fe,
Fray Joseph Yrigoien
Notario del Santo Oficio [rúbrica]

En conformidad de hallarse enfermo Miguel de Quintana, determinó dicho Reverendo Padre Comisario pasar a la casa del dicho y lo ejecutó hoy día veinte y tres de enero de mil setecientos y treinta y siete, por la mañana como a las nueve, y hallándolo en su sano y enterezo juicio le notificó de parte del muy santo y recto tribunal de la Inquisición: por ante mí el infraescrito notario que se dejase de revelaciones ridículas y de publicarlas so pena de que sería castigado como embustero, pertinaz y rebelde, y se le señaló después de reprehenderlo ásperamente por confesor que dirigiese su espíritu al Reverendo Padre Fray Joseph Yrigoien, Ministro de la Misión de Santa Clara, que es el más inmediato a la morada de[35] dicho Miguel de Quintana, y a todo responde: que todo lo que se le ordena obedece y obedecerá sin faltar en nada y que siente de sus revelaciones y escritos lo que siente el Santo Tribunal y que le pesa mucho el haberlo hecho y creído en tales disparates. Prometió el secreto y lo

[f. 470v]

firmó con dicho Reverendo Padre Comisario ante mí el infraescrito notario en dicho día, mes y año, en la Villa Nueva de Santa Cruz.

Fray Joseph Antonio Guerrero [rúbrica]
Comisario del Santo Oficio

Miguel de Quintana [rúbrica]

Pasó ante mí
Joseph Yrigoien
[Al pie de la página, una rúbrica parecida a la de Yrigoien]
Notario del Santo Oficio

Document 16. April 17, 1737. Letter from Quintana to Father Juan de la Cruz, asking his reaction to new poems and prose he has written

[f. 474r]

++

Muy Reverendo Padre Predicador Jubilado Fray Juan de la Cruz:

Amantísimo Padre y Dueño mío, saludo a Vuestra Paternidad con tal voluntad que siempre deseando su buena salud. En ambos huesos[36] yo quedo con alguna mejoría, a Dios las gracias, y muy a las órdenes de Vuestra Paternidad, a quien remito los inclusos métricos y demás cláusulas, sujetándolas a la censura y concepción de Vuestra Paternidad en orden a lo que me envió a decir Vuestra Paternidad con mi comadre Gertrudis Xirona. Interin quedo pidiendo a su Divina Majestad me guarde a Vuestra Paternidad muchos años para mi consuelo de ésta su casa, abril 17 de 1737.

Beso su santa mano de
Vuestra Paternidad Reverenda,
Su más humilde siervo que le estima,
Miguel de Quintana [rúbrica]

Document 17. April 24, 1737. A report by Fray Juan Joseph Pérez [de] Mirabal on how he took possession of the new poems and prose by Quintana mentioned in the preceeding document. Those writings by Quintana are included

[f. 471r]

Digo yo, Fray Juan Joseph Pérez de Mirabal, Padre Jubilado y Ministro de esta jurisdicción de la Villa Nueva de Santa Cruz, que el día veinte y cuatro de abril de mil setecientos y treinta y siete años, habiendo pasado dicho día en dicha jurisdicción como a las tres de la tarde a visitar al Reverendo Padre Jubilado Fray Juan de la Cruz, hallé que a su Paternidad le había escrito Miguel de Quintana, vecino de dicha Villa de Santa Cruz una papeleta en verso y prosa que es como se sigue:

Jesús, María y José
El supremo Director
que sólo lo es Jesucristo,
soberano Rey del Cielo
a quien adoras rendido
es, Miguel, el que te guía
con su poder infinito.

La luz que llevas es clara
y tan libre de peligro
Cuanto mi amor fue de darte
por más pobre y abatido.

De mi clemencia la gozas
y mal puede ser delito
el que de mi gracia goces
es grande beneficio.

No le temas al demonio
que en ti no tiene dominio
ni lo tendrá su soberbia,
su confusión ni su abismo.

Que si de sabio se precia
de discreto y entendido
todo lo entiende al revés
y así Dios lo ha confundido.

Y el que a tu casa o persona
se osare y fuere atrevido
tendrá de mi fuerte brazo
un riguroso castigo.

No tengas miedo, Miguel.
Prosigue con tus escritos
que con ellos vas seguro
y muy libre de peligros.

Esa variedad que sientes
de pensamientos distintos
no los temas que son todos
de mi amor bien dirigidos.

Mira mi causa y no temas
que no te vendrá castigo
confusión, daño ni afrenta
por lo que llevas escrito.

Que si los hombres te estrechan
en sus limitados juicios
Dios tu corazón dilata
con celestiales arbitrios.

La luz interior que gozas
es, Miguel, de Jesucristo
y no ilusión del demonio
como los hombres te han dicho.

Y si por mi fino amor
te ves, Miguel, perseguido,
sígueme que no habrá quien
te estorbe ese camino.

Es un grandioso interior
el que del poder divino
gozas por humilde y pobre
de gran concepto y sentido.

Cree, Miguel, con viva fe
que Dios no te ha confundido
ni su divina grandeza
está enojado contigo.

[Escrito entre columnas:]
Miguel, no hayas miedo. Cree que quien te ha movido y mueve es la divina omnipotencia de Dios. Cree que tus letras han de causar a los que te han mofado horror, confusión y espanto. Esos agudos dolores que te afligen se te quitarán. Ten paciencia que muy poquito falta.

[f. 471v]

Cree, Miguel, que eres movido, amparado, auxiliado y favorecido de la inmensa majestad, poder y sabiduría de Dios único, Dueño y Señor absoluto de todas las cosas y quien tiene dominio y poder sobre todos, el mismo a quien adoras, reverencias y confiesas por tu Dios, por tu Rey, por tu Rendentor, por tu Padre y Bienhechor en el sagrado madero de la cruz. No hayas miedo ni temor que no se perderá tu alma. Prosigue, escribe, que Dios es Dios y, pues, el Reverendo Padre

Predicador Jubilado Fray Juan de la Cruz, tu amigo, doliéndose de tu aflicción te envió a decir que escribieses lo que sentía y siente tu interior. Escribe y no te hagan fuerza esos pensamientos que sientes y la Divina Majestad de Dios te determina que su Divina Majestad, como maestro de la sabiduría y que sabe enmendar a los más sabios, se vale de los instrumentos más débiles y de los pobrecitos a quien el mundo abate y persigue por instrumentos de su Divina Justicia, permitiendo en ellos muchas culpas para castigo de otras mayores. El Reverendo Padre Comisario del Santo Oficio y su notario te han venido, Miguel, a dar gatazo[37] con pretextos frívolos vestidos de sus pasiones, haciéndote cargo y calificándote culpa donde no la tienes ni venial. Fíate de Dios que si pretenden quitarte la vida o hacerte perder el juicio, no lo conseguirán porque Dios que es Dios te la conserva con su poder santísimo. Miguel, es Dios Dios, Dios es el que te inspira, no es el demonio. Prosigue, escribe, que es su santísima voluntad que escribas, que si te han privado de que escribas, amenazándote con un severo castigo por el Santo Oficio, no ha de ser lo que sus paternidades quieren, y sólo ha de ser lo que Dios quisiere y fuere servido de darte. Y te dará su gloria su Divina Majestad como quisiere y fuere de su santísima voluntad y a tu modo de entender, como a su Divina Majestad le diere mucha gana y no a gusto ni paladar de ningún individuo, pues puede su alta grandeza darte de sus inmensos tesoros lo que quisiere sin que haya quien se lo impida a su Divina Majestad y eso en ti, Miguel, no puede ser culpa. Alégrate, Miguel, en Dios, consuélate en su grandeza, en su divina sabiduría y amor santísimo, el más perfecto, el más fino y el más seguro que no habrá poder humano que a tus letras ponga la más mínima tacha. No te mueres que Dios conserva tu vida y has de escribir a pesar de todo el infierno porque es voluntad de Dios. Muy breve te verás sano de esa dolencia

[f. 472r]

que padeces, y si el Padre Guerrero te ha estrechado y puesto precepto de que sólo con su notario te has de confesar y no con otro, es injusticia e insolencia y aun asco el que tal escribas materias muy dignas de reparo porque eres católico cristiano y no te han de probar ninguna herejía ni cosa que se oponga a la católica fe que profesas. Confiésate con quien quisieres, que su Divina Majestad te dio tu albedrío libre para que así lo hagas, que Dios no impone preceptos imposibles a ninguna de sus criaturas ni quiere que las almas se enreden con escrúpulos. Descansa y no quemes esas letras aunque te veas afligido. Remíteselas al Reverendo Padre Fray Juan de la Cruz, que su paternidad reverenda pondrá los medios para tu alivio, y no te dé, Miguel, cuidado de nada. Fíate, Miguel, de Dios, que Dios es Dios, quien te guía y dilata tu pobrecito y afligido corazón y teniendo a su Divina Majestad no te puede faltar nada. Ríndele a su Divina Majestad tu pobrecito y sencillo corazón que la interioridad que por su alta disposición gozas no te la podrá estorbar todo el poder del infierno que se te oponga. Ni el Reverendo Padre Comisario del Santo Tribunal ni su notario se meterán contigo en bueno [ni] en malo como lo verás, ni por esa vía serás afligido más. Escribirás con sosiego, quietud y tranquilidad, gozando de mi poder, amor y clemencia santísima, las luces y soberanos auxilios que yo te diere para confusión de muchos que se precian de discretos y entendidos. Descansa y remite al Reverendo Padre Predicador Jubilado esas letras como tienes prevenido y no te dé cuidado nada, que caminas seguro y muy seguro, y serás muy breve consolado. No es, Miguel, cosa de chanza lo que tienes entendido. Fíate de Dios y no temas que de Dios eres movido. Su soberana grandeza te ofrece un grandioso alivio dentro de muy breve tiempo, como lo verás cumplido. Espérale que es muy padre, muy discreto y muy benigno. No temas el perecer viviendo a su amor rendido. Miguel, tus trabajitos, aflicciones y congojas de tu espíritu y los de tu pobrecita mujer los tiene Dios asentados de buena letra en su divino acatamiento. Algo hubiera dado y hoy diera el Reverendo Padre

[f. 472v]

Comisario del Santo Oficio por no haber venido a tu casa con su celoso notario. Remite tus letras sin recelo ninguno que ni lo justo ante Dios dejará de ser justo, ni lo injusto injusto, porque Dios tiene espada para todos.

____[38]

Mirabal Mirabal Mirabal [tres rúbricas]

Concuerda con su original de donde yo, Fray Juan Joseph Pérez Mirabal saqué la sobredicha copia para hacer entrega de ella al Reverendo Padre Predicador general jubilado exdicreto de esta Santa Custodia, notario al padre párroco de la Provincia del Santo Evangelio, sus custodias y misiones y notario del Santo Oficio, Fray Joseph de Yrigoien, ministro de la Misión de Santa Clara, para que como oficial del muy Recto y Santo Tribunal de la Inquisición hoy ponga lo que convenga y para que conste y haga fe. Lo firmé en este convento de la Villa Nueva de Santa Cruz en el sobredicho día veinte y cuatro de abril de mil setecientos y treinta y siete años.

Fray Juan Joseph Pérez Mirabal [rúbrica]
Ministro de la Villa Nueva [de Santa Cruz]

Document 18. April 25, 1737. Letter to Quintana from Juan de la Cruz, responding to Quintana's most recent writings

[f. 475r]

++

Miguel de Quintana:

Muy Señor mío, recibí el documento con su inclusa que en realidad de verdad debo decir a Vuestra Merced que ni lo entendí ni sus cláusulas alcancé ni penetré, motivo por qué remitiéndoselo a Vuestra Merced, como incluso va en ésta, podrá conocer mi incapacidad e insuficiencia de censor de su obra. Pues *veo videro* [que] pide fundamentos más eruditos que lo que alcanza mi ignorancia. En lo que Vuestra Merced [pregunta] de Gertrudis Xirona, le digo lo que le dije. Fue que atento lo dilatado de su enfermedad con sus circunstancias en un hombre de negocios como ha estado en la presente *litis* Vuestra Merced y otras ocupaciones—que en lo civil siendo casi secretario perpetuo de los alcaldes mayores—fuera cosa acertada y en lo moral de gran seguridad para su conciencia examinar y reexaminarla para ver si había algún gravamen en ella

[f. 475v]

que o por fragilidad u otros motivos. En lo moral de las conciencias cada día se tocan y experimentan hacer alguna declaración de lo que conociese Vuestra Merced estar su conciencia lastimada, pues si algo hay lo estará hecho en materia de sacramentos. Es nulo y debe reiterarse si Vuestra Merced no siente, hecha dicha diligencia, ningún estímulo de justicia ni conciencia, [entonces] cumplió en su obligación como buen cristiano y entonces con fundamento de[39] intrínseca probabilidad podrá Vuestra Merced deponer todo escrúpulo *i hic et nunc.*[40] Obrar con toda licitud de conciencia es lo que yo quisiera decir a Vuestra Merced con la referida[41] dicha. Atento la diversidad de accidentes que tengo noticia de su enfermedad de Vuestra Merced que Dios guarde y dé perfecta salud muchos años. San Juan, abril 25 de 1737.

Besa su mano de Vuestra Merced,
su afecto capellán,
Fray Juan de la Cruz [rúbrica]

Document 19. April 30, 1737. Yrigoien testifies how he obtained a copy of Quintana's latest writings through Father Mirabal

[f. 473r]

++

En la villa de Santa Fe, capital del Reino de la Nueva México, en treinta días del mes de abril del año de mil setecientos treinta y siete por la mañana, como a las diez del día, ante el Reverendo Padre Comisario del Santo Oficio de este dicho reino pareció sin ser llamado y juró en forma que dirá verdad un religioso de Nuestro Seráfico Padre San Francisco, hijo de la Provincia del Santo Evangelio de México que dijo llamarse Fray Joseph Yrigoien, notario apostólico y actual del Santo Oficio, el cual para descargo de su conciencia dice y denuncia que el día veinte y cuatro de este dicho mes de abril, estando en la Villa Nueva de Santa Cruz en negocios que se le habían ofrecido, en el convento de dicha villa como a la oración de la noche llegó el Reverendo Padre Ministro de dicha villa, Fray Juan Joseph de Mirabal, y le dijo que necesitaba de su persona a solas por la cual despidió a los que en su compañía estaban y que dicho padre prosiguió diciéndole que venía escandalizado de visitar al Reverendo Padre Fray Juan de la Cruz porque su paternidad lo había llamado para leerle una papeleta que contenía unos versos y prosa escrita por Miguel de Quintana, y remitida a dicho Reverendo Padre Fray Juan de la Cruz para que su paternidad la aprobara y que habiendo visto en ella muchas proposiciones disonantes, y contra el recto y libre ejercicio del Santo Oficio, le dijo al dicho Reverendo Padre Fray Juan de la Cruz que había de delatar al Santo Tribunal y que dicho padre dijo que no entendía la papeleta, que él le escribiría a Miguel de Quintana y se la devolvería. Y que mientras dicho Reverendo Padre Fray Juan de la Cruz le escribía a dicho Quintana, se apartó a otro cuarto con la papeleta y suplicó le diesen tinta y papel y sacó un manuscrito firmado de su mano, el que a mí, Fray Joseph Yrigoien, entregó como a notario del Santo Oficio para que lo presentase como lo hago hoy día de la fecha y tiene un pliego de papel escrito por las cuatro llanas menos un pedazo de la última. Y juntamente me dijo dicho Reverendo Padre Fray Juan de Mirabal[42] que si quería haber[43] a las manos el original y la carta que respondía dicho Reverendo Padre Fray Juan de la Cruz, pasase a casa de Manuel de la Rosa, vecino de la dicha Villa Nueva de la Santa Cruz, que era el portador que pudiera ser no lo hubiera entregado a dicho Miguel de Quintana, por lo cual con toda diligencia pasé a casa de dicho

[rúbrica]

[f. 473v]

Manuel de la Rosa y le pregunté que si llevaba una carta que enviaba el Reverendo Padre Fray Juan de la Cruz a Miguel de Quintana, y me respondió que sí y le dije que como a notario del Santo Tribunal me la entregase, lo que ejecutó luego al punto y le encargué el secreto que prometió verbalmente y hago entrega de dicha carta rotulada para dicho Miguel de Quintana, cerrada con pan y marcada con las uñas, y habiendo hecho mi regreso al dicho convento de la Nueva Villa [de Santa Cruz] como a las ocho de la noche, me dijo el

Reverendo Padre Fray Juan de Mirabal que si quería coger el papel que escribió dicho Miguel de Quintana al dicho Reverendo Padre Fray Juan de la Cruz en que le pide la aprobación de dicha papeleta que pasase a la madrugada a la posada del dicho Reverendo Padre Fray Juan de la Cruz y se la pidiese, lo cual ejecuté por parecerme así conveniente y a las seis de la mañana del día veinte y cinco pasé a la posada de dicho Reverendo Padre Fray Juan de la Cruz, y le dije a su paternidad que me entregase como a Ministro del Santo Oficio un papel que en su poder tenía de Miguel de Quintana, el que me dio y presento ante dicho Reverendo Padre Comisario. Tiene una cuartilla de papel escrita por un lado y firmada de dicho Miguel de Quintana, y que ésta es la verdad, so cargo del juramento que hecho[44] tiene, que no lo dice por odio ni mala voluntad. Prometió el secreto y siéndole leído dijo estar bien escrito, que no tenía que añadir ni quitar y la firmó con dicho Reverendo Padre Comisario ante mí el infraescrito notario nombrado en dicho día mes y año.

Fray Joseph Antonio Guerrero [rúbrica]
Comisario del Santo Oficio

Joseph Yrigoien [rúbrica]

Pasó ante mí,
Fray Joseph de Eguía
Notario Nombrado [rúbrica]

DOCUMENTACION ADICIONAL

Document 20. 1737. Quintana's Retraction

From the Franciscan Archives, Mexico City—#982,
box 15, no. 260 (7r–v, 8r–v)

Descripción/sinopsis: Carta abierta de Miguel de Quintana en que se retracta de ciertas acusaciones que hizo contra los misioneros franciscanos de Nueva México: Villa Nueva de Santa Cruz de Nueva México, 2 noviembre 1737. Antecedida de solicitud de certificación que hace Fray Juan Antonio de Ezeiza y de auto de Henrique de Olavide y Michelena, Gobernador de Nueva México, Villa de Santa Fe, 22 noviembre 1737.

[Al margen:]
Escrito 11/23/1737

Señor Gobernador y Capitán General:

Fray Juan Antonio de Ezeiza, actual vice-custodio en estas misiones de la Santa Custodia de la Conversión de San Pablo de la Nueva México, parezco ante Vuestra Señoría en la mejor forma que haya lugar en derecho, y al mío convenga, y digo que por cuanto por lo que a nuestro crédito mira, estando perdido o en peligro manifiesto de perderse (como hoy lloramos todos los misioneros de esta santa custodia) no se debe omitir ocasión en que pueda subsanarse, trayéndose el caso a las manos esta carta abierta, que ante Vuestra Señoría presento, pido y suplico dos tantos de ellas, me mande sacar, y testimoniados en manera que hagan fe, me los devuelva para recurrir donde el derecho me permite. Protestando como protesto ante mi escrito no ser de malicia alguna y en lo necesario, etc. = Fray Juan Antonio de Ezeiza.

[Al margen:]
Auto

En la Villa de Santa Fe, capital de este Reino de la Nueva México, el veintidós del mes de noviembre de mil setecientos treinta y siete años, se presentó esta petición; y por mí, Gobernador y Capitán General de este dicho Reino y sus provincias, vista, la hube por presentada y mandésela dar a esta parte el testimonio que pide de la carta que presenta en pública forma y manera que haga fe. Así lo procesé, mandé y firmé actuando por reciprocía con testigos de asistencia a falta de Señor notario real y público, que no lo hay en dicho reino. Henrique de Olavide y Michelena, testigo, Juan Joseph Moreno, testigo, Pedro Joseph de León.

[Al margen izquierdo:]
Carta

Ilustrísimo Señor Doctor Don Martín de Elizacochea, por la gracia de Dios, y de la Santa Sede Apostólica, dignísimo obispo de este obispado, mi Señor.

Ilustrísimo Señor:

Con el mayor rendimiento que debo a la alta dignidad de Vuestra Señoría Ilustrísima, como pobre y humilde notario de Vuestra Señoría Ilustrísima en esta Villa Nueva de Santa Cruz de este Reino de la Nueva México, escribo ésta a Vuestra Señoría Ilustrísima y digo Señor: que por cuanto tengo escritas varias cartas al Señor Don Joseph Bustamante, Vicario Juez Eclesiástico que fue de este reino, y estas resultan en descrédito de los religiosos, hijos de mi Seráfico Padre San Francisco, siendo católico cristiano por la gracia de Dios, y solicitando la salud de mi alma y satisfacer como debo a su Divina Majestad, el daño que de ellas puede resultar contra dicha sagrada religión de mi Padre San Francisco, debo decir, y digo, que como hombre flaco, pobre y forzado de mi necesidad, por buscar un pan para mis hijos, las escribí por adulación, que con humildad confieso: y así de todo lo que en ellas está depuesto, me deniego y digo que los reverendos padres ministros cumplen exactamente con su obligación en la administración de los santos sacramentos; y sus doctrinas han sido dirigidas al bien espiritual de las almas, conociendo que el Reverendo Padre Predicador Fray Joseph de Yrigoien y el Reverendo Padre Predicador Fray Joseph Antonio Guerrero, en sus acciones, y proposiciones, y consejos han solicitado mi bien espiritual, y temporal, y yo vestido de mi amor propio y mis pasiones, los he recibido por agravios, entendiendo las han obrado por razón de notario de Vuestra Señoría Ilustrísima y así para que en todo, y por todo, se les satisfaga su crédito así a los dichos, como a todos los demás, pongo en la alta comprehensión de Vuestra Señoría Ilustrísima todo lo clausulado, y expresado en ésta; pidiendo a Vuestra Señoría Ilustrísima me perdone el mal ejemplo que por dichas cartas de cualquier manera que las haya escrito, por amor de Dios y de su Santísima Madre la Virgen María, Nuestra Señora, y de nuestro Padre San Francisco, el que todo ceda a mayor honra y gracia de su Divina Majestad, a quien humildemente pido prospere y guarde la muy importante vida de Vuestra Señoría Ilustrísima por muchos años en su mayor prosperidad. Hecha en esta Villa Nueva de Santa Cruz de la Nueva México a dos días del mes de noviembre de mil setecientos treinta y siete años = Ilustrísimo Señor, está a los pies de Vuestra Señoría Ilustrísima, su más digno siervo y notario.

Miguel de Quintana [firma]

Concuerda con su original, que le devolví a la parte de donde se sacó este testimonio, el que va corregido y concertado, y fielmente sacado, a lo cual fueron testigos Don Juan Joseph Moreno, Pedro Joseph de León y Salvador de Santistevan. Y para que conste donde convenga, doy el presente actuando por reciprocía con testigos de asistencia a falta de Señor notario real y público, que no lo hay, formado de mi nombre en esta Villa de Santa Fe de la Nueva México en veintitrés días del mes de noviembre de mil setecientos treinta y siete años =

En testimonio de verdad hago mi firma acostumbrada.

Henrique de Olavide y Michelena [firma]

Ilustrísimo Señor Pedro Joseph de León [rúbrica]	Juan Joseph Moreno [rúbrica]

Appendix One: Quintana's Lawsuit over Stolen Horses

Spanish Archives of new Mexico, no. 178, fr. 627–29, (Twitchell, *The Spanish Archives of New Mexico*, vol. 2, no. 178)

[frame 627]

Jesús, María y José Villa Nueva de la Santa Cruz, Año de 1712

Demanda puesta por Miguel de Quintana a Joseph Trujillo por haberle hurtado unos indios, el uno sirviente suyo, dos caballos

[frame 628]

[Parte de la página está rota, indescifrable]

Miguel de Quintana, natural de la ciudad de México y vecino de la Villa Nueva de Santa Cruz. En la mejor vía y forma que haya lugar en derecho y al mío convenga, ante la grandeza de Vuestra Señoría parezco y digo que pasó el día trece del pasado mes de julio hicieron fuga tres apaches cristianos, el uno del capitán Joseph Trujillo, el otro del muy Reverendo Padre Custodio, y el otro Cristóbal, el criado que fue de Diego Martín, y hoy se halla en su libertad. Pues, como estaba o se había ido a acomodar con dicho Capitán Joseph Trujillo, y habiendo ejecutado su fuga, resultó contra mi suma pobreza, llevándome dos caballos de camino y _____ mansos de rienda, el uno tordillo que tenía yo persogado cerca de mi casa, el cual me llevaron cortándome la persoga con cuchillo. Y hallando así el pedazo que dejaron, presumí me lo hubiese hurtado alguno para venir a esta villa. Y, yendo yo para casa del dicho Joseph Trujillo por un caballo alazán que me tenía en su caballada de camino y manso de rienda para hacer diligencia de buscar el otro, supe [que] de casa de Cristóbal Torres se habían huido los dichos tres apaches y se habían llevado dos caballos, un rosillo y un alazán. Para verificar si había sido el mío, pasé a ver al dicho Joseph Trujillo y me dijo habérselo llevado amarrado a su corral, lo cual había hecho porque no se me extraviara. Y con esta razón me vine a mi casa considerando mi suma desgracia, pues después de hallarme como me hallo, cargado de siete hijos, tenía en dichos dos caballos el alivio de conducir un poco de bastimento y leña y salir a mis diligencias. Cuando tenía más perdidas las esperanzas de resarcirlas, fue Dios Nuestro Señor servido de que se hayan vuelto dos de ellos, que son Cristóbal y Andrés, éste criado del susodicho Joseph Trujillo, a quien con buenas razones le dije que el caballo alazán que tenía en su poder le tocaba hacérmelo bueno, pues los ladrones habían sido de su casa y ya se habían vuelto a ella, a lo cual me respondió que los cobrase yo, puesto que era mío y que no

[frame 629]

____ hecho obligación de pagármelo si se perdía y hec____ ya no habían sido enemigos los que se lo llevaron de este ____ como medio conveniente representar mi justicio _____ ante la grandeza de Vuestra Señoría para que atendiéndome como por estar cargado de hijos, y eran mis pies y manos los dichos dos caballos, se me restituyan, pues cualquiera de los tres fugitivos cooperantes en mi entera restitución. Por todo lo cual a Vuestra Señoría pido y suplico con todo rendimiento y obediencia se sirva de que me paguen mis dos caballos, tales cuales eran, que en ellos recibiré merced con justicia que pido y juro por Dios Nuestro Señor e Hijo en la Cruz no ser mi escrito de malicia y en lo necesario

Miguel de Quintana [rúbrica]

Appendix Two: Lugarda Quintana's Will

Spanish Archives of New Mexico (SANM), Series I, Land Records of New Mexico, no. 968, rollo 5, fr. 717–20. Lugarda Quintana, Testamento, 1749.

In Die Domini, amen.

En el nombre de Dios, Todopoderoso, Padre, Hijo y Espíritu Santo; tres personas distintas, y un solo Dios verdadero; y de la Virgen María, Nuestra Señora; el bien aventurado San Miguel Arcángel, San Juan Bautista, apóstoles San Pedro y San Pablo; mi patrona, Santa Lugarda, y el santo angel de mí querido. Yo, Lugarda Quintana, natural de este reino y vecina de esta Villa de Santa Cruz, hago esta memoria, testamento, estando enferma en cama de la enfermedad que Dios, Nuestro Señor, ha sido servido de darme, estando en mi entero juicio y conocimiento por la divina gracia.

Primeramente, protesto y digo que creo fiel y verdaderamente en el misterio de la Santísima Trinidad, Padre, Hijo y Espíritu Santo, tres personas distintas y un solo Dios verdadero y en todos los demás misterios que cree y confiesa nuestra Santa Iglesia Católica Romana en la cual murieron todos los santos y que en esta fe quiero vivir y morir como católica cristiana por la divina gracia.

Item: mando mi alma a Dios que la creó y reanimó con su preciosísima sangre y el cuerpo a la tierra de cuyo linaje fui formado.

Item: mando a mi albacea, para cuyo efecto nombro a mi compadre, Pedro Sánchez, que si Dios, Nuestro Señor, fuere servido de llevarme de esta vida a la otra, que por estar mi esposo ausente y no saber donde se halla, le elijo por tal albacea, [y que] sea mi cuerpo sepultado en la iglesia parroquial de la Villa de Santa Cruz en la parte que quisiera el dicho albacea.

Item: mando a las mandas forzosas a personas cada una con glosa por lo de mis bienes.

Item: declaro que soy casada según orden de nuestra Madre, la Santa Iglesia, con Asencio Archuleta, de cuyo matrimonio

[fol. 1v]

tuvimos y procreamos tres hijos: una mujer y dos hombres, que son Cristóbal, Juana Josefa y Nicolás Marcos Archuleta, a quienes dejo con mi esposo por herederos.

Item: declaro que si Dios me llevare de esta vida, por mi entierro y funeral lo dejo a la voluntad de mi albacea.

Primeramente, declaro por mis bienes cuatro bueyes mansos y dos toros bueyes.

Item: declaro tener una vaca de vientre y una ternera de dos años.

Item: declaro haberle comprado a Luis de Archuleta un pedazo de tierra por precio y cantidad de treinta y cinco pesos, los que fue el ajuste de dicha tierra, y queda el dicho Luis de Archuleta satisfecho y que el dicho queda con la obligación de hacerme la venta pagando a la justicia los derechos que son doscientos y diez y ocho varas de largo y de once hasta la acequia madre.

Item: más otro pedazo de tierra que le cupo de herencia a mi esposo con parte de la casa que por no estar repartido entre sus hermanos no se sabe con claridad hasta que la justicia lo reparta. Sí declaro que en dicha tierra tengo fabricado un huerto de diez varas que sólo llamo mío las paredes y techo.

Item: dejo una coa vieja y dos cavadoras viejas, más otra coa pequeña, una hacha pequeña, una azuela y escoplo, un asador, una cuchara, una barrena, un cazo viejo; que también declaro dejar tres puntas pequeñas; el cazo es de lo que buscó mi marido, una cadereta vieja, un cuchillo viejo de rescate.

Item: tres cajas con sus cerraduras, dos chiquitas ["más tres" superimpuesto] y una grande vieja.

Y un acanalador, una guitarra, dos ventanas y una silleta, una ortesita.

Item: dejo una enaguas de sarga nuevas y otras viejas, un par de faldillas, cuatro varas de encaje entre fino y otras varas de lo dicho de pita, dos mantellinas, una con forro y otra sin él, un paño de media seda nuevo, un par de zapatos de hombres, dos palios, cuatro varas de listón, una gargantilla de corales chochos y platillos revueltos, unos pulseros de esmalte azul, unos zarcillos de perlas finas con berruecos, todo grueso, cuatro mechitos de seda encarnados con más dos madejas de seda anteadas, unas medias de lana nuevas y unas calcetas de algodón nuevas.

[fol. 2r]

Dos pares de agujas de medias, tres posuelos, dos finos y uno ordinario, cuatro tecomatitos chicos, un pedazo de fleco viejo, un jarrito de alcorzar o bocadito, una tela de cedazo blanco, unos manteles pequeños y una servilleta, un ceñidor de Sonora de dos varas y media, una jícara nueva, tres puertas todas de una mano, dos cerrojos con una llave.

Item: catorce efigies de santos, todos pequeños, y un Santo Cristo de bronce.

Item: un colchón con tres sábanas y trece varas de sayal, un caballo de rienda, una carreta aviada—las ruedas las marqué yo.

Item: declaro tener ciento y diez cabezas de ganado menor que de unas reses que traje de herencia de mi padre; las troqué por borregos con ocho cabras que mi esposo compró por su parte y de estos se han multiplicado en lo dicho. Cuatro cueros de vacas.

Item: declaro tener tres aves hembras y dos gallos y siete ristras de chile, dos en ramillete viejo, un libro de San Antonio viejo. A Juan Manuel un carnero debo. [palabras tachadas]

Item: debo tres pesos y cuatro reales a Antonia Trujillo, los tres pesos. . . .

Item: declaro que me deben diez cabezas de ganado que esos van inclusos en el número de los ciento y diez arriba expresados; que los de don Gerónimo, el indio que era del difunto Antonio Martín, de dichas cabras, el cacique debe una borrega y una cabra; Juan, el de Marcos Martín, debe una cabra, Ma[g]dalena, la india, una cabra; Eusebio Durán, un carnero; Miguel Martín otro carnero [Francisca, la india, debe una misa]; Miguel Trujillo una borrega; Juana Lobato debe una borrega; la debe por albacea de Antonio Martín, que el dicho difunto la debía a mí. Un toro que debe Juan Esteban [palabras tachadas] de tres años. Francisca de Herrera, un peso, más cinco pesos que debe Pedro Cisneros. Maria Josefa López, un peso; dos carneros que debe Miguel Trujillo. Y habiendo ya herederos y albacea y declarado todos mis bienes y ditas, supliqué al Capitán Hilario Archuleta, teniente de alcalde mayor y capitán a guerra de esta Villa Nueva de Santa Cruz y su jurisdicción, interpusiese su autoridad y que esta mi última voluntad se guarde y cumpla de la manera y forma que la tengo declarada y declaro que no tengo hecho ningún otro testamento,

[fol. 2v]

ni memoria ni codicilo y que de [a]parecer otro alguno lo revoco y anulo y quiero que ésta mi voluntad se guarde y cumpla. Y yo, dicho teniente de alcalde mayor, lo autoricé por no hallarse el alcalde mayor a la presente y ser el caso forzoso, según las partes me dicen, siendo testigos instrumentales Eusebio Durán y Luis de Archuleta. Otrosí declaro que de lo declarado mando que después de pagados mis funerales se haga lo que quedase un conjunto y se haga un conjunto por entero, dos partes, la una para mis hijos y la otra a mi marido y que a una sobrinita mía que tengo le separo de mi ganadito, mando se le dé seis cabecitas de ganado y una caja. Siendo testigos de mi asistencia, yo, dicho teniente, nombré a Francisco Valdés y al Capitán Miguel Martín y no lo firmó la testadora por no saber. Y es hecho en doce de mayo de mil setecientos cuarenta y nueve en el presente papel porque el sellado no corre en estas partes. Ut supra, etcétera.

Ante mí, de que doy fe.
Hilario Archuleta [rúbrica]
Testigo, Francisco Valdés [rúbrica]
Testigo, Miguel Martín Serrano [rúbrica]

[escrito verticalmente al pie de la página]
Año de 1749, Testamento de Lugarda Quintana

Notes

Part One

1. During the years of the Quintana case, the Franciscans in New Mexico were very much on the defensive. Inspection visits by church officials from farther south continued to find their conduct substandard, and the bishops of the Diocese of Durango had been seeking to take jurisdiction for the region away from the Franciscan Order. Jim Norris writes: "In 1734, [Franciscan administrator] Custos Fray José Ortiz de Velasco, based in El Paso, inspected the northern missions . . . [and] found many of the old problems still in place. . . . Ortiz closed with a passionate plea for the missionaries to live 'according to the examples set by St. Francis and St. Paul.' . . . Concern over the reports coming out of New Mexico, including the negative assessments from the [??] Crespo and [Don Martín de] Elizacochea visits, evoked a further response from the Franciscan hierarchy." *After "The Year Eighty": The Demise of Franciscan Power in Spanish New Mexico* (Albuquerque: University of New Mexico Press, 2000), 101.

2. Enlightenment philosophical ideas of French origin would, in fact, arrive in Mexico, but not for another fifty years at the earliest. Richard E. Greenleaf observes that "the Mexican clergy rejected the new thought of the Age of Science and the Age of Reason and cooperated in ferreting out heretics" (171), but he writes in the context of the 1790s and later. Similarly Karl Schmitt studies the question in the "last quarter of the eighteenth century" (153). See Richard E. Greenleaf, "The Mexican Inquisition and the Enlightenment, 1763–1805," in *The Roman Catholic Church in Colonial Latin America*, ed. Richard E. Greenleaf, 164–76 (New York: Knopf, 1971) and Karl Schmitt, "The Clergy and the Enlightenment," 152–63, in the same collection of essays.

3. Enrique R. Lamadrid has pointed out that *Los Comanches*, a New Mexican folk play probably originating in the late eighteenth century and still staged today, strengthens Chicano Studies' search for cultural roots that manifest "a counterhegemonic discourse." Quintana's writings are similar in this regard but more explicit in their challenge to hegemonic authority. See "*Los Comanches*: Text, Performance, and Transculturation in an Eighteenth-Century New Mexican Folk Drama," in *Recovering the U.S. Hispanic Literary Heritage*, eds. María Herrera-Sobek and Virginia Sánchez Korrol (Houston: Arte Público Press, 2000), 3:173.

4. *Intrahistoria* is the concept of capturing daily activities and emotions generally not thought of as worthy of historical consideration. Spanish philosopher and literary giant Miguel de Unamuno popularized it in the early twentieth century as a way of understanding cultures and their literature from within.

5. Establishing the connection to Spanish literary tradition of what has seemed primarily a document from New Mexican social history is similar to the work of Barbara de Marco regarding accounts of the 1680 Pueblo Revolt. She writes that "the official documents and correspondence which comprise the historical record contain echoes of hagiographic narratives which are so integral a part of the literary history of Spain." See "Cantaron la Victoria: Spanish Literary Tradition and the 1680 Pueblo Revolt," in *Recovering* (see note 3), 3:163.

6. Luis Leal, "California Colonial Literature," in *In Retrospect: Essays on Latin American Literature*, ed. Elizabeth S. Rogers and Timothy Rogers, 24–39 (York, SC: Sp. Lit. Pubs. Co., 1987.

7. Often the reference is to "el vasto norte de las provincias internas," or "the vast north of the Provincias Internas."

8. The title varies depending on the historian. The work is sometimes referred to as *Naufragios*, but most assuredly the title given here is an abbreviation of the exceedingly long and exuberant Renaissance original. A recent novel detailing the life of Cabeza de Vaca sets him in his historical context with care. See Alfred Rodríguez, *Plus Ultra: The Life and Times of Alvar Núñez Cabeza de Vaca* (Lincoln, NE: Iuniverse, 2001). An exhaustive listing of books by and about this explorer and writer is found at http://www.library.txstate.edu/swwc/cdv/further_study/books.html.

9. The text is available in *Colección de los documentos inéditos, relativos al descubrimiento, conquista . . .* , ed. Joaquín Pacheco and Francisco Cárdenas, 42 vols. (Madrid, 1864–65), 3:325–50.

10. The Spanish text was published in Marco de Nizza, *Nuevo México* (Mexico City: Consejo Nacional para la Cultura y las Artes, 1995).

11. Zárate Salmerón's compilation of early accounts of exploration was first published in 1856. A more recent Spanish edition is entitled *Noticias sacadas de un mss. intitulado Relaciones de todas las cosas que en el Nuevo México se han visto y sabido, así por mar como por tierra desde el año 1538 hasta el de 1626*, ed. José Fernando Ramírez (Mexico City: Vargas Rea, 1949). An English translation is *Relaciones*, trans. Alicia Ronstadt Milich, with a foreword by Donald C. Cutter (Albuquerque: Horn & Wallace, 1966).

12. The original Spanish text was published for the first time in *Missionalia Hispánica*, edited by Clark A. Colahan and Alfred Rodríguez, under the title "La relación de Fray Escobar de la expedición de Oñate a California (1604)" (Madrid: Consejo Superior de Investigaciones Científicas) 43 (1986): 373–94. The English translation is found in Herbert E. Bolton's "Father Escobar's Relation of the Oñate Expedition to California," *The Catholic Historical Review* 5 (April 1919–January 1920): 19–40.

13. Such a work (Boston: D. Lothrop & Co., 1885) served multiple purposes, most centrally the recruitment of Anglo settlers and entrepreneurs to the region. The oddity at first glance is contained in the usage of the Aztec myth of Aztlán, but the contemporary discovery of the "Aztec" ruins in northwestern New Mexico at the end of the nineteenth century seems to justify, albeit romantically, such a connection with the Aztec world.

14. It is worth noting that *México* in Spanish can refer to both the capital and the country, depending on the context. Whenever there is any doubt, the city is designated by D.F. (Distrito Federal).

15. See his "Chronicles of Exploration and Discovery: The Enchantment of the Unknown," in *Pasó Por Aquí: Critical Essays on the New Mexican Literary Tradition, 1542–1988*, ed. Erlinda Gonzales-Berry, 14–46 (Albuquerque: University of New Mexico Press, 1989). Other scholarly contributions to concentrate on New Mexico are: A. Gabriel Meléndez in *So All Is Not Lost: The Poetics of Print in Nuevomexicano Communities, 1834–1958* (Albuquerque: University of New Mexico Press, 1997); Genaro M. Padilla in *My History, Not Yours: The Formation of Mexican American Autobiography* (Madison: University of Wisconsin Press, 1993); Doris Meyer in *Speaking For Themselves: Neomexicano Cultural Identity and the Spanish-Language Press, 1880–1920* (Albuquerque: University of New Mexico Press, 1996); and Francisco A. Lomelí, Víctor A. Sorell,

and Genaro M. Padilla, *Nuevomexicano Cultural Legacy: Forms, Agency and Discourse* (Albuquerque University of New Mexico Press, 2002).

16. For further information on the expeditions mentioned, consult the thorough explanation Ralph Emerson Twitchell provided in "Spanish Colonization in New Mexico in the Oñate and De Vargas Periods," *Historical Society of New Mexico* 22 (1919): 3–39. Among the Oñate colonizers, 125 settlers are accounted for, excluding the friars and lay brothers. Among the first Vargas expedition there were 186 colonists in addition to some of the returning settlers from the 1680 Pueblo Revolt, most of whom were temporarily residing in El Paso del Norte and surrounding areas, thus accounting for almost 800 persons in all.

17. John L. Kessell comments that "Almost all the male heads of household proudly bore the casta distinction *español*, as did their wives and children. At the baptismal font, during prenuptial investigations, and at their weddings, this group of future New Mexicans was almost uniformly placed in this highest casta. Perhaps for this reason, once established in New Mexico, children of the Velasco-Farfán colonists tended to intermarry." See John L. Kessell, Rick Hendricks, and Meredith D. Dodge, eds., *To the Royal Crown Restored: The Journals of don Diego de Vargas, New Mexico, 1692–94* (Albuquerque: University of New Mexico Press, 1995), 9–10. Esquibel makes a similar point: "The viceroy's request at Mexico City for colonizers was not aimed at the aristocratic families of Nueva España, and his request very purposefully excluded racially mixed families as well as Indians, Africans and Filipinos. The viceroy's intent was to recruit Españoles, people of Spanish background, who were married legitimately within the church and of good character. The responding families were those of moderate means, non-aristocratic, and law abiding citizens." In particular, people with practical craft skills were sought. See "Mexico City to Santa Fe: Spanish Pioneers on the Camino Real, 1693–94," in *El Camino Real de Tierra Adentro*, ed. José A. Esquibel (Santa Fe: Bureau of Land Management, 1999), 5.

18. Upon comparing the Páez Hurtado muster list of 1695 with the 1693 Vargas muster list, it is revealing to note that the former no longer upheld Spanish origin as a requirement, consequently permitting many mestizos and mulattoes to enlist. Such a change appears to have definitely facilitated the recruitment of colonists willing to venture north. See John B. Colligan, *The Juan Páez Hurtado Expedition of 1695: Fraud in Recruiting Colonists for New Mexico* (Albuquerque: University of New Mexico Press, 1995).

19. See Clive Hallenbeck, *The Land of the Conquistadores* (Caldwell, ID: Caxton Printers, 1950), viii.

20. Ibid., p. viii.

21. For further information, consult Reed Anderson's "Early Secular Theater in New Mexico," in *Pasó Por Aquí* (see note 15), 101–26.

22. Russell Martin, "A Sagebrush School of Literature," *Los Angeles Times*, April 1, 1990.

23. The first translation was Gilberto Espinosa's *History of New Mexico* (Los Angeles: Quivira Society, 1933) but the most comprehensive and authoritative is by Miguel Encinias, Alfred Rodríguez, and Joseph P. Sánchez, *Historia de la Nueva Mexico, 1610, Gaspar Pérez de Villagrá. A Critical and Annotated Spanish/English Edition* (Albuquerque: University of New Mexico Press, 1992). Among other critical studies, see Luis Leal's "The First American Epic: Villagrá's *History of New Mexico*," in *Pasó Por Aquí* (see note

15), 47–62; and María Herrera-Sobek's "Contemporary Critical Theories and the Pérez de Villagrá Epic," in *Recovering (see note 3), 3:154–62.*

24. *See John L. Kessell, ed., Remote beyond Compare: Letters of don Diego de Vargas to His Family from New Spain and New Mexico, 1675–1706* (Albuquerque: University of New Mexico Press, 1989).

25. See Fray Angélico Chávez, "The Mad Poet of Santa Cruz," *New Mexico Folklore Record* 3 (1948–49): 10.

26. For more details on the *indita* see Arthur León Campa, *Spanish Folk-Poetry in New Mexico* (Albuquerque: University of New Mexico Press, 1946), 92, and Enrique R. Lamadrid, "History, Faith, and Intercultural Relations in Two New Mexican Inditas: 'Plácida Romero' and 'San Luis Gonzaga,'" in *Nuevomexicano Cultural Legacy: Forms, Agencies, and Discourse*, ed. Francisco A. Lomelí, Victor Sorell, and Genaro Padilla, 164–84 (Albuquerque: University of New Mexico Press, 2002). The indita is a culturally hybrid folk musical genre that sometimes contains elements of captivity narratives. Others, however, may be devotional, but a common element is their first-person narration. Although there do exist inditas in Mexico, the New Mexican indita is distinguished by its indigenous chanting quality. In other words, it reads like a corrido, but its rhythmic qualities clearly reveal an indigenous influence.

27. *Recuperación* is the term used by Carlos de Sigüenza y Góngora in the *Mercurio Volante* published at Mexico City in 1693. See Kessell, Hendricks, and Dodge, *To the Royal Crown Restored*, 7.

28. For a thorough history of the Penitentes, see Marta Weigle, *Brothers of Light, Brothers of Blood: The Penitentes of the Southwest* (Santa Fe, NM: Ancient City Press, 1989).

29. These folios of the Quintana archival manuscript range from 446 to 477 accounting for approximately thirty-two pages, but representing more in total. There are forty-seven pages if we count numbered pages but fifty-seven if we count every side of a page. Such discrepancies in the numbering system are significant in that various persons more than likely handled the original documents at different stages of the investigation. It appears that those in charge of such a compilation at times found themselves altering page numbers or simply adding pages, even haphazardly or hastily, without numbering them, depending on the availability of documents collected. In other instances, pages were erroneously marked. Some of the inaccuracies will be corrected by establishing a sequence and by indicating omissions or errors in the pagination. We have also made every attempt to clarify the order of such documents by reordering them chronologically as much as possible. The rampant confusion is principally the result of the chaotic "organization" or lack thereof.

30. The glaring omission, which we will discuss later, is Quintana's final recantation, which was sent directly to the bishop of Durango on November 22, 1737. Such a critical piece of evidence in the case survived thanks in the Archivos Franciscanos in Mexico City, which failed to add it to the collection of Inquisition papers for unknown reasons. The only plausible explanation is that the letter arrived after the case had been officially closed by April 1737, having been held in Durango, Mexico, or elsewhere, probably because of its contents. The retraction, containing Quintana's bitter criticism of his ecclesiastic accusers, may have fueled the ongoing rounds of mutual recrimination of the time between the civil government and the Franciscans in New Mexico.

31. The pertinent studies are: France V. Scholes, *Troublous Times in New Mexico,*

1659–1670 (New York: AMS Press, 1942, 1977) and *Church and State in New Mexico, 1610–1650* (Albuquerque: University of New Mexico Press, 1937); John L. Kessell, *Kiva, Cross, and Crown: The Pecos Indians and New Mexico, 1540–1840* (Washington, D.C.: National Park Service, U.S. Department of the Interior, 1979); Robert J. McCloe, "The Holy Office of the Inquisition: Its Role in New Mexico," in *Thetian*, ed. Arch O. Egbert (Provo: Phi Alpha Theta, 1967); and Richard E. Greenleaf, "The Mexican Inquisition and the Enlightenment," and *The Mexican Inquisition of the Sixteenth Century* (Albuquerque University of New Mexico Press, 1969).

32. See Scholes, *Church and State in New Mexico.*

33. See Kessell, Hendricks, and Dodge, *To the Royal Crown Restored*, 245–49. Of the 275 individuals recruited (61 families and 2 single men), 235 (now 67 families and 1 single man) actually left Mexico City on the original expedition. It is not altogether clear why only 186 figure in the official muster in Vargas's report, organized by Fray Francisco Farfán, also the procurator general of the expedition. The only explanation is that the distance and hardship of the trek produced attrition at a somewhat high rate, including desertions, deaths, possible changes of mind, and other circumstances. Also consult the Vargas report contained in Twitchell, "Spanish Colonization." The qualifier provided is that the list only contains settlers and excludes names of soldiers, officers, priests, and those returning after the 1680 revolt.

34. We are able to determine from the archives that another brother of Miguel, José de Quintana, lived in New Mexico, specifically in Santa Cruz de la Cañada, by 1695. He married Antonia Luján in that same year and made his living as a scribe primarily in Santa Fe and Bernalillo. Fray Angélico Chávez and José A. Esquibel believe he traveled in the same expedition as Miguel and Gertrudis as a soldier. For unknown reasons, no muster rolls exist for the soldiers who served as security for the expedition, but at a scant fourteen years old, it is doubtful he actually made that trip. A middle-class family was probably not inclined to allow a son with some formal education to join as a soldier. He more than likely joined a later caravan once news of the success of the resettlement traveled to Mexico City, subsequently settling initially in Santa Cruz de la Cañada, where his older brother Miguel already lived. More than likely he entered New Mexico in the Juan Páez expedition of 1695, given that earlier strict requirements for the recruitment process had become more relaxed by seeking able-bodied men to join such expeditions, even dropping marriage status and Spanish descent from the strict criteria. John L. Kessell, Rick Hendricks, and Meredith D. Dodge, in *Blood on the Boulders: The Journals of Don Diego de Vargas, New Mexico, 1694–97* (Albuquerque: University of New Mexico Press, 1998), list José among the colonists who entered from Sombrerete, Zacatecas, or the kingdoms of New Galicia and New Biscay, a fact that tends to confirm Esquibel's proposed entry date of 1695, but not necessarily as a soldier.

35. According to Ralph Emerson Twitchell, this included "not more than one half of the Spaniards who had been driven out thirteen years before, as, all told, in 1693, soldiers and settlers with De Vargas did not exceed eight hundred souls." See "Spanish Colonization," 28.

36. "In Mexico City the news of the successful restoration of New Mexico to the crown ignited celebrations among the city dwellers. To show his support for the accomplishment of Governor don Diego de Vargas, the viceroy of Nueva España, don Gaspar de la Cerda, Conde de Galve, initiated the recruitment of additional colonists for New Mexico with a decree that was read in all customary places in the City of

Mexico. The proclamation stated that provisions and transportation would be provided at the crown's expense for those families who enlisted to settle in New Mexico, and they would be accorded the honors and privileges of colonizers and granted land in the name of the king." José A. Esquibel, "The People of the Camino Real: A Genealogical Appendix," in *The Royal Road: El Camino Real from Mexico City to Santa Fe*, by Douglas Preston and José Antonio Esquibel, with photographs by Christine Preston, 145–76 (Albuquerque: University of New Mexico Press, 1998).

37. The only variation of his name found in the archives involves the "de" between his other names. People who know him well always refer to him as Miguel de Quintana.

38. His baptism took place at the Cathedral of Mexico in Mexico City, and his godfather was Joseph Gallegos de Velasco. See Esquibel, "The People of the Camino Real," 151.

39. Fray Angélico Chávez, in *The Origins of New Mexico Families in the Spanish Colonial Period in Two Parts: The Seventeenth (1598–1693) and the Eighteenth (1693–1821) Centuries* (Santa Fe: The Historical Society of New Mexico, 1954), offers a different interpretation of a hole or dimple in the chin. See 261.

40. The original Spanish is: "En veinte y ocho de febrero de mil seiscientos y setenta y siete años con licencia del cura Semo bauticé a Miguel Mathías, hijo de José de Quintana y de Doña Nicolasa de Valdez [*sic*] Altamirano. Fue su padrino el Capitán don Agustín Flores Urrutia de Vergara, Caballero del Orden de Santiago, Alguacil Mayor del tribunal. Dr. Antonio de la Torre y Arrellano [rubric]." See José A. Esquibel, "Mexico City Roots: Baptismal Records of Miguel de Quintana Valdés y Altamirano y Cervantes and José de Quintana Valdés Altamirano y Cervantes," *Genealogical Society of Hispanic America* 4, no. 2 (1992): 41–42.

41. His burial notice reads as follows: "En nueve de abril de mil setecientos y cuarenta y ocho años, murió recibidos los santos sacramentos Don Miguel de Quintana de edad de setenta años, poco más o menos, casado con [Gertrudis de Trujillo]. Está enterrado su cuerpo en esta excelentísima iglesia. Conste lo firmé en dicho día, mes y año, ut supra. Fray Antonio Gabaldón." (On April 9, 1748, having received the holy sacraments, don Miguel de Quintana died at age seventy, more or less, married to [Gertrudis de Trujillo]. His body is buried in this most excellent church. Let it be of record that I signed on that day, month, and year as shown above). From Archives of the Archdiocese of Santa Fe, Burials of Santa Cruz, 1726–1768, reel 39.

42. Gertrudis's physical features are described in the muster roll thus: "Gertrudes [*sic*] de Trujillo, wife of the above [Miguel], daughter of Nicolás, native of Mexico City, fifteen years of age, medium height, aquiline face, large eyes, and small nose" (Twitchell, "Spanish Colonization," 36). The phrase "aquiline face," according to Twitchell in *Spanish Archives*, suggests "a long face having an aquiline or hooked nose" (92).

43. Esquibel pinpoints with considerable accuracy the likely time of Miguel and Gertrudis's marriage. On the muster roll between July 7 and July 15, 1693, Gertrudis appears as single, but on the September 1, 1693, muster roll they are described as a married couple, suggesting that they celebrated their nuptials between July 15 and September 15, 1693. Gertrudis was born July 23, 1675, in Mexico City, making her eighteen years old instead of the fifteen the official secretary of the caravan recorded.

44. We have been unable to locate the actual decree that delineates all the privileges for the settlers, but a common formula, drafted as "Title of Hidalgo for New Mexico's Conquistadors, July 8, 1602," appears in part in Gaspar Pérez de Villagrá's *Historia de la Nueva México*:

> Those who pledge to establish settlements and have done so, fulfilling the terms of their contract, we name them and their legitimate descendants hidalgos of noble lineage in order to honor them and their descendants and so that they may leave a laudable memory as first settlers; and so that, in the town they have established, or anywhere else in the Indies, they may be considered as hidalgos of noble lineage and may enjoy all the honors and prerogatives and act as do all other hidalgos and caballeros in the kingdoms of Castile, in accordance with the laws and customs of Spain.

Cited in George P. Hammond and Agapito Rey, *Don Juan de Oñate, Colonizer of New Mexico, 1595–1628,* Part 2 (Albuquerque: University of New Mexico Press, 1953), 974.

45. *For the qualities sought in potential members of the expedition, see Esquibel, "The People of the Camino Real," 152.*

46. Founded before the 1680 revolt, this town, like Santa Fe, was designated as a villa to underscore its relative centrality and importance in the region. A villa was a chartered municipality superior in size, status, and privilege to a pueblo, but inferior to a ciudad, or city. There were only three New Mexican villas at the moment of Vargas's colonization; the other was El Paso del Norte. Quintana's hometown experienced various name changes in a process that constantly shortened the name from the one Vargas gave to Villa Nueva Santa Cruz de la Cañada to Santa Cruz de la Cañada to today's Santa Cruz. The Tano Indians had overrun the town after the Spanish expulsion of 1680, so Vargas needed to negotiate tactfully a way to remove them in favor of the new settlers.

47. See Myra Ellen Jenkins, "Settlement of the Jurisdiction of La Cañada," in folder "Settlement and Irrigation in the Santa Cruz-Quemado Watershed," at the Spanish Archives of New Mexico, CD3.

48. This represents an old Spanish form of a "dry measure of more than 1.5 to more than 2.5 bushels, according to the locality." See Eleanor B. Adams and Fray Angélico Chávez, *The Missions of New Mexico, 1776: A Description by Fray Francisco Atanasio Domínguez with Other Contemporary Documents* (Albuquerque: University of New Mexico Press, 1956, 1976), 355.

49. See Kessell, Hendricks, and Dodge, *Blood on the Boulders,* 1153, representing information from Spanish Archives of New Mexico, Series II, no. 65, roll 3, frame 73, entitled "De Vargas, Diego, Santa Fe, Mayo 1, 1697, Repartimiento hecho por Don Diego de Vargas a la vecindad del Nuevo México de los géneros recib[id]os así como ganado" (De Vargas, Diego, Santa Fe, May 1, 1697, Distribution made by don Diego de Vargas to the residents of New Mexico of goods received, such as cattle).

50. "Petición presentada por los españoles de México de la Villa Nueva de Santa Cruz," in *The New Mexico Archives* as part of the Archivo General de la Nación in the "Historia" section: 39, part 4, folios 446–47. This also appears in Kessell, Hendricks, and Dodge, eds., *Blood on the Boulders,* as "Petition the Spaniards from Mexico of Villa Nueva de Santa Cruz Presented," 642–44. Without double-checking redundancies, there are forty names but the actual number is thirty-two. The petitions contain vivid remarks that poignantly depict the living conditions, especially when they state: "[W]e ask and beg for all these reasons that you continue to give us the necessary sustenance until we plant, harvest, and provide ourselves with seeds, because although it is true we have planted, we are going to harvest even less than we planted. This has not been for

lack of cultivation, because many of us have given everything we had in order to pay Indians to cultivate our fields, so that our physical labor would not be lacking, since we have attended to the milpas from dawn to dusk" (Kessell, Hendricks, and Dodge, *Blood on the Boulders*, 642–43).

51. Vargas noted the deteriorating condition of the villa when he observed that "at this said Villa of Santa Cruz, which I inspected and visited, I found it depopulated and in ruins, with only the new structure of its chapel, which serves as a church, and not in the part first settled." See Myra Ellen Jenkins, "Settlement of the Jurisdiction of La Cañada," in the folder "Settlement and Irrigation in the Santa Cruz–Quemado Watershed," no. 194, folder CD3. See also Spanish Archives of New Mexico, Series II, no. 71, frames 640–43.

52. Combining data from José A. Esquibel, Larry Miller (from the Vargas Project at the University of New Mexico), and our own findings, we have pieced together a chronological and relatively comprehensive summary of Quintana's activity in the *diligencias matrimoniales* (designated here by DM), or prenuptial investigations. His signature appeared between 1704 and 1736, but it should be pointed out that the bulk of activity was concentrated between 1705 and 1725:

(category, date, number, application, location)
1. DM 1704, Oct. 16 (no. 1), Gonzales de la Rosa, Santa Cruz.
2. DM 1705, Jan. 7 (no. 1), Martín, Santa Fe.
3. DM 1705, May 10 (no. 16), S. Cruz, Santa Cruz.
4. DM 1705, June 4 (no. 4), Góngora, Santa Fe.
5. DM 1705, Sept. 18 (no. 17), Martín, Santa Cruz.
6. DM 1705, Nov. 5 (no. 20), Alba, Santa Cruz.
7. DM 1708, Mar. 6 (no. 3), Santa Fe.
8. DM 1709, [no month given] (no. 20), Vásquez, Santa Cruz.
9. DM 1709, Aug. 29 (no. 6), Márquez, Santa Cruz.
10. DM 1709, Nov. 7 (no. 14), Trujillo, Santa Cruz.
11. DM 1710, Dec. (no. 24), Martín, Santa Cruz.
12. DM 1710, May 30, Santa Cruz.
13. DM 1711, Oct. 16 (no. 2), Trujillo, Santa Cruz.
14. DM 1712, Dec. 25 (no. 3), Torres, Santa Fe/Santa Cruz.
15. DM 1714, Apr. 14 (no. 1), Bejarano, Santa Cruz.
16. DM 1714, May 5 (no. 19), Tafoya, Albuquerque.
17. DM 1714, July 28, Vásquez, Santa Fe.
18. DM 1714, Aug. 16 (no. 21), Valenzuela, Santa Cruz.
19. DM 1714, Sept. 28 (no. 20), Martín, Santa Cruz.
20. DM 1714, Oct. 1 (no. 4), Martín, Santa Fe.
21. DM 1715, Feb. 20 (no. 10), Maese de Campo, Santa Cruz.
22. DM 1715, Mar. 10 (no. 6), Trujillo, Santa Cruz.
23. DM 1715, Mar. 20 (no. 14), Griego, Santa Cruz.
24. DM 1716, [no month given], (no. 21), Martín, Santa Cruz.
25. DM 1716, Aug. (no. 3), Durán, Santa Cruz.
26. DM 1716, Apr. 18 (no. 28), Barrera, Santa Cruz.
27. DM 1716, Nov. 4 (no. 29), Luján, San Ildefonso.
28. DM 1716, Nov. 8 (no. 13), Trujillo, Santa Cruz.

29. DM 1717, Feb. 17 (no. 11), Martín, Santa Cruz.
30. DM 1717, Apr. 8 (no. 6), Romero, Santa Cruz.
31. DM 1717, Apr. 9 (no. 16), Medina, Santa Cruz.
32. DM 1718, Mar. 4 (no. 14), Fernández, Santa Cruz.
33. DM 1718, May 9 (no. 24), Jurado, Santa Cruz.
34. DM 1718, Sept. 14 (no. 15), Cortés, Santa Cruz.
35. DM 1718, Nov. 14. (no. 20), Montoya, Santa Fe.
36. DM 1718, Nov. 17 (no. 22), Martín, Santa Fe.
37. DM 1719, Apr. 19 (no. 7), Trujillo, Santa Cruz.
38. DM 1719, Apr. 22 (no. 1), Balbeinci, Santa Cruz.
39. DM 1719, May 8 (no. 16), Naranjo, Santa Cruz.
40. DM 1719, Jun. 23 (no. 9), Tafoya, Santa Cruz.
41. DM 1720, Jan. 8 (no. 1), Mestas, Santa Cruz.
42. DM 1720, Jan. 20 (no. [number not given]), Santa Cruz.
43. DM 1720, Feb. 5 (no. 8), Martín, Santa Cruz.
44. DM 1720, May 7 (no. 14), Sandoval, Santa Cruz.
45. DM 1720, Sept. 20 (no. 10), Cortés, Santa Cruz
46. DM 1721, Jan. 10 (no. 2), [no name given] Santa Cruz.
47. DM 1721, Jan. 12 (no. 6), [no name given] Santa Fe.
48. DM 1721, Oct. 29 (no. 1), Martín, Albuquerque.
49. DM 1722, Jan. 12 (no. 6), Salazar, Santa Fe.
50. DM 1723, Aug. 11 (no. 1), Jirón, Santa Cruz.
51. DM 1723, Aug. 30 (no. 9), Martín, Santa Cruz.
52. DM 1723, Sept. 8 (no. 5), Domínguez, Santa Cruz.
53. DM 1723, Sept. 8 (no. 16), Rosas, Santa Cruz.
54. DM 1723, Sept. 23 (no. 6), [no name given] Santa Cruz.
55. DM 1725, Sept. 15 (no. 9), Martín, Santa Cruz.
56. DM 1736, Jan. 13 (no. 1), Martín, Santa Fe.

The summary can potentially be more extensive, but a number of archival documents have been lost or destroyed, thus limiting us in providing a complete listing. Nonetheless, it serves to illustrate Quintana's professional activities.

53. Examples of these cases include the following documents: "Rivera is [suing] claiming damages from Trujillo" (Santa Fe, 1711); "Civil and criminal case of Juan de Dios Romero against Juan Antonio López," Spanish Archives of New Mexico, Series II (Santa Fe, June 20–July 3, 1720), roll 5, frames 1032–49; "Junta de guerra proceedings regarding campaign against Comanchas [*sic*] for attacks on Jicarillas" (November 8, 1723); "Criminal proceedings against Francisco Afán de Rivera for wounding Joseph Atienza and son," Spanish Archives of New Mexico, Series II (Santa Cruz, June 28–July 27, 1724), roll 6, frames 199–262); "Settlement of estate of Francisco Afán de Rivera," Spanish Archives of New Mexico, Series II (May 13, 1736), no. 355, roll 5, frames 739–76; "Criminal proceedings against Francisco Xavier Romero for sodomy," Spanish Archives of New Mexico, Series II, (Santa Cruz, June 9, 1734); and "Criminal case against Joseph Naranjo for wounding Lorenzo Jaramillo," Spanish Archives of New Mexico, Series II (Santa Clara, September 1–July 17, 1734), roll 6, frames 917–39. A valuable document exists illustrating one occasion when Miguel de Quintana accepted serving as scribe, equivalent to his renewing a license since he had already served as one prior to that:

Aceptación de notario
Digo, Miguel de Quintana, que acepto el oficio de notario para estas informaciones y juro a Dios, Nuestro Señor, y la señal de la cruz de hacer fiel y legalmente mi oficio y lo firmé en cinco días del mes de junio de 1710 años.
Miguel de Quintana
[signature]

Acceptance as scribe
I, Miguel de Quintana, state that I accept the position as scribe for these investigations, and I swear to God, our Lord, by the sign of the cross to carry out faithfully and legally my position, and I signed it on the fifth day of the month of June, 1710.
Miguel de Quintana
(signature)

54. Archival historians disagree regarding the number of Quintana family members. For example, Fray Angélico Chávez in *The Origins of New Mexico Families* cites seven children (Nicolás, Micaela, Lugarda, Juan, Francisco, José, and Antonia), while José A. Esquibel and John B. Colligan in *The Spanish Recolonization of New Mexico: An Account of the Families Recruited at Mexico City in 1693* (Albuquerque: Hispanic Genealogical Research Center of New Mexico, 1999) mention only four (María, Micaela, Lugarda, and Nicolás), but Esquibel later lists nine members in "The Family of Miguel de Quintana y Valdés Altamirano" (submitted to us personally by the author): (María, Micaela, Gertrudis, Lugarda, Nicolás, Juan, José, Francisco, and Manuel). Esquibel may be confusing Miguel with his brother José. To complicate the issue, Ida R. Foraci in *The Quintana's* counts ten known children (José, María Antonia, Francisco, Micaela, Juan Antonio, Gertrudis, Lugarda, Nicolás, Manuel, and Francisco) (3). Since it is doubtful Miguel and Gertrudis stopped bearing children by 1712, part of the confusion can be attributed to when the children are counted.

55. The document appears as "Pleito de Miguel de Quintana contra Joseph Trujillo," Spanish Archives of New Mexico, Series II (August 8–October 24, 1712), roll 4, frames 627–44. This Joseph Trujillo might be the same Joseph Damián Trujillo who made the trek from Mexico City with the Vargas caravan in 1693 and was possibly a relative of Quintana's through marriage. Described as seven years old in 1693, he would have been twenty-six at the time of the suit.

56. The complete though partially indecipherable statement is found on 175, in appendix one.

57. The authorship of this folk play, like that of *Los Comanches*, is uncertain, unsurprising in a society lacking a printing press and in which oral tradition and manuscript copies were the vehicles of literary transmission. Enrique R. Lamadrid points out that the family of don Pedro Bautista Pino, New Mexican delegate to the 1810 constitutional convention in Cádiz, claimed him as the author of *Los Comanches*. In the case of *Los pastores*, we have Quintana's autograph statement that he authored plays on the same general subject. In neither case do we know to what extent the surviving text, whether passed down orally or in handwriting, has evolved from Pino's and Quintana's hypothetical original versions through changes introduced by actors,

directors, and copyists. See Lamadrid, "*Los Comanches,*" 176.

58. *See Juan B. Rael, The Sources and Diffusion of the Mexican Shepherds' Plays* (Guadalajara: Librería la Joyita, 1965).

59. He has also been known as Arrellaga.

60. Owen Francis Da Silva, OFM, *Mission Music of California, A Collection of Old California Mission Hymns and Masses* (Los Angeles: Warren F. Lewis, 1941), 22.

61. Hubert Howe Bancroft, *California Pastoral 1769–1848* (San Francisco: The History Company, 1888), 429.

62. Cited in Auspicius van Corstanje, OFM, *The Third Order for Our Time* (Chicago: Franciscan Herald Press, 1974), 31.

63. See Benedictines of Solesmes, eds., *Liber Usualis* (Tournai, Belgium: Society of St. John the Evangelist, 1938), 1644.

64. See *The Writings of St. Francis of Assisi,* trans. Benen Fahy, OFM (Chicago: Franciscan Herald Press, 1964), 99.

65. See Thomas J. Steele, SJ, "The Spanish Passion Play in New Mexico and Colorado," *New Mexico Historical Review* 53, no. 3 (1978): 239–59.

66. Benet A. Fonck, *New Ritual for Public Functions: [of the] Franciscan Third Order* (Chicago: Franciscan Herald Press, 1973), 76–77.

67. For the complete text of the hymn and its ties to María de Agreda, see Clark A. Colahan and Alfred Rodríguez, "A New Mexican *Alabado* about María de Jesús de Agreda: Reflections on its Popular Retention and Transmission," *The Liberal and Fine Arts Review* 5 (1985): 4–14.

68. María de Jesús de Agreda, *Mística ciudad de Dios: Vida de María,* ed. Celestino Solaguren et al. (Madrid, 1970). This voluminous work is readily available in English translation. See María de Agreda, *City of God: Popular Abridgment of the Divine History and Life of the Virgin Mother of God; Manifested to Mary of Agreda for the Encouragement of Men,* trans. Fiscar Marison (Albuquerque, NM: Corcoran Publishing Co., 1949), Book 1, p. 19.

69. Marcelino Menéndez y Pelayo, *Historia de los heterodoxos españoles,* 2nd ed. (Madrid: Librería General de Victoriano Suárez, 1933), 242–43.

70. All references will be to the following edition: *Guía espiritual,* ed. José Angel Valente (Barcelona: Barral, 1974).

71. Heinrich Denzinger and Clementem Bannwart, SJ, *Enchiridion Symbolorum (Freiburg: Herder, 1922), 362, no. 53.*

72. The origins of New Mexico's penitential brotherhood are still the subject of debate, including the extent of the influence of the Third Order of St. Francis. On that subject see E. Boyd's well-documented study, "The Third Order of St. Francis and the Penitentes of New Mexico," in Popular Arts of Spanish New Mexico (Santa Fe: Museum of New Mexico Press, 1974), 440–500. For a full discussion of the movement, including information on other roots of the brotherhood, see Marta Weigle, *Brothers of Light.*

73. For the Franciscan roots of many alabados see William R. Fisher, *A Study of the Historical Background of New Mexican Alabados* (Albuquerque: University of New Mexico Press, 1952). See also Thomas J. Steele, SJ, ed. and trans., *The Alabados of New Mexico* (Albuquerque: University of New Mexico Press, 2005).

74. The members of the Penitente confraternity, as part of the rituals in their moradas/chapels, often used the following oral formula incorporating internal rhyme in order to ground their prayers:

¿Quién a esta casa da luz? Jesús	[Who to this house gives light? Jesus]
¿Quién la llena de alegría? María	[Who fills it with happiness? Mary]
¿Quién la conserva en la fe? José	[Who preserves it in faith? Joseph]

Aurelio M. Espinosa cites this in "The Folklore of Spain in the American Southwest," in *Traditional Spanish Folk Literature in Northern New Mexico and Southern Colorado*, ed. J. Manuel Espinosa (Norman: University of Oklahoma Press, 1985), 109. Quintana's frequent use of this same cluster of sacred names may echo this specific practice, as though asserting his orthodoxy in the most traditional New Mexican way.

75. See Juan Bautista Rael, *The New Mexican Alabado*, Stanford Language and Literature Series 9, no. 3 (1950), 22.

76. See Appendix Two, titled "Lugarda Quintana's Will, 1749," Spanish Archives of New Mexico, Series I, 968, roll 5, frames 717–20. It is also very likely that some of the agricultural objects and tools mentioned in the will were originally Miguel de Quintana's.

77. See the letter Sánchez de Tagle signed from March 1, 1735, fol. 467r.

78. The expression he used, "embustero, pertinaz y rebelde," is a formula typically stated in Inquisition investigations but its colorful, hyperbolic value cannot be overlooked.

79. See Document 20 from the Archivos Franciscanos (#982, box 15, no. 260 [7r–v, 8r–v]) in the Additional Documentation section.

80. Cited in J. P. Magunagoicochea, "Octavio Paz: Encuentro con el Premio Cervantes 1981," *Los Angeles La Opinión*, Sunday Supplement, August 1, 1982, 13.

Part Two

1. See note 29 in part one, which explains the haphazard organization in paginating the folios and how the Quintana materials actually represent more pages than what the numbers suggest. We have reordered the contents in chronological order to provide a clearer impression of the unfolding events and subsequent actions. For practical reasons we modernized the orthography and punctuation of the original Spanish for easier reading, making every attempt to closely respect and reproduce it as is, including a "layering effect" whereby various anonymous persons inserted comments or marked in the margins or other sections. These we point out in footnotes to show the immediate reaction of external readers visibly apprehensive about certain contents of what and how Quintana wrote. Another important explanation is necessary: the designation of folio numbers accompanied by an *r* (recto, or front side) or a *v* (verso, or back side) corresponds to a conventional system of pagination for old manuscripts. The original text, aside from presenting problems with paleography and at times a poor state of preservation—or undecipherable stitched edges—was as challenging as unraveling a giant puzzle.

2. It has been standard practice in the Hispanic Roman Catholic world to introduce a page with either a single or double cross as a way of rendering a blessing or invoking a religious association.

3. The term used is *vecino*, which means more than simply a resident, and was distinguished from more temporary inhabitants of a place called *residentes* or *moradores*. The term referred to a permanent citizen who maintained a home and establishment and was the highest social designation.

4. The expression in Spanish suggests a dubious or immoral set of propositions or proposals loosely defined even though ecclesiastical authority was considered absolute and went unchallenged, particularly on the frontier where social harmony and spiritual homogeneity were viewed as necessary ingredients for Spanish colonization. Frequently these *proposiciones* involved a wide range of unsanctioned activities such as witchcraft heresy or unorthodoxy, dementia, polygamy, and any religious rituals contrary to church practice.

5. *Fray* as a title means "Brother" and was used in the Spanish empire to refer to a member of the Franciscan Order.

6. Norris (*After "The Year Eighty"*) documents regarding Fray Manuel José de Sopeña: "criollo, native of Mexico City. Father: Francisco de Sopeña, native of Vizcaya. Mother: Doña Francisca de Velarde, native of Mexico City. Professed at San Francisco de México in 1707 at age 20" (173).

7. A *comisario*, or commissary, who functioned like an agent for the Inquisition since no independent court existed in New Mexico, was required "to receive the denunciations and testifications of this nature that may be offered . . . examining the conflicting statements that witnesses may make, and validating both before honorable persons, in accordance with the use and instructions of the Holy Office." McCue, "The Holy Office of the Inquisition," 14.

8. The reference indicates that the denouncing friar was from the Franciscan Order. There are three orders of St. Francis, the first to which Fray Joseph Manuel Sopeña belonged—composed of friars—the second of Poor Clare nuns, and the third, to which Miguel de Quintana and Cervantes belonged, of lay persons. Such a distinction is important here.

9. Known as *acuarterón*, or a fourth of a regular folio and measuring 4.5 by 6.5 inches, this refers to small sheets of paper in the form of a personal notebook or pad where Quintana was collecting his poetry combined with prose. There were initially nine such pages turned in as evidence for the case and approximately six near the end, some of which appear as rewrites of the first batch. Quintana makes frequent references to his writings in a variety of generic terms: *trabajitos* (little works or sufferings), *letras* (writings), and *hojas (pages)*.

10. *I*n the sense of maintaining confidentiality.

11. Referring to Yrigoien.

12. *The rúbrica*, used throughout the Hispanic world, is similar to a person's signature, but differs in that the letters in the name take on a highly stylized shape far removed from their normal appearance, thus making forgery difficult.

13. Norris, *After "The Year Eighty,"* provides considerable biographical information on the Franciscan priest José de Yrigoien, all of which points to a person of talent and strong will: "(1724–1760), criollo, native of Puebla. Father: Don Pedro de Yrigoien, a *gachupín* [i.e., a Spaniard] from Navarra. Mother: Doña Rosa Irrieta y Maulean, native of Puebla. Paternal grandparents were also from Navarra, and were described as 'from noble descent.' The maternal grandparents were from Vizcaya, but he was described as an *alcalde ordinario* of Puebla. Professed at San Francisco de Puebla in 1716 at age 17" (170). Yrigoien was extraordinarily good at the native languages, credited with having "mastered the various Tanoan subgroups, despite being transferred often among these Puebloans" (99). In the 1740s he extended the range of his missionary work by traveling to the Hopis and the Navajos (105–6). In that same decade he was apparently going to

be ordered to leave New Mexico, for unknown reasons, to judge by the fact that in 1748 he requested, and was granted, that letters calling for his removal by several Franciscans and the governor of the region be removed from his career file with the Franciscan Order; see Archivos Franciscanos #30-591.1, abril 16, 1748. Then two years later, in 1750, along with his friend Custos Andrés Varo, he was charged with soliciting women from the confessional and removed from his post at Albuquerque (Norris, *After "The Year Eighty,"* 127). A few years later, however, he was begged to return to New Mexico and was reinstated with honors, "premiándole sus servicios en lo que son acreedores por todo lo que ha hecho" (rewarding his services, as they testify to all that he has done); in the Archivos Franciscanos in Mexico City see #30-591.1, Nuevo Mexico, 1756.

Fray Angélico Chávez, in *Archives of the Archdiocese of Santa Fe* (249), found documents linking him to fourteen different pueblos in a missionary career that spanned thirty-three years in New Mexico, from 1725 to 1758. His frequent presence in Santa Cruz de la Cañada is reflected in documents that place him there at the following times: April–June 1732; March 1734; March, May, and October 1735; September–November 1737; and October 1738–March 1741. He had a reputation for getting things done, as reflected in his assignment to the parish at Santa Cruz because the church there was badly cracked, and he was to have a new one built. See Kessell, *Kiva, Cross, and Crown,* 89n3. Because he had not observed the legal formalities required by the viceroy, the governor had refused his petition for Indian workmen. Nonetheless, that same year a license to build was issued from Mexico City, and in 1744 Father Menchero mentioned that he was building "a sumptuous church." He was cited for extraordinary bravery in his missionary work at Sandia Pueblo; see a letter by Fray Manuel Bermejo in #177-590 of the Archivos Franciscanos.

14. Although marked 462 in the original, the order dictates it to be 463.

15. Generally suggesting a blessing or the invocation of divine inspiration, the two-cross figure might actually allude to Santísimo Tribunal (Most Holy Tribunal, referring to the Inquisition). Because the abbreviations would be *SS*, by crossing them it resembles a two-cross figure, a convenient emblem for the purpose of such religious-legalistic proceedings.

16. *Convento,* or convent, was the term then used to designate the residence of Franciscan friars.

17. The inserted underlining seems to have been done by Lic. don Diego Mangado y Clavijo, one of the first Inquisition authorities in Mexico City to review the case in 1734, almost two years after it began in New Mexico. He then apparently submitted it to higher channels for further consideration. The emblematic *"nota bene"* or *"Nota bene"* in the margins shows the first "spontaneous" response by an Inquisition official.

18. New Mexico was originally referred to as El Reino de la Nueva México, or the Kingdom of New Mexico. Note the variant of Nueva (new), which through time has become Nuevo.

19. Another principal duty of the commissary was to "publish the general edicts of faith and the letter of anathema at the time when you are ordered to do so and not in any other manner." McCue, "The Holy Office of the Inquisition," 15. The edicts required all Christians to inform the Inquisition of heretical ideas being expressed or put into practice in the local community. This explains the phrase found in the denunciations by Sopeña and Yrigoien that they are making statements about Quintana's behavior "in order to unburden their conscience, not out of malice."

20. Guerrero represents a key player at the regional level in the Quintana case because, as the commissary or agent for the Inquisition in Santa Fe, he was responsible for gathering denunciations and forwarding them to Mexico City. Although he claims to simply carry out his duties, there is an element of possible collusion with Yrigoien, which is explained in the introduction. John L. Kessell indicates he was born in Mexico City and first professed on January 1, 1706, and died after 1742 (*Kiva, Cross, and Crown*, 499). According to Fray Angélico Chávez in *Archives of the Archdiocese of Santa Fe*, he served as a priest in varying capacities in seven towns between 1714 and 1742, having served in Santa Cruz the following times: July–September 1721, May 1734, and March 17[illegible]. Adams's and Chavez's findings, however, suggest that he served in nine towns between 1714 and 1742 while serving in Santa Cruz in July–September 1721 and as commissary visitor in 1723, secretary of visitation in 1724, *vice-custos* and visitor in 1725, and visitor general in 1727. The records consulted by Adams and Chávez supposedly show that Guerrero was granted a *jubilación de hebdómada*, a kind of temporary sabbatical after seven years of service to recharge his batteries, on July 5, 1730—a refutable fact given his active participation in the 1730s. He also served as chaplain in Santa Fe in 1732 and most important, as commissary of the Holy Office during the entire investigations of Quintana from 1732 to 1737. According to the Archivos Franciscanos in Mexico City, Guerrero was a *juez eclesiástico* (ecclesiastical judge) in 1729 (see Archivos Franciscanos #26-503). In 1721 it was pointed out that various priests wrote in favor of Guerrero, the guardian and priest of the convent and parish of the Villa de Santa Fe, who later served as vice-custos and chaplain of the Villa Nueva de Santa Cruz. Norris supplies additional information: "Father: Juan Clemente Guerrero, native of Madrid. Mother: Doña Josefa Martínez de la Vega, native of Mexico City. No information was offered on paternal grandparents, but maternal grandparents were natives of Mexico City and he was described as being involved in mining. Professed at San Francisco de México in 1694 at age 16" (*After "The Year Eighty,"* 169). In 1731, while vice-custos, he unsuccessfully requested the governor to overturn the appointment of Santiago Roybal to a position as New Mexico vicar of Bishop Crespo of the Diocese of Durango and as the ecclesiastical judge of the region (90).

21. The designation of such secondary pagination is intended to indicate what folios were written by Miguel de Quintana (MQ plus the number to indicate the sequence) in his own handwriting. This allows pinpointing the number of pages attributed to him.

22. Throughout Quintana's poetry, he resorts to the more archaic and/or more literary form of *aquese(a)* (both masculine and feminine for "that") and *aqueste* (this), rarely used today.

23. Quintana uses a shortened in-group referent for his town, now known as Santa Cruz.

24. The priest mentioned figures as Quintana's favorite local priest with whom he had a fairly close religious affiliation. This Tagle should not be confused with the other Tagle (don Pedro Anselmo Sánchez de Tagle), whose signature appears in a few documents originating from the Holy Office in Mexico City. Regarding the former, Norris, *After "The Year Eighty,"* finds that he, like Yrigoien, came from a noble Spanish family. An ardent defender of Franciscan rights against attacks by the civil government, he served both as custos and vice-custos, and the details of his leadership role in the New Mexican church are given by Norris in chap. 6, "Conflict." Regarding his family and missionary efforts, Norris writes that he

> was a native of San Vincente de Barquiera, Spain, and born to a family of some stature, since his parents were addressed as Don and Doña in Spanish records. It is unclear when he came to New Spain, but he professed his vows at twenty years of age. . . . His first recorded assignment was to San Ildefonso in 1701, and he remained the mission father there until his time in the colony ended in 1726. Tagle seems to have been at least a competent missionary. That he labored only at San Ildefonso for a quarter of a century suggests some degree of harmony between Tagle and his neophytes. In addition, there are no extant records of any irregularities or complaints associated with his administration of that mission. (58)

Quintana's close friendship with him, which he recalls with nostalgia, must have been nurtured by the proximity of San Ildefonso to Santa Cruz. Tagle became involved with Governor Peñuela in a disagreement over the extent to which the Pueblo Indians should be allowed to retain their traditional dress and practices. A strong liberal in this regard, he was accused by the governor of extravagant behavior, such as going from pueblo to pueblo and encouraging the residents to dance. Peñuela even alleged that one of Tagle's Franciscan associates had encouraged Taos Pueblo to construct two kivas (Kessell, *Kiva, Cross, and Crown*, 311). Whatever the truth of these accusations may have been, it is quite apparent that Tagle favored greater religious tolerance than most church officials in the region. For this reason, it is not surprising to discover the close personal friendship with Quintana, or at least the confidence and trust the latter felt toward Tagle. That might help explain in part Quintana's vision of Tagle's ghostly apparition precisely when the poet felt under pressure to conform to the other authorities' demands and wishes.

25. The verb construction used by Quintana is *veile*, a popular variant for "I saw him," which we converted into the more modernized *vile*, or equivalent to *le vi* (I saw him).

26. The author creates an ambiguous metaphor that is perhaps not meant to be taken literally, for *capilla calada* connotes a chapel recently whitewashed with lime. Here the image may suggest the priest's common form of wearing his cowl over his face.

27. The reference is apparently to Fray Manuel de Sopeña, minister of the church at Santa Cruz. The argument could be made that Quintana's narration of the vision is designed to suggest, on the part of Sopeña, a jealousy of Miguel's close friendship with the late and influential Tagle.

28. Such a cryptic and metaphorical allusion may refer to the time when priests wear red robes, but the coincidence that blood is mentioned along with the name of Sopeña, his accuser, cannot be overlooked.

29. Quintana uses the term *cuidaditos* (little hardships) interchangeably with *trabajitos* (little sufferings or little labors). The diminutive form expresses humble acceptance of his sufferings and perhaps an element of affection toward his writings that have been the outcome.

30. The file of Quintana's letters, poetry, and essays contains repeated insertions of *ojo* (nota bene or notice) throughout to indicate or highlight a warning sign of the text's potential subversive quality. It is useful to pay close attention to such insertions because another reader—usually anonymous—at some point in the Inquisition's process has designated the "dangerous" or questionable sections. It is not always clear who writes them, but handwriting analysis seems to indicate either Yrigoien or Guerrero as the

most likely candidates, a likely supposition given their official positions and their accusing point of view on the case.

31. The underlining was probably added by Clavijo or Guerrero, again, as part of the review process.

32. The Latin ecclesiastical phrase *secundum canones sanctae ecclesiae catholicae apostolicae Romanae* means "in conformance with the doctrines of the Holy, Catholic, Apostolic, Roman Church."

33. The reader of the file here is perhaps Mangado y Clavijo.

34. The tablets consist of small chocolate bars, a highly prized item, along with sugar, in such remote areas of the northern Mexican provinces where it was not produced locally.

35. Here, the Virgin Mary speaks directly to Quintana while providing instructions, guidance, and encouragement.

36. The implication here is that Miguel does write out of arrogance.

37. The example cited demonstrates the technique of Quintana dialoguing with the Virgin Mary in his verses. Such a direct approach probably stirred some sense of concern among the priests who were unaccustomed to parishioners acting on their own, unless it was through prayer.

38. A sizable and recognizable rúbrica by Fray Joseph Yrigoien appears next to this verse.

39. This represents yet another example of Quintana's thinking that to the local priests might have seemed deviant. Describing God as being Greek must have seemed to them a bit farfetched as a description. "Greek" is used in the classical sense, referring to rational thinking and equanimity in reaching final judgments. This was a literary expression used principally among the learned of the time.

40. The poet's admission of being moved by a spirit—underlined by one of the censors and accompanied by the nota bene warning—shows a double concern, keeping in mind the dangers of being possessed by something.

41. The date is underlined for emphasis perhaps to point to the beginnings of Quintana's potential hallucinations, thus making a case for repeated behavior.

42. This folio displays a number of dividing lines between each item, which is written as if prose, but can easily be organized into verse form. It is quite clear Quintana deliberately made such separations.

43. *Soli Deo honor et gloria* is a Latin phrase meaning "Honor and glory are due to God alone."

44. Quintana resorts to the rhetorical tool of the diminutive to minimize his writings, which he refers to here as *letritas*, or "little letters."

45. Latin for "chosen from before the beginning of time." The italics do not figure in the original.

46. Another annotation in the form of nota bene by one of the censors is inserted in the left margin.

47. Here appears another clear visual marker with a line between passages that Quintana for some reason felt compelled to separate, which we reproduce for the effect he desired.

48. The sorrowful mysteries are one section within the cycle of prayers contained in the rosary.

49. At this point, the pagination system becomes quite confusing, even erratic. The

present folio constitutes a continuation of Quintana's writings, but for some unknown reason it is not paginated properly. Nonetheless, it ends up being compensated for at the end in the final pagination provided by the Inquisition papers. Either the original compilers (understood as one of the priests or Inquisition authorities) or archivists confused the pagination at the beginning while the denunciation was in process or after the Inquisition collected the documents. Instead of providing two folios numbered 457 (a and b), we opted for following the sequential order, which accounts for the lack of correspondence in the pagination from this point forward.

50. Part of the reason these remarks seem almost undecipherable is that they appear between the saddle stitch of the text between the two pages, thus obscuring some of the key words.

51. Quintana seems to have a difficult time writing this sentence that contains "strayed" and "deceived" because he crosses it out and rewrites at least twice, signaling some hesitation. The redundancy in the same phrase may be accidental; we detect some nervousness on the author's part.

52. We again find in this folio two divisions, appearing as lines, intentionally put in by Quintana to separate either paragraphs or blocks of ideas.

53. The present folio is actually marked as 458, but we make the adjustment with the newly accounted folios.

54. Yrigoien's signature appears along the margins next to this sentence.

55. Here Quintana uses a popular command form that in standard Spanish would be *apiádate* (from *apiadarse*, "to feel pity").

56. Another voice, this time God, speaks directly to Quintana, indicating how he should proceed, how he should defend himself, and where he stands in terms of piety and rights.

57. The term used here is the archaic *albor* (*árbol* in modern Spanish), which more closely resembles the Latin *arbor.*

58. Quintana once again tries to separate prose from poetry.

59. The foreboding ojo, or nota bene, included in the margin, along with the rúbricas in the page, resembles more that of Yrigoien, suggesting a disagreement with the poet. The priest may glimpse heresy in the encouragement visible in Jesus Christ's words.

60. Referring to his poems.

61. A poetic voice, none other than God, speaks directly again while interceding on Quintana's behalf.

62. Yrigoien insists on inserting his signature without any commentary next to this verse in addition to two other occasions in this folio.

63. *Redondas* is a popular Spanish verse form of ABCB while the quartet represents a rhyme scheme of ABBA. Quintana's allusion to such poetic meters is significant because it displays his awareness of poetic forms.

64. The word *siempre* in the original Spanish appears as *spr~e*, an abbreviated form.

65. This excerpt and the following inserted in between the columns are more prosaic than poetic in their composition.

66. Quintana appears to anticipate the denunciations. By mentioning a venial fault, he circumvents the possibility of it being a worse offense, or mortal sin, thus minimizing the charge.

67. The original in Spanish is *maestro*, which can be understood somewhere between master and teacher, both applying almost equally, given the Biblical connotations.

68. The term *agasajo* in Spanish suggests a token of esteem or appreciation.

69. *O quan incomprensibilia sunt judicia eius* is Latin for "Oh, how unfathomable are his decisions." Quintana establishes a key point in his defense and indictment against those who hound him for unjustified reasons. The double-edged statement, containing a bit of ambiguity, gains greater resonance in Latin, thus appearing as a defense of fighting fire with fire.

70. At this point, we find the poet in the midst of his best rhetorical flair in defending his viewpoint. It is no wonder that one of the censors or agents of the Inquisition has inserted "ojo" to again point out a questionable section in Quintana's writings.

71. This folio is marked in the original as 461.

72. God is attributed a poetic voice, speaking to Quintana from the first person.

73. More than likely, the reservation revolves around Quintana's audacity to put words in God's mouth in his defense, suggesting he only has to be accountable to God and no one else.

74. A third-person poetic voice takes over for the God-narrator almost midstream.

75. There was a popular belief in colonial New Mexico that membership in the Third Order of St. Francis greatly increased the chances of escaping damnation.

76. Quintana daringly states here that one does not have to form part of the Third Order of St. Francis to be saved, opting instead to adhere to a superior divine order, in this case holy Mary of Carmen.

77. There are three important observations to make here. First, this folio is unmarked but corresponds to the number we designate if we follow our aforementioned order. Second, this folio was incorporated into the general body of the documents, but it is unclear when, except perhaps when all the floating Quintana papers were finally collected into one place. Third, whereas the Inquisition documents initially allude to Quintana's writings as consisting of nine or ten pages, we encounter more pages that augment the overall collection of his writings. For that reason, we continue the numbering system pertaining to actual pages written by Quintana himself by using "MQ," in contrast to letters penned by other authorities.

78. The two references here to direct points of contention related to the Inquisition and heresy are fundamental to Quintana's arguments about the persecution he was suffering and why an individual had latitude to act on his own regarding very intimate religious and aesthetic (also understood as philosophical) questions.

79. In Franciscan New Mexico a guardian priest of a church was the regular priest of a convento.

80. The word used in Spanish, *presentada*, indicates a feminine antecedent such as *denuncia* (denunciation or formal accusation).

81. The priests mentioned in this folio are inquisitors of various ranks from the Holy Office in Mexico City, representing a chain of command ranging from prosecutor to censor, and so forth, and who were responsible for reviewing and coordinating the case with Commissary Guerrero in Santa Fe. Judging from the comments inserted by the various priests, it is clear they appear quite removed from the case, at times making outlandish statements. It should be noted that many of the notes on the margins were incorporated into the text after the entire collection of poetry and essays.

82. The note would seem to provide a preliminary conclusion on the case before it was completed and corresponds to the final verdict. That such a note is included without a specific date contributes to some conjecture.

83. Note the contradictory statement when juxtaposed with the previous annotation on the same page, both of which have been added to the folio after the original document was written.

84. This refers to the two original accusers, Fray Manuel de Sopeña and Fray Joseph Yrigoien.

85. It can be assumed that "him" refers to the New Mexico commissary, Guerrero, responsible for coordinating and gathering evidence in the case.

86. The prosecutor for the Inquisition, who resided in Mexico City, was not the same person as the Inquisition's commissioners, who were the institution's agents in various parts of New Spain.

87. Although the same accusation today might seem minor, or at best an anachronism, this expectation of compliance is indicative of the influence and authority the church and its agents exercised in daily life at the time. Such failures to comply were viewed as transgressions against morality, that is, as violations of societal practices and religious rituals that were intrinsically tied to each other.

88. The term in Spanish, *secreto*, here specifically refers to a kind of court or chamber of the Inquisition where highly secretive investigations, deliberations, and decisions were conducted. In this way leaks were avoided or at least other outside considerations prevented from influencing the proceedings.

89. Licentiate in the Hispanic world is a title of an individual who holds a university degree in law.

90. Since this document refers to 1732 as the prior year, and since that was the year in which the charges were originally filed, the accuracy of the same date appearing here becomes questionable.

91. This official appears as the main intermediary through which all paperwork on the investigations passed, thus coordinating the other authorities to respond and act accordingly.

92. Though we have no information on the charges against María Domínguez, the comments made here—probably by the two inquisitors in Mexico City who also oversaw the Quintana investigation—strengthen the impression given in the latter's case that they were more circumspect, more willing to give the accused the benefit of the doubt, than were their agent and his notary in Santa Fe.

93. The second paragraph of this folio represents an almost exact replica of what appears in folios 450r and 450v, thus we do not reproduce it here. The only minor difference consists of the omission of the signatures of Frays don Pedro Navarro de Ysla, Pedro Anselmo Sánchez de Tagle, and Agustín González Ramírez de Zárate in the second version.

94. The word here designating a priest, *prete* or *preste*, often refers to one whose responsibility it is to celebrate mass.

95. Picurís Pueblo is not far from Santa Cruz.

96. The custodia was an ecclesiastical administrative unit administered by a custos and a vice-custos. According to Eleanor B. Adams and Fray Angélico Chávez, such a unit was created by St. Francis when his followers became too numerous, thus requiring a division into groups. With time, the larger groups adopted the term "province" while using "custody" for smaller groups. As they add, "This was the Custody of the Conversion of St. Paul in N.[ew] M.[exico], which was dependent on the Province of the Holy Gospel in Mexico City for more than two centuries." *The Missions of New*

Mexico, 1776, 354–55. In addition, they clarify: "The eighteenth-century title of *custos* is equivalent to the modern commissary" (355).

97. A Fray José de Eguía y Lumbre arrived at Santa Cruz by 1732, but little else is known about him. See Kessell, *Kiva, Cross, and Crown*, 500. Norris lists his dates in New Mexico as 1732–1743; see *After "The Year Eighty,"* 168. According to Chávez's *The Archives of the Archdiocese of Santa Fe*, this priest served in Santa Cruz from November 1732 to June 1733; at Santa Clara from December 1732 to May 1733 and also July 1734; at Nambé from June 1733 to August 1734; in Santa Fe from August 1734 to July 1735 and January 1736, as well as from August 1738 to July 1739; then at Pecos from September 1739 to June 1740; and finally at Zia in August 1735 (246). His presence, like that of Cressa, at this hearing of the Inquisition apparently was designed to add credibility to the testimony given.

98. The words used in an archaic variant of the time are *foxas* and *hojas*, meaning sheets and pages.

99. The Latin expression *ad perpetuam rei memoriam* means "as a permanent record of the matter."

100. As notary to the alcaldes mayores (magistrates) who exercised ordinary jurisdiction in Santa Cruz, Quintana seems to have held a position of some social stature. His post bespeaks his mental prowess.

101. It is a body of judges within the ecclesiastical ranks, referred to in Spanish as *judicatura eclesiástica*. So, Quintana participated in both civil and ecclesiastical law, judging from his position in assisting both sectors mentioned.

102. *Discreto*, which appears in the original as *dicreto*, was the person chosen to aid the superior in the administration of a religious order.

103. Norris documents Fray Juan Antonio Ezeiza in New Mexico from 1730 to 1762. He was a Spaniard, "native of Vizcaya. Father: Domingo de Ezeiza, native of Vizcaya. Mother: Bernarda de Almasorrayon, native of Vizcaya. Professed at San Francisco de México in 1724 at age 22" (*After "The Year Eighty,"* 168). Ezeiza's signature appears on New Mexico documents from 1730 through 1760. Documents place him at Santa Cruz March 26 through April 15, 1734, according to Adams and Chávez in *The Missions of New Mexico, 1776* (332). On June 28, 1762, he was declared "incapacitated" by Governor Vélez Cachupín. Fray Bravo Lerchundi, born in Puebla, Mexico, first arrived in Acoma by 1730 and served at Pecos Mission during 1733 and 1734–35 (Kessell, *Kiva, Cross, and Crown*, 501).

104. Either confusion abounds in this statement or the writer of such a document is unclear in his writing. It would perhaps make more sense to say "haberle pedido lo dicho" (having asked of him the herein mentioned document).

105. Note that this folio becomes 464 to adhere to our continuous numbering system but has no back side.

106. The Latin expression *iten*, used three times in the present folio, is equivalent to "and also" or "and then."

107. Again, the writer of this document, Fray Joseph Antonio Guerrero, resorts to another Latin word, *próxime*, to refer to "last."

108. Fray Juan Mingues was killed by Pawnees after fourteen years of mission work in New Mexico, while accompanying soldiers on an expedition to the Platte River in 1719. See Norris, *After "The Year Eighty,"* 86. If so, then Quintana had been writing and distributing poetry for some years prior to the opening of the Inquisition investigation

against him. The only New Mexican friar with the surname of Pino at this time who has come to light is Juan Jorge del Pino, who came to New Mexico between 1715 and 1719. He was the chaplain on the 1719 expedition to the Platte River. See pp. 86, 92. In fact, by 1717 he was at San Ildefonso, close to Quintana's ranch at Santa Cruz. Kessell notes that "For some reason, Father Pino used consistently the English form George instead of the Spanish form Jorge." See Kessell, *Kiva, Cross, and Crown*, 499, 541n33. Perhaps the two ambiguous letters following "Juan" stand for "George."

109. Such a reference means they are Franciscans or part of the Order of St. Francis.

110. The author of this letter also uses the Latin expression *iten* for "and then" or "and also."

111. As an interesting side note, it is not altogether clear how damaging or incriminating such a statement might be against Quintana.

112. There is a small cross inscribed anonymously next to the annotation to indicate that a word was left out in the text.

113. Although more than one feast day in honor of the Virgin Mary is celebrated in September, the reference here is probably to the eighth of September—the Nativity of Mary, Our Lady of Charity.

114. Reenacting the steps of Christ through the Via Crucis during Easter time is regarded as one of the most intensively spiritual experiences of suffering, sacrifice, and contemplation for Christians. Quintana's writings take on a crescendo quality in this section because he provides a glimpse into his mental state of "hearing the steps" of the Passion but likewise insists he is not delirious or imagining anything.

115. Fray Juan de la Cruz, who served in New Mexico from 1719 to 1746, was a Spaniard who had arrived in New Spain in 1717. See Norris, *After "The Year Eighty,"* 167.

116. This town is considered the first Spanish town in New Mexico in 1598 in the upper Río Grande Valley, located near the confluence of the Río Grande and the Río Chama.

117. This statement was highlighted by one of the censoring agents, believed in this case to be Yrigoien, who is pointing out to the Inquisition officials, both regional and in Mexico City, the specific, allegedly heretical assertions of Miguel de Quintana.

118. The insinuation is of a potential procedural error whereby Guerrero, and possibly other authorities, did not give the accused due process.

119. The added annotations in the margins here clearly demonstrate how the Inquisitorial process worked relative to Quintana's case. Note that the original document, originally from November 10, 1734, was considered by the authorities in Mexico some four months later on March 15, 1735, showing some degree of expediency. In addition, the remarks in the margins allow us to directly observe the censors' tentative judgments as they were unfolding. The judicial procedure appears painstaking and exhibits careful documentation by the authorities in the process of creating a case against Quintana.

120. The number on the original document was folio 465.

121. Aside from Quintana's accusers, one of the Inquisition agents in Mexico City, Fray Pedro Anselmo Sánchez de Tagle, expresses with harsh, blunt language his impression of the extreme scenario in the case with an outright condemnation shrouded with threats.

122. The original folio number is marked 466.

123. Again, the time lapse between the original document and the annotation on the

margin indicates a difference of around five months, which seems consistent with other exchanges.

124. The expression is a formal part of the decree added onto the letter ex post facto once the Inquisition reviewers have read it and determined what part of the process it constitutes.

125. An edict involves a formal decree or proclamation issued by an authority. Specifically, edicts of faith were published as letters of anathema or ecclesiastic bans to discourage certain unauthorized behavior. Such edicts called on all Christians to inform the Inquisition of heretical ideas being expressed or being put into practice in the local community. This explains the phrase found in the denunciations by Yrigoien and Sopeña that they are making statements about Quintana's behavior "in order to unburden their conscience, not out of malice."

126. Confusion in the pagination at this point abounds and becomes even more perplexing. Originally marked as 467, it was later scratched as 469, which now matches our sequence perfectly. Such changes indicate the many adjustments made by someone (or various persons) in trying to put the entire body of documents together.

127. This folio, originally numbered 468, was later scratched out and marked with a superimposed 470, where someone was attempting to make some sense of the sequence of the documents. There is no concrete indication as to when or why the pagination was altered except to assume that either carelessness was exercised at some time or a few documents were inserted after a tentative count had been made.

128. This is the only occasion when Yrigoien includes the "de" in his name in referring to himself. All other signatures and references omit it, including his signature at the end of this short letter.

129. It is of interest to see Quintana's dwelling or home be referred to as *morada*, which should not be confused with the ceremonial place of the Penitentes. The word is the same, but the more specialized connotation in New Mexico has almost become reserved for a religious place of worship. Either way, morada generally represents a fairly simple dwelling, even ascetic in nature, which might indicate the point where the two meanings diverged.

130. The Spanish reads *reprehendello*, an archaic form for *reprehenderlo*, meaning to "admonish him." Curiously, the silent *h* is used here although other comparable educated words are transcribed with the colloquial form of an aspirated *g* sound common in popular speech.

131. The numbering corresponds to the original as 477 even though the number 474 was crossed off. Considerable confusion in the numbering here becomes exacerbated at this point in the documents because various hands appear to have contributed to it, and because the brief letter by Quintana himself was inserted out of order. Originally marked as folio 474, someone later superimposed the number 477. The latter would indicate it should figure at the very end of the collection of documents since that is the last page of the Inquisition documents on Quintana as presently found. The principal reason for such confusion rests on the fact that this folio was attached to the other folios either as an afterthought or simply because it was made available much later after the others had been collected. Either way, this folio in particular represents a small-sized page about half the size of a normal page and seems to have been attached quite haphazardly.

The numbering to account for the continuing documents by Quintana is important here because there are more than what the different participants claim, partly because of the repetition of some of those documents that were apparently recopied.

132. Officially known as Fray Juan Sánchez de la Cruz, he was born in an unknown location in Spain and came to New Spain in approximately 1717, according to Kessell in *Kiva, Cross, and Crown* (499), then died after 1746. Very little is known about this priest except that he was a chaplain in Santa Cruz near the end of the time of Quintana's encounter with the Inquisition. He provided him friendship, confidence, and counsel.

133. We discover why Quintana is ailing at the time that he is unable to personally answer the charges before the commissary of the Holy Office. Quintana uses the archaic form *fuesos* for *huesos*, or "bones."

134. *Comadre* embodies an important kinship as part of the extended family concept, specifically a midwife or godparent of one's child. Given the strong Hispanic traditions of maintaining familial ties and the hardships of the frontier, having such extensions in family affiliations provided greater security and denotes close friendship and/or relations.

135. Quintana here resorts to a common adage of extreme courtesy in Spanish, *mi casa es su casa* (my home is your home).

136. Norris supplies information that points to the senior standing of Fray Juan José Pérez de Mirabal within the Franciscan community in New Mexico, where he lived for many years (1722–62). He was Spanish, a "native of Antequerra, Málaga. Father: Don Juan Alonso Pérez Mirabal, native of Antequerra. Mother: Doña Angela Ramírez Portilla, native of Antequerra. Admitted to San Francisco de México as a novice, he was a graduate of a seminary in Antequerra. Fray Juan was custos for at least one term" (*After "The Year Eighty,"* 172). He served as minister of Villa Nueva de Santa Cruz in 1737, coinciding with the end of the Inquisitorial process of Quintana.

137. This folio is characterized by faulty markings in the pagination, reflecting either the compiler's confusion, the constant shuffling of documents, or both. It was labeled as 469, but we have changed it to 471.

138. It is significant to note that the verses and prose included here represent essentially the same as before, which were in Quintana's own handwriting. A few discrepancies from the previous collection appear in the subsequent pages because Father Pérez de Mirabal copied them by hand to insert in the record.

139. The archaic term in Spanish used here is *adbitrios* for *arbitrios*, or "provisions," related to choices freely made.

140. The word *enojado* for "angry" is another example where the poet associates two subjects in the same stanza with some ambiguity. Instead of modifying the closest noun (*grandeza*, or "might," requiring a feminine modifier), the adjective *enojado* actually reverts to the distant masculine noun, *Dios*, or "God." This exemplifies some poetic virtuosity, opting for having the noun of grander reputation finish the thought, Quintana again underscoring a sense of righteousness vis-à-vis his censors.

141. The expression *a dar gatazo* used by Fray Juan Joseph Pérez [de] Mirabal is most interesting for various reasons. First of all, it may simply refer to an object of torture, the cat-o'-nine-tails, a type of whip that left markings similar to a cat's scratches. It may also, however, suggest a conspiracy. If the origin of the expression is the verb *catear*, the implication is that ecclesiastical authorities have come to inspect or monitor Quintana with the intention to unlawfully search his house or spy on him. It can also mean to swindle or impose a trick of deception. All these usages imply some type of harassment or intended hurt.

142. This folio is not paginated in the original Inquisition documents as most others. We therefore insert the 472 to continue our sequential order. Such discrepancies in not paginating suggest that certain pages were added to the body of the text after the first round of pagination had taken place.

143. The back side of this folio has the number 469 inserted haphazardly, further confusing the numbering system used.

144. Fray Juan Joseph Pérez [de] Mirabal not only inserts this line of demarcation in the original but also includes just below it three personal rúbricas.

145. The assumption seems to be that Pérez [de] Mirabal is being very precise about all of Yrigoien's current and past ecclesiastical titles. As with the earlier reference to the post of discreto, advisor to the head of a religious order, the original text shows "dicreto."

146. The reference in general alludes to the newly constructed mission and not to an actual convent per se.

147. We note that his name does not include the "de" between Perez and Mirabal in his signature, contrary to the way others refer to him.

148. The original folio shows markings of 471 and later 474 but corresponds to the order we follow, or 475. This confusion was attributed to the handling of the documents by various individuals at various times.

149. The Spanish/Latin phrase seems to mean "I see, I will see." Fray Juan de la Cruz is unable to find anything suspicious contained in Quintana's writings. The censor sees only so much and waits to see whether there is anything else that Quintana's writings might contain.

150. This Latin expression literally means "that is, here and now" or "that is, this very day and moment."

151. We are extrapolating meaning here from the context because the Spanish original appears as an abbreviation (*izuie.a* or *iruie.a*), possibly meaning *iría a* (going to) or *quisiera* (wishing) or an act of wishful thinking. Such ambiguity does not seem shocking because the writer of the letter appears uncomfortable with the message he is transmitting as well as the written language to which he is resorting. We are not sure whether he is being a clever spin doctor on exonerating Quintana or his incoherence is grounded on carelessness.

152. This folio was originally numbered 470 but was later corrected or changed to 473, which corresponds to the sequential order we are following.

153. Note the variation of his name from the documents, which he signs as "Fray Joseph Pérez Mirabal," also signing as "Fray Juan Joseph Perez de Mirabal."

154. This individual does not appear in the Farfán-Velasco muster list of the 1693 expedition, perhaps being the son of Francisco de la Rosa, who had traveled with the early colonists.

155. The step taken here suggests close collaboration between the civil and ecclesiastical authorities.

156. The allusion is to the pope or the Vatican.

157. Quintana's expression would appear to be key insofar as bearing a cryptic notion of possible (false) modesty. It may also be used to infer two other points: that his adulation for Bustamante is in direct contrast to what he feels toward Sopeña and Yrigoien and that he was counting on Bustamante's support. The latter's stature and his concern about Franciscan inadequacies in New Mexico, even though he had no

direct authority over the friars, may have been seen by Quintana as a possible source of political support.

158. Note the none-too-indirect discourse of justification as well as indictment, strongly suggesting that the two priests conspired against and harassed him because of jealousy or envy toward his position as notary for the ecclesiastic authorities in Santa Cruz. It becomes quite apparent that Quintana recalls such a perspective from past troubles, affirming once again that he still believes it in the most recent present (1737).

159. This phrase, which we have discussed earlier, seems to take on here a connotation similar to the English declaration, "I swear to tell the truth, the whole truth, and nothing but the truth."

160. In colonial New Mexico, members of Indian nations not under Spanish control, primarily the Apaches and Comanches, often lived with the Spanish settlers as servants known as *genízaros*, a name taken from the Janissaries who served as royal guards. The word derived from the settlers' perception of such Christianized Indians, who in addition to living with the Spaniards had their own communities located between the Christian area and those exposed to hostile indigenous peoples as a buffer or protection against attack.

161. This clearly stipulates their social standing as genízaros.

162. The letter ends here, but in the following document one finds that a deposition by one of the Apaches was ordered. In it he states that he had been invited to return to Apache country by an Indian servant of the custos, Fray Juan de Tagle. Such a return was a crime under Spanish law.

163. Latin for "On the day of the Lord."

164. A vara was between 31 and 34 inches.

165. The term in Spanish refers to an old agricultural instrument that has no real equivalent in English. It can resemble something between a hoe and a shovel: it is straight on one side, curved on the other with a sharp point and a long wooden handle. The tool was principally used for digging and cultivating.

166. It is possible that the manuscript is in error here and should have read, instead of *guitarra*, *guijarra*, a small stone from a river bed that could have been used as a pestle. That implement would be more in line with the other items in the list.

167. Baroque pearls are irregular, not perfectly spherical.

168. Although it may seem strange for Lugarda to refer to Gerónimo, an Indian, with the honorific title of "don," it is probably used here out of respect, for he seems to have taken care of Antonio Martin before his death. Gerónimo was probably a caretaker or even a mayordomo for the deceased man, accompanying him to the very end. That, in Lugarda's mind, may well have demanded respect or some degree of praise surpassing social class differences. And she, like her father, may have been of an egalitarian persuasion. All this, and the possibility that Gerónimo was by this time of an advanced age, may have contributed to Lugarda's respectful reference.

Part Three

1. It is unclear who wrote this ojo, or warning, on the margin to take note of what Fray Joseph Yrigoien claims about Quintana's reasons for not attending mass. The poet's apparent lack of blind obedience to church, and its agents the priests, suggests a freethinker or possible rebel who resorts to divine arguments in his favor.

2. The Latin ecclesiastical phrase *secundum canones sanctae ecclesiae catholicae*

apostolicae Romanae means "in conformance with the doctrines of the Holy, Catholic, Apostolic, Roman Church."

3. This folio or page contains numerous divisions placed by Quintana himself to separate ideas or fragments of his arguments and justifications. It is not altogether clear why he chose the format that oscillates between poetry and prose.

4. Latin for "To God alone, honor and glory."

5. From Latin, meaning "chosen from before the beginning of time." The italics do not figure in the original but the phrase is highlighted thus because it is an expression from a foreign language.

6. The marker indicates another natural demarcation inserted by Miguel de Quintana himself. He obviously felt some kind of need to separate the two paragraphs and for that reason we reproduce it as is.

7. The reason this statement is presently undecipherable is that it appears between the saddle stitch of the text, obscuring some of the key words.

8. Perhaps Miguel de Quintana reveals a bit of hesitation in writing "since you are not in error" twice as if in the third person, having scratched it out the first time and inserting it again. As is evident, the redundancy in the same phrase in the following sentence fails to be coincidence but is instead a technique of echoing that sentiment in multiple ways.

9. The poet offers another "natural" division of his ideas by separating one section of his text from the other with a line from margin to margin. We reproduce it to illustrate the visual means by which Miguel de Quintana organized or presented his text, including his ideas.

10. This line marks another "natural" demarcation in the text by Quintana.

11. The form used here by Quintana is *piédete*, colloquial for the more standard verb of *apiadarse*, meaning to have or to fill with pity.

12. This is another attempt to divide the text.

13. This is still another marker to divide the text into sections.

14. We find another foreboding "ojo," or "watch out," on the margin by one of the authorities who apparently disagrees with the poet or suspects some signs of subliminal heresy. Judging from the rather innocuous statement, the warning sign is probably indirectly questioning Quintana's insistence on being sanctioned by Jesus Christ.

15. Regarded as a significant reference to poetry meters, it reveals Quintana's overt awareness of poetic forms and how he develops his writing within that tradition.

16. Quintana appears to be fully anticipating what others might accuse him of. By mentioning a "venial fault," he essentially circumvents the possibility of it being a mortal sin, thus minimizing the charge.

17. A division the poet provided.

18. Another division Quintana inserted.

19. The Latin expression encompasses a key defense against and indictment of those who hound the New Mexican poet. It means "Oh, how incomprehensible are his judgments," where the "his" could be interpreted, as in the Bible, as referring to God or sarcastically in the writer's personal context, to the censorious priest. The double-edged statement is given greater weight by quoting in Latin, acting as a defense by fighting fire with fire.

20. At this point, we find the poet in the midst of his best rhetorical flair in defending his position. It is no wonder that someone, perhaps the commissary or one of the two

denouncing priests, inserted "ojo," or "watch out," in this section.

21. Here we encounter another inserted "ojo," or "look," to whoever is reading the poet's text. More than likely, the concern revolves around Quintana's audacity to put words in God's mouth in his defense, suggesting he alone has to be accountable to God and no one else.

22. Quintana daringly states that one does not have to form part of the Third Order of St. Francis to be saved, opting instead to adhere to a superior and divine order, in this case that of Holy Mary of Carmen.

23. The expression *dar sangre en flux* (in the original *enflús*) might refer to the luck involved in God's giving of His blood to Quintana or simply be a way of stating that God's blood flowed for him. Quintana could have used *flujo* in more modern Spanish, but it would have ruined his rhyme scheme, and thus the Latin version.

24. Quintana inserts this internal division within the text for unknown reasons.

25. Here we find yet another marker by Quintana himself to separate ideas in a single document.

26. Either confusion abounds in this statement or the writer of this document is unclear in his writing, which contributes to further confusion in attempting to decipher meaning. It would make more sense to say "haberle pedido lo dicho" (having asked of him the herein mentioned document).

27. Latin for "as a permanent record of the matter."

28. Latin, meaning "furthermore."

29. The author of the document uses *próxime* (recent) in the singular, even though the grammatical context requires plurality. It might be an oversight on the part of the writer or a colloquial usage of the term.

30. The author of this letter writes *incurria*, though the noncolloquial form is *incuria*.

31. In the margin someone writes or observes *dice* (he says) and places a small handwritten cross next to it as a way of adding sanctity to the observation.

32. Reenacting the steps of Christ's *via crucis* during Easter time is regarded as one of the most intensive spiritual experiences for the close followers of the Bible. Quintana's writings take on a crescendo quality in this section because he provides a glimpse into his mental state of "hearing the steps" of the Passion but likewise insists he is not delirious or imagining anything.

33. This unknown rúbrica is probably by an official of the Inquisition in Mexico City, judging by the date and the lack of similarity to any of the New Mexican signatures found in the case documents.

34. Instead of *concierte*, the text has *concite*, which we take to be a mistranscription.

35. The term *morada* refers simply to Quintana's dwelling or home and should not be confused in this case with the morada, or ceremonial place, of the Penitentes. Obviously, the words are similar in origin but different in their usage in Spanish.

36. Another archaism is used here in the original, *fuesos*, or "bones," for the more modernized version of *huesos* with a silent *h*.

37. The expression *a dar gatazo* used by Fray Juan Joseph Pérez Mirabal is most interesting for various reasons. First of all, it suggests a conspiracy by someone against Miguel de Quintana. If the origin of the expression is the verb *catear*, the implication is that ecclesiastical persons have come to check Quintana out and with the intention to unlawfully search someone's house or spy on the individual. If it is understood more

literally, then it could suggest swindling someone or imposing an uninvited trick of deception. Either usage implies some type of harassment or intended hurt.

38. Immediately below this demarcation line, the author of this document, Fray Juan Joseph Pérez Mirabal, includes three of his rúbricas at the beginning of this section.

39. Written on margins is a small cross and the observation *de accidente*, or "by accident."

40. It comes from Latin, meaning "that is, here and now."

41. An annotation is included in the left margin that says *"de accidentes,"* accompanied by a small cross to bless the statement. Here, it probably alludes to Quintana's state of health or complications resulting from his illness.

42. Note a variation of his name from the documents in which he signs "Fray Juan Joseph Pérez Mirabal."

43. The verb used in Spanish, *haber*, also means *tener*, or "to have," at a time when they were sometimes used interchangeably.

44. The author still uses the more archaic form *fecho*, which we have modernized into *hecho*, or "done."

Bibliography

Adams, Eleanor B., and Fray Angélico Chávez. *The Missions of New Mexico, 1776: A Description by Fray Francisco Atanasio Domínguez with Other Contemporary Documents.* Albuquerque: University of New Mexico Press, 1956, 1976.

Agreda, María de Jesús. *Mística ciudad de Dios: Vida de María.* Edited by Celestino Solaguren et al. Madrid, 1970.

———. *City of God: Popular Abridgment of the Divine History and Life of the Virgin Mother of God; Manifested to Mary of Agreda for the Encouragement of Men.* Translated by Fiscar Marison. Albuquerque: Corcoran Publishing Co., 1949.

Anderson, Reed. "Early Secular Theater in New Mexico." In *Pasó por Aquí: Critical Essays on the New Mexican Literary Tradition, 1542–1988.* Edited by Erlinda Gonzales-Berry, 101–27. Albuquerque: University of New Mexico Press, 1989.

Anonymous. *La iglesia de Santa Cruz de la Cañada, 1733–1983.* Santa Cruz, NM, 1983.

Bancroft, Hubert Howe. *California Pastoral 1769–1848.* San Francisco: The History Company, 1888.

———. *History of Arizona and New Mexico, 1530–1888.* San Francisco: The History Company, 1889.

Bandelier, Adolph F. A., and Fanny R. Bandelier. *Historical Documents Relating to New Mexico, Nueva Vizcaya, and Approaches Thereto 1773.* Vol. 1. Washington, DC: Carnegie Institution of Washington, 1923.

Benedictines of Solesmes, eds. *Liber Usualis.* Tournai, Belgium: Society of St. John the Evangelist, 1938.

Boyd, E. "The Third Order of St. Francis and the Penitentes of New Mexico." In *Popular Arts of Spanish New Mexico,* 440–500. Santa Fe: Museum of New Mexico Press, 1974.

Bunting, Bainbridge. *Early Architecture in New Mexico.* Albuquerque: University of New Mexico Press, 1976.

"Burials of Santa Cruz." Reel 39 (1748). *Archives of the Archdiocese of Santa Fe.*

Campa, Arthur Leon. *Spanish Folk-Poetry in New Mexico.* Albuquerque: University of New Mexico Press, 1946.

———. "The Spanish Folksong in the Southwest." In *The University of New Mexico Bulletin* 4, no. 1 (1933): 1–67

———. "Spanish Religious Folktheatre in the Spanish Southwest (First Cycle)." In *The University of New Mexico Bulletin* 5, no. 1 (1935).

———. "Spanish Religious Folktheatre in the Southwest [Second Cycle]." In *The University of New Mexico Bulletin* 5, no. 2 (1934).

———. *Hispanic Folklore Studies of Arthur L. Campa.* New York: Arno, 1976.

Chávez, Fray Angélico. *Archives of the Archdiocese of Santa Fe, 1678–1900.* Washington, DC: Academy of American Franciscan History, 1957.

———. "The Mad Poet of Santa Cruz." In *New Mexico Folklore* 3 (1948–49): 10–17.

———. *The Origins of New Mexico Families in the Spanish Colonial Period in Two Parts:*

The Seventeenth (1598–1693) and the Eighteenth (1693–1821) Centuries. Santa Fe: The Historical Society of New Mexico, 1954.

Colahan, Clark A. "Chronicles of Exploration and Discovery: The Enchantment of the Unknown." In *Pasó Por Aquí: Critical Essays on the New Mexican Literary Tradition, 1542–1988.* Edited by Erlinda Gonzales-Berry, 14–46. Albuquerque: University of New Mexico Press, 1989.

———. "A Forerunner of Chicano Literature: Miguel de Quintana." In *Dictionary of Literary Biography; Chicano Writers,* 2nd series. Edited by Francisco A. Lomelí and Carl R. Shirley, 329–32. Detroit: Gale Research, 1992.

Colahan, Clark A., and Francisco A. Lomelí. "Miguel de Quintana: An Eighteenth-Century New Mexico Poet Laureate?" In *Pasó Por Aquí: Critical Essays on the New Mexican Literary Tradition, 1542–1988.* Edited by Erlinda Gonzales-Berry, 65–78. Albuquerque: University of New Mexico Press, 1989.

Colahan, Clark A., and Francisco A. Lomelí. "Miguel de Quintana, poeta nuevomexicano ante la Inquisición, con muestras de su obra." Working Paper 102. Albuquerque: Southwest Hispanic Research Institute, 1983.

Colahan, Clark A., and Alfred Rodríguez. "A New Mexican *Alabado* about María de Jesús de Agreda: Reflections on its Popular Retention and Transmission." In *The Liberal and Fine Arts Review* 5 (1985): 4–14.

Colligan, John B. *The Juan Páez Hurtado Expedition of 1695: Fraud in Recruiting Colonists for New Mexico.* Albuquerque: University of New Mexico Press, 1995.

Corstanje, Auspicius van, OFM. *The Third Order for Our Time.* Chicago: Franciscan Herald Press, 1974.

Da Silva, Owen Francis, OFM. *Mission Music of California, A Collection of Old California Mission Hymns and Masses.* Los Angeles: Warren F. Lewis, 1941.

Denzinger, Heinrich, and Clementem Bannwart, SJ. *Enchiridion Symbolorum.* Freiburg Herder, 1922.

Domínguez, Fray Francisco Atanasio. *The Missions of New Mexico, 1776: A Description by Fray Francisco Atanasio Domínguez, with Other Contemporary Documents.* Edited and translated by Eleanor B. Adams and Fray Angélico Chávez. Albuquerque University of New Mexico Press, 1956.

Escobar, Francisco. "La relación de Fray Escobar de la expedición de Oñate a California." Edited by Clark A. Colahan and Alfred Rodríguez. In *Missionalia Hispánica* Madrid: Consejo Superior de Investigaciones Científicas 43 (1986): 373–94.

Espinosa, Aurelio M. "The Folklore of Spain in the American Southwest." In *Traditional Spanish Folk Literature in Northern New Mexico and Southern Colorado.* Edited by J. Manuel Espinosa. Norman: University of Oklahoma Press, 1985.

Espinosa, J. Manuel. *Crusaders of the Río Grande: The Story of Don Diego de Vargas and the Reconquest and Refounding of New Mexico.* Chicago: Institute of Jesuit History, 1942.

Esquibel, José A. "The Family of Quintana y Valdés Altamirano." Unpublished manuscript used by permission of author, 1998.

———. "Mexico City Roots: Baptismal Records of Miguel de Quintana Valdés Altamirano y Cervantes and José de Quintana Valdés Altamirano y Cervantes." In *Genealogical Society of Hispanic America* 4, no. 2 (1992): 41–42.

———. "Mexico City to Santa Fe: Spanish Pioneers on the Camino Real, 1693–94." In *El Camino Real de Tierra Adentro.* Edited by José A. Esquibel, 3–18. Santa Fe, NM: Bureau Of Land Management, 1999.

———. "The People of the Camino Real: A Genealogical Appendix." In *The Royal Road: El Camino Real from Mexico City to Santa Fe,* 145–76. Albuquerque: University of New Mexico Press, 1998.

———. *Remembrance/Recordación: The Spanish Colonists that Arrived in Santa Fe, 23 June 1694.* Denver: Genealogical Society of Hispanic America, 1994.

Esquibel, José A., and John B. Colligan, *The Spanish Recolonization of New Mexico: An Account of the Families Recruited at Mexico City in 1693.* Albuquerque: Hispanic Genealogical Research Center of New Mexico, 1999.

Fergusson, Edna. *New Mexico: A Pageant of Three Peoples.* Albuquerque: University of New Mexico Press, 1951.

Fisher, William R. *A Study of the Historical Background of New Mexican Alabados.* Albuquerque: University of New Mexico Press, 1952.

Fonck, Benet A. *New Ritual for Public Functions: [of the] Franciscan Third Order.* Chicago: Franciscan Herald Press, 1973.

Foraci, Ida R. (Ramonsita Adelaida Quintana [Cordova]). *The Quintana's.* 23 vols. N.p., 1992.

Francis of Assisi. *The Writings of St. Francis of Assisi.* Translated by Benen Fahy, OFM. Chicago: Franciscan Herald Press, 1964.

Gonzales-Berry, Erlinda, ed. *Pasó Por Aquí: Critical Essays on the New Mexican Literary Tradition, 1542–1988.* Albuquerque: University of New Mexico Press, 1989.

Greenleaf, Richard E. "The Mexican Inquisition and the Enlightenment, 1763–1805." In *The Roman Catholic Church in Colonial Latin America.* Edited by Richard E. Greenleaf, 164–76. New York: Knopf, 1971.

———. *The Mexican Inquisition of the Sixteenth Century.* Albuquerque: University of New Mexico Press, 1969.

Hallenbeck, Cleve. *The Land of the Conquistadores.* Caldwell, ID: Caxton Printers, 1950.

Hamilton, Alastair. *Heresy and Mysticism in Sixteenth-Century Spain: 'Los Alumbrados.'* Toronto: University of Toronto Press, 1992.

Hammond, George P., and Agapito Rey. *Don Juan de Oñate, Colonizer of New Mexico, 1595–1628.* Part 2. Albuquerque: University of New Mexico Press, 1953.

Herrera-Sobek, María. "Contemporary Critical Theories and the Pérez de Villagrá Epic." In *Recovering the U.S. Hispanic Literary Heritage.* Edited by María Herrera-Sobek and Virginia Sánchez Korrol, 154–62. Vol. 3. Houston: Arte Público Press, 2000.

Jenkins, Myra Ellen. "Settlement of the Jurisdiction of La Cañada." Folder "Settlement and Irrigation in the Santa Cruz–Quemado Watershed." Spanish Archives in Santa Fe. #CD 3.

Jiménez Rueda, Julio. *Herejías y supersticiones en la Nueva España (los heterodoxos en México).* Mexico City: Imprenta Universitaria, 1946.

Kamen, Henry. *The Spanish Inquisition.* New York: New American Library, 1965.

Kessell, John L. *Kiva, Cross, and Crown: The Pecos Indians and New Mexico, 1540–1840.* Washington, DC: National Park Service, U.S. Department of the Interior, 1979.

———, ed. *Remote Beyond Compare: Letters of Don Diego de Vargas to His Family from New Spain and New Mexico, 1675–1706.* Albuquerque: University of New Mexico Press, 1989.

Kessell, John L., Rick Hendricks, and Meredith D. Dodge, eds. *Blood on the Boulders: The Journals of Don Diego de Vargas, New Mexico, 1694–97.* Albuquerque: University of New Mexico Press, 1998.

Kessell, John L., Rick Hendricks, and Meredith D. Dodge, eds. *To the Royal Crown Restored: The Journal of Don Diego de Vargas, New Mexico, 1692–1694.* Albuquerque: University of New Mexico Press, 1995.

Lamadrid, Enrique R. "History, Faith, and Intercultural Relations in Two New Mexican Inditas: 'Plácida Romero' and 'San Luis Gonzaga.'" In *Nuevomexicano Cultural Legacy: Forms, Agencies and Discourse.* Edited by Francisco A. Lomelí, Víctor Sorell, and Genaro Padilla. Albuquerque: University of New Mexico Press, 2002.

———. "*Los Comanches*: Text, Performance, and Transculturation in an Eighteenth-Century New Mexican Folk Drama." In *Recovering the U.S. Hispanic Literary Heritage.* Edited by María Herrera-Sobek and Virginia Sánchez Korrol, 173–85. Vol. 3. Houston: Arte Público Press, 2000.

Leal, Luis. "California Colonial Literature." In *In Retrospect: Essays on Latin American Literature.* Edited by Elizabeth S. Rogers and Timothy Rogers, 24–39. York, SC: Spanish Literary Pubublications Company, 1987.

———. "The First American Epic: Villagrá's *History of New Mexico.*" In *Pasó Por Aquí: Critical Essays on the New Mexican Literary Tradition, 1542–1988.* Edited by Erlinda Gonzales-Berry, 47–62. Albuquerque: University of New Mexico Press, 1989.

———. "Pre-Chicano Literature: Process and Meaning (1539–1959)." In *Handbook of Hispanic Cultures in the United States: Literature and Art.* Edited by Francisco A. Lomelí, 62–85. Houston: Arte Público Press, 1992.

Lomelí, Francisco A., and Clark A. Colahan. "Miguel de Quintana, poeta nuevomexicano ante la Inquisición." In *Revista Chicano-Riqueña* 7, no. 2 (1984): 51–68.

Lomelí, Francisco A., Víctor Sorell, and Genaro M. Padilla. *Nuevomexicano Cultural Legacy: Forms, Agencies and Discourse.* Albuquerque: University of New Mexico Press, 2002.

Magunagoicochea, J. P. "Octavio Paz: encuentro con el Premio Cervantes 1981."In *La Opinión, Los Angeles,* Sunday Supplement, August 1, 1982.

Marco, Barbara de. "Cantaron la Victoria: Spanish Literary Tradition and the 1680 Pueblo Revolt." In *Recovering the U.S. Hispanic Literary Heritage.* Edited by María Herrera-Sobek and Virginia Sánchez Korrol, 163–72. Houston: Arte Público Press, 2000.

Márquez, Antonio. *Literatura e Inquisición en España (1478–1834).* Madrid: Taurus Ediciones, 1980.

Martin, Russell. "A Sagebrush School of Literature." In *Los Angeles Times,* April 1, 1990.

McCue, Robert J. "The Holy Office of the Inquisition: Its Role in New Mexico." In *Thetian.* Edited by Arch O. Egbert. Provo, UT: Phi Alpha Theta, 1967.

Medina, José Toribio. *Historia del Tribunal del Santo Oficio de la Inquisición en México.* Mexico City: Ediciones Fuente Cultural, 1905.

———. *La primitiva Inquisición americana (1493–1569).* Santiago, Chile: Imprenta Elzeviriana, 1914.

Menéndez y Pelayo, Marcelino. *Historia de los heterodoxos españoles.* 2nd ed. Madrid: Librería General de Victoriano Suárez, 1933.

Molinos, Miguel de. *Guía espiritual.* Edited by José Angel Valente. Barcelona: Barral, 1974.

Niza, Marcos de. Descubrimiento de las siete ciudades por el Padre Fray Marcos de Niza. In vol. 3 of *Colección de los documentos inéditos, relativos al descubrimiento, conquista. . . .* Edited by Joaquín Pacheco and Francisco Cárdenas, 325–50. 42 vols. Madrid, 1864–65.

———. *Nuevo México.* Mexico City: Consejo Nacional para la Cultura y las Artes, 1995.

Norris, Jim. *After "The Year Eighty": The Demise of Franciscan Power in Spanish New Mexico.* Albuquerque: University of New Mexico Press, 2000.

Núñez Cabeza de Vaca, Alvar, and Roberto Ferrando. *Naufragios y comentarios.* Madrid: Historia 16, 1984.

Ortego, Philip D. "Backgrounds of Mexican American Literature." PhD diss., University of New Mexico, 1971.

Pérez de Villagrá, Gaspar. *Historia de la Nueva México.* Alcalá de Henares, 1610.

———. *Historia de la Nueva México, 1610. Gaspar Pérez de Villagrá; A Critical and Annotated Spanish/English Edition.* Edited and translated by Miguel Encinias, Alfred Rodríguez, and Joseph P. Sánchez. Albuquerque: University of New Mexico Press, 1992.

"Petición presentada por los españoles de México de la Villa Nueva de Santa Cruz." *The New Mexico Archives,* Archivo General de la Nación, Mexico City. Section 39, part 4, folios 446–47.

Preston, Douglas, and José A. Esquibel. *The Royal Road: El Camino Real from Mexico City to Santa Fe.* Albuquerque: University of New Mexico Press, 1998.

Quintana, Miguel de. "Nuevo Mexico. Año de 1734. El S[eñ]or Inq[uisid]or fiscal de este S[ant]o Oficio de Méx[i]co c[ontra] Miguel de Quintana de estado casado, vecino de la Villa Nueva de S[an]ta Cruz. Por proposiciones." In Archivo General de la Nación—Mexico. Documentos de la Inquisición. Vol. 849, no. 2. Folios 446–76. Lecumberri, Mexico City.

Rael, Juan B. *The New Mexican Alabado.* New York: AMS Press, Stanford University Publications University Series, 1967.

———. *The New Mexican Alabado.* With transcription of music by Eleanor Hague. Stanford Language and Literature Series 9, no. 3 (1950).

———. *The Sources and Diffusion of the Mexican Shepherds' Plays.* Guadalajara: Librería la Joyita, 1965.

Ritch, William. *Aztlan: The History, Resources, and Attractions of New Mexico.* Boston: D. Lothrop & Co., 1885.

Rodríguez, Alfred. *Plus Ultra: The Life and Times of Alvar Núñez Cabeza de Vaca.* Lincoln, NE: Iuniverse, 2001.

Roth, Cecil. *The Spanish Inquisition.* New York: W. W .Norton & Company, 1964.

Schmitt, Karl. "The Clergy and the Enlightenment." In *The Roman Catholic Church in Colonial Latin America.* Edited by Richard E Greenleaf, 152–63. New York: Knopf, 1971.

Scholes, France V. *Church and State in New Mexico, 1610–1650.* Albuquerque: University of New Mexico Press, 1937.

———. *Troublous Times in New Mexico, 1659–1670.* New York: AMS Press, 1942, 1977.

Steele, Thomas J., SJ. “The Spanish Passion Play in New Mexico and Colorado.” In *New Mexico Historical Review* 53, no. 3 (1978): 239–59.

Steele, Thomas J., SJ., ed. and trans. *The Alabados of New Mexico.* Albuquerque: University of New Mexico Press, 2005.

Twitchell, Ralph Emerson. *The Spanish Archives of New Mexico.* 2 vols. Cedar Rapids, IA: The Torch Press, 1914.

———. “Spanish Colonization in New Mexico in the Oñate and De Vargas Periods.” In *Historical Society of New Mexico* 22 (1919): 3–39.

Weigle, Marta. *Brothers of Light, Brothers of Blood: The Penitentes of the Southwest.* Santa Fe, NM: Ancient City Press, 1989.

Zárate Salmerón, Gerónimo de. *Noticias sacadas de un mss. intitulado Relaciones de todas las cosas que en el Nuevo México se han visto y sabido, así por mar como por tierra desde el año 1538 hasta el de 1626.* Edited by José Fernando Ramírez. Mexico City: Vargas Rea, 1949.

———. *Relaciones.* Translated by Alicia Ronstadt Milich. Albuquerque: Horn & Wallace, 1966.

Index

Note: Page numbers for figures appear in italics.